Index
to
Associators *and* Militia
of
Cumberland County
Pennsylvania

AN INDEX TO
Pennsylvania Archives
FIFTH SERIES
VOLUME VI

Jane Dickens

HERITAGE BOOKS
2010

HERITAGE BOOKS

AN IMPRINT OF HERITAGE BOOKS, INC.

Books, CDs, and more—Worldwide

For our listing of thousands of titles see our website
at
www.HeritageBooks.com

Published 2010 by
HERITAGE BOOKS, INC.
Publishing Division
100 Railroad Ave. #104
Westminster, Maryland 21157

Originally published 1998
by Family Line Publications

International Standard Book Numbers
Paperbound: 978-1-58549-480-4
Clothbound: 978-0-7884-8562-6

INTRODUCTION

This is an index to *Pennsylvania Archives*, Fifth Series, Volume VI: Associators And Militia for Cumberland County. The Fifth, Sixth, and Seventh Series consist primarily of lists of names, the Fifth collecting all available muster and militia rolls for the earlier periods of the French and Indian Wars and the Revolution, while the Sixth covers, in general, later militia rolls, those for the years of peace and for the War of 1812-14.[1] The Seventh Series consists exclusively of a five-volume index to the sixth Series. The indexing to the Fifth Series is covered by Volume XV of the Sixth Series, in two parts (books) consisting of 2515 pages. In order to provide the reader with a smaller index which pertains only to Volume VI of the Fifth Series, this book was prepared.

The names appear in various spellings - much more than even an experienced researcher of colonial records would expect. In some cases I have combined or cross referenced different spellings.

Many of the major libraries of the U.S. have copies of the *Pennsylvania Archives*.

This work contains various muster rolls. Some of these are muster rolls taken when the units were activated. Others are merely rolls in which classes were determined or confirmed. Each member was assigned to a class, 1 through 8. In many instances only certain classes were called up; this disallowed the depletion of the men of an entire company. Because companies were formed by local regions, no one region was drained of its manpower. Thus class number has no value to the typical researcher.

Most of the abbreviations used by original clerk or scribe as recorded in the original book are obvious in meaning. The less obvious ones are the following:

B.S. = blacksmith
corp. = corporal
creek = lived near a creek
mountain = lived near mountain
took up a deserter = was taken up as a deserter ??

---

1 For a thorough treatment of the Pennsylvania Archives see Henry Howard Eddy, *Guiide To The Published Archives of Pennsylvania covering the 138 volumes of Colonia Records and pennsylvania Archives Series I-IX*, published by Division of Public Records, Pennsylvania historical And Museum Commision, Harrisburg, 1949.

The following abbreviations were used in this index:

Adj. = Adjutant
Capt. = Captain
Col. = Colonel
Cpl. = Corporal
Ens. = Ensign
Gen. = General
Lt. = Lieutenant
Lt. Col. = Lieutenant Colonel
Maj. = Major
Pvt. = Private
Sgt. = Sergeant
Sub. Lt. = Sub. Lieutenant

F. Edward Wright
Westminster, Maryland
1998

-A-

ABERCROMBY, William (Pvt.) 160
ABERCRUMBIE, William (Pvt.) 195, 617
ABRAHAM, Noah (Capt.) 12, 17, 19, 21, 28, 43, 51, 53, 59, 60, 62, 85, 86, 120, 121, 127, 128, 138, 140, 383, 387, 515, 603, 609, 620, 626
ACISAN, Thomas (Pvt.) 409
ACKELS, Daniel (Pvt.) 296
William (Pvt.) 296
ACKISON, Thomas (Pvt.) 394
ACKMAN, John (Pvt.) 133, 436
Thomas (Pvt.) 134, 437, 656
William (Pvt.) 133, 402, 437
ACRE, William (Pvt.) 519
ADAIR, Abram (Pvt.) 206
James (Pvt.) 350, 357, 472, 478, 484
Joseph (Pvt.) 214
Robert (Pvt.) 625
Samuel (1st Lt.) Died by 6 Feb 1778. 453, 469
ADAM, Albert (Qtr. Master) 451
James (Capt.) 609
Stephen (Pvt.) 94
Stophel (Pvt.) 116
Thomas 606
ADAMS, Abraham (Pvt.) 221
Abram (Pvt.) 227
David (Pvt.) 74, 88, 119, 329, 523, 527, 538, 546, 623
Gaven (Pvt.) 402, 419
Jacob (Pvt.), 329, 553, 624, 646, 650
Jacob (Sgt.) 489
James (Capt.) 6, 320, 324, 597
James (Pvt.) 330, 597, 624
John (Pvt.) 141, 515
Joseph (Pvt.) 325, 646, 650
Mathew (Pvt.) 187, 588
Matthew (Pvt.) 195
Matthew (Sgt.) 647
Robert (Pvt.) 458
Samuel (Pvt.) 221, 227, 305
Samuel (Sgt.) 79, 101
Thomas (Pvt.) 181, 195, 251, 457, 493, 496
William (Pvt.) 64, 79, 101, 107, 141, 147, 196, 323, 346, 356, 366, 458, 481, 497, 502, 515, 569, 574, 578, 646, 648
ADAMSON, John (Pvt.) 278, 287, 311, 589
ADAMSTON, John (Pvt.) 54, 62, 395,

421, 433
ADAMSTONE, John (Pvt.) 57
ADARE, James (Pvt.) 619
ADDAMS, James (Capt.) 333
James (Lt.) 550
John (Capt.) 326
ADMESTON, John (Pvt.) 136
ADMISTON, John (Pvt.) 51
AGNEW, Samuel (1st Lt.) 204, 210, 213
Samuel (Capt.) 235, 237
Samuel (Pvt.) 616
William (Pvt.) 209
AGNUE, Samuel (Pvt.) 221
William (Pvt.), 221
AIKENS, James (Pvt.) 23
Robert (Pvt.) 499
AIKIN, William (Pvt.) 56, 632
AIKINS, Alexander (Pvt.) 466
AIKMAN, John (Pvt.) 8, 418
Thomas (Pvt.) 66
William (Pvt.) 26, 419
AIRBUCKLE, William (Ens.) 252
AKEMAN, James (Pvt.) 392
John (Pvt.) 10
AKENS, Robert (Pvt.) 474
William (Pvt.) 572
AKER, William (Pvt.) 524
AKINS, Alexander (Pvt.) 454
AKISON, Thomas (Pvt.) 424, 442
ALBRIGHT, George (Pvt.) 252, 483, 485, 501, 651
Peter (Pvt.) 80, 101
ALDER, David (Pvt.) 31
Joseph (Pvt.) 39
Matthew (Pvt.) 326
William (Ens.) 22, 51
ALENDER, Joseph (Pvt.) 92, 576, 583
ALENDOR, Joseph (Pvt.) 138
ALEXANDER, David (Pvt.) 558, 650
Francis (Pvt.) 554, 556, 558, 650
Hugh (Pvt.) 186, 588
James 28
James (Pvt.) 22, 25, 120, 141, 323, 384, 515
John (Pvt.) 77, 82, 111, 126, 343, 548, 555, 559, 625, 630, 655
Joseph 605
Joseph (Cpl.) 545
Joseph (Pvt.) 87, 123, 391, 403, 404, 419, 437, 538, 589, 590, 641
Joshua (Pvt.) 118
Nathaniel (Pvt.) 88, 98
Patrick (Pvt.) 82, 110, 125

Robert, (Pvt.) 120, 140, 428, 515, 650
Samuel (Pvt.) 558, 570, 578, 648
Thomas (Capt.) 321, 324, 331, 335
Thomas (Pvt.) 650
William (2nd Lt.) 13, 15, 16, 44, 46, 48,
   55, 135, 588
William (Lt.) 628
William (Pvt.) 395, 421, 427, 432, 582,
   634, 636
ALEXANDOR, Samuel (Pvt.) 574
ALFORD, John (Pvt.) 330, 567
John (Sgt.) 581, 635
ALFRED, John (Pvt.) 563
ALICE, Nicles (Pvt.) 305
ALINDER, Joseph (Pvt.) 76
ALINE, David (Pvt.) 632
ALIS, Francis (Pvt.) 651
ALISON, Mathew (Pvt.) 222
ALLBRIGHT, George (Pvt.) 510
ALLEN, David (Pvt.) 122, 162, 177, 477,
   502, 573, 638, 639
George (Pvt.) 350, 357
James (Pvt.) 37, 39, 200, 515
John (Pvt.) 64, 81, 109, 110, 125, 392,
   403, 419, 437, 477, 502, 552, 647,
   653, 654, 656
Jonathan (Pvt.) 129
Josiah (Pvt.) 279, 312
Josias (Pvt.) 288
Peter (Pvt.) 331, 566, 630
Robert (Pvt.) 64, 145, 439
William (Pvt.) 478, 490, 504
ALLESON, Robert (Pvt.) 650
ALLEXANDER, Francis (Pvt.) 577
James (Pvt.) 128
Joseph (Pvt.) 58
Robert (Pvt.) 85, 127
Thomas (Pvt.) 130
William (2nd Lt.) 57
ALLICE, Nicolls (Pvt.) 298
ALLIN, John (Pvt.) 147
Robert (Pvt.) 147
ALLING, John (Pvt.) 564
Peter (Pvt.) 564
ALLIS, Nicholas (Pvt.) 274
ALLISON, --- 5
Andrew (Pvt.) 267, 279, 280, 290, 302,
   309
Charles (Pvt.) 280, 290
Hugh (Ens.) 369, 377
Hugh (Pvt.) 280, 291
James (Pvt.) 280, 290, 624
John (Col.) 5

John () 4
John (Ens.) 317
John (Pvt.) 15, 17, 68, 79, 133, 586, 631
Matthew (Pvt.) 209, 228, 365
Robert (Pvt.) 336, 558, 570
Tate (Pvt.) 279, 289
Thomas (Light Dragoon) 640
Thomas (Pvt.) 68, 375
William (Pvt.) 81, 98, 102, 130, 160
ALLISTER, William (Pvt.) 618
ALLON, David (Pvt.) 56
Hugh (Pvt.) 152
James (Pvt.) 41, 141
ALLONDER, Joseph (Pvt.) 104
ALLOT, John (Pvt.) 645
ALLSBACK, Henry (Pvt.) 501
ALSBAUGH, Henry (Pvt.) 502
ALSWORCH, Andrew (Sgt.) 148
ALSWORTH, Andrew (Pvt.) 151, 436
Andrew (Sgt.) 631
Benjamin (Pvt.) 435, 450
James (Pvt.) 416, 449
ALTECK, Daniel (Pvt.) 590
ALTER, Jacob (Pvt.) 193
ALTICK, Daniel (Pvt.) 58, 136
ALTIG, Daniel (Pvt.) 389, 396, 421
ALTIGER, Christn. (Pvt.) 396
Christopher (Pvt.) 389
Christr. (Pvt.) 433
ALWORTH, Andrew (Pvt.) 390, 450
James (Pvt.) 425, 434, 636
ANDERSON, Abraham (Pvt.) 400
Adam (Pvt.) 133
Daniel (Pvt.) 249, 472, 475, 486, 500,
   619
David (1st Lt.) 11, 15, 16, 43, 46, 48,
   55, 60, 131
David (Lt.) 626
George (Pvt.) 65, 68, 108, 118, 135,
   151, 400, 413, 439, 445, 447, 572
James (Pvt.) 236, 238, 289, 303
John 565, 606
John (Pvt.) 27, 35, 37, 39, 41, 62, 79,
   91, 102, 103, 109, 132, 137, 160,
   250, 251(2), 252, 328, 414, 442, 472,
   475, 480, 492(2), 495, 554, 556, 561,
   565, 573, 574, 575, 577, 578, 582,
   618, 619, 630, 500
John (Sgt.) 408, 423, 620, 648
Joshua (Pvt.) 51, 54, 61, 62, 131, 409,
   423, 442
Oliver (Pvt.) 269, 275, 282, 373
Robert (Pvt.) 269, 283, 311, 330

Samuel (Pvt.) 325, 560
Thomas (Pvt.) 26, 35, 208, 220, 223, 250, 353, 358, 480, 487, 494, 618, 621
William (Pvt.) 327, 418
ANDREW, David (Pvt.) 359, 363, 622
John (Ens.) 87
John (Pvt.) 538
John 537
Jonathan (Ens.) 118
Robert (Pvt.) 275
ANDREWS, James (Pvt.) 546
John (Capt.) 5
John (Ens.) 70
John (Pvt.) 538
John 545
Robert (Pvt.) 283
ANESLOW, James (Pvt.) 263
ANSLEY, James (Pvt.) 643
ANSLOW, James (Pvt.) 268, 303
ANSMINGER, Nichles (Pvt.) 102
ANTHONY, Phillip (Pvt.) 142
ANTINGER, Christy (Pvt.) 58, 590
APLEBEE, William (Pvt.) 248
APPLEBY, Thomas (Pvt.) 160
William (Pvt.) 159, 396, 421, 433
ARBUCKLE, James (2nd Lt.) 241
John (Pvt.) 481, 490, 497, 506
Samuel (2nd Lt.) 250, 255
Samuel (Ens.) 241
William (Ens.) 255
ARCHER, Zacariah (Pvt.) 438
Zacharia (Pvt.) 420
Zechariah (Pvt.) 64, 147
ARCHIBALD, David (Pvt.) 292
William (Pvt.) 292, 296
ARDERY, James (Pvt.) 409, 455, 466
John (Pvt.) 457
ARDLEY, Calib (Pvt.) 188
ARDREY, James (Pvt.) 365, 423, 442
ARDRY, James (Pvt.) 355, 364
John (Pvt.) 358
ARDY, John (Pvt.) 353
ARES, George (Pvt.) 219
ARFORD, Dewilt (Pvt.) 231, 235
ARIS, George (Pvt.) 225
ARMITAGE, John (Pvt.) 185, 191
ARMOR, William (Pvt.) 158
ARMSBEY, Mathew (Pvt.) 141
ARMSBY, John (Pvt.) 85
ARMSTRONG, --- 5, 316
--- (Pvt.) 128
Alexander (Pvt.) 174, 178, 193, 346, 366
Andrew (Pvt.) 206, 214
David (Pvt.) 86, 121, 128, 141, 384, 393, 515
George (Cpl.) 242, 259
George (Pvt.) 56, 479, 491, 573, 632
James (Pvt.) 27, 250, 326, 478, 481, 483, 497, 618, 644
James (Sgt.) 35
John 607
John (COO) 4
John (Lt.) 3
John (Pvt.) 142, 482, 492, 497, 566
Joseph (Col.) 5, 316, 317, 318
Joseph (Pvt.) 278, 287, 311, 380, 604
Joshua (Pvt.) 214
Josiah (Pvt.) 206
Robert (Pvt.) 637, 647
Thomas (Pvt.) 206, 230, 234, 480, 494
William (Pvt.) 86, 121, 128, 160, 174, 178, 187, 200, 325, 327, 365, 407, 481, 497, 563
ARREL, David (Pvt.) 390
ARROL, David (Pvt.) 430
ARSBALD, William (Pvt.) 313
ARTHERS, Richard (Pvt.) 566
ARTHUR, Richard (Pvt.) (Scout) 652
ARTHURS, Thomas (Pvt.) 597
ARTINGER, Christey (Pvt.) 657
ARTLEY, Caleb (Pvt.) 195
ASH, John (Pvt.) 490
ASKEY, Alexander (Allexander) (Pvt.) 57, 135, 395, 420, 432, 589
James (Pvt.) 409
Thomas (Capt.) 6, 9, 23, 27, 43, 47, 49, 52, 60, 131, 387, 408, 410, 412, 422, 424, 441, 442, 609, 614, 626, 630
Thomas (Pvt. - a substitute employed by James Hambleton) 24
ASKINS, Thomas (Capt.), 11
ASPEY (Aspie), George (Pvt.) 176 185, 617
ASQUE, Alexander (Pvt.) 415
ASSPY, Thomas (Pvt.) 635
ASTEN (Aston), Owen (Pvt.) 81, 547
Owen (Qtr. Master) 109
ATCHINSON, Alexander (Pvt.) 158
Jacob (Pvt.) 159, 168, 248
ATCHISON, Edward 196
Jacob (Pvt.) 195
James (Pvt.) 617
Nathaniel (Pvt.) 395
Thomas (Pvt.) 347

4

Timothy (Pvt.) 177, 196
ATHINGER, Cristn. (Pvt.) 421
ATKINSON, Charles (Pvt.) 360
Cornelius (Pvt.) 359, 622
James (Pvt.) 360, 622
ATKISON (Atkerson, Atherson), George
(Pvt.) 219, 225, 229, 232
William (Pvt.) 643
ATLIN, John (Pvt.) 328
ATTINGER, Christy (Pvt.) 136
AUTER, Samuel (Pvt.) 573
AUTOR, Abraham (Pvt.) 572, 632
Samuel (Pvt.) 632

-B-
BACHOS (Backhouse, Bakehous) Daniel
(Pvt.), 205, 236, 237
BAGEE, Samuel (Pvt.) 618
BAGLE, James (Pvt.) 62
BAHANAN, Robert (Pvt.) (Scout) 652
BAILEY (Baily), Charles (Pvt.) 312
Cotral (Cottrel, Cottial) (Pvt.) 278, 287,
311
James (Pvt.) 329, 629
John (Pvt.) 200(2), 311
Robert (Pvt.) 278
BAIR, James (Pvt.) 478
BAIRD, Andrew (Pvt.) 381
David (Pvt.) 455, 466
Hugh (Pvt.) 560, 650
Isaac (Pvt.) 300
John (Pvt.) 200, 206, 227 (Aug 1780 -
dead), 337, 373, 374, 648, 650
Richard (Pvt.) 298, 305
Samuel (Pvt.) 646
Thomas (Clerk) 545
Thomas (Pvt.) 227, 523
William (Pvt.) 227, 318, 323, 336, 646,
650
BAIRFIELD, George (Pvt.) 474, 653
BAKER, George (Pvt.) 117
Henry (Pvt.) 93, 116, 122
Jacob (Pvt.) 89, 112, 124
James (Sgt.) 541
John (Pvt.) 90, 98, 113, 457
Samuel (Pvt.) 37, 39, 52, 132, 414, 440
BALDRADGE (Baldrige), Thomas (Pvt.)
620, 631
BALDRIDGE, Alexander (Pvt.) 267,
302, 309, 450
BALE, David (Pvt.) 505
BALF, Dennis (Dinis) (Pvt.) 291, 313
BALL, Andrew (Pvt.) 52

Robert (Pvt.) 275
BALM, Frederick (Pvt.) 630
Jonas (Pvt.) 328
BALMER, William 605
BALRIDGE, Thomas (Pvt.) 393
BAM, Frederick (Pvt.) 579
John (Pvt.) 554
BAMER, Frederick (Ens.) 155
BANBRICK, Peter (Pvt.) 108
BANCORD (Bancourt, Barncurt,
Bancurts, Barncourt), Jacob (Pvt.)
298, 301, 306, 576, 583
Peter (Pvt.) 297, 304, 297, 305
BANLAY, John (Pvt.) 395
BAR, Alexander (Pvt.) 405, 436
Thomas (Pvt.) 435
William (Pvt.) 406
BARBER, David (Pvt.) 180, 197
BARCLAY, Hugh (Pvt.) 519
John (Pvt.) 96, 420, 432
BARD, John (Pvt.) 374, 382
Richard (Pvt.) 382
Robert (Pvt.) 372
William (Pvt.) 382, 582, 634, 636
BARDE, John (Pvt.) 74, 88, 92
William (Pvt.) 91, 568
BARDEE, Richard (Pvt.) 266
BARE, Alexander (Pvt.) 66
BAREFIELD, George (Pvt.) 488
John (Pvt.) 621
BARIAHILL, John (Pvt.), 405 (for James
McCune)
BARICKMAN, Christopher (Pvt.) 618
BARK, David (Pvt.) 475
BARKER, John (Pvt.) 353, 358, 362,
456, 467
William (Pvt.) 205, 353
BARKHAM(M)ER (Barkhimer), Leonard
(Lennard) (Pvt.) 74, 89, 118
Ludwick (Loudwick) (Pvt.) 74, 90, 108,
119, 586
BARKLEY, Hugh (Pvt.) 540
John (Pvt.) 415
BARLAND, James (Pvt.) 600
BARLEY, James (Pvt.) 342
BARN, Fredrick (Pvt.) 574
BARNCOURT, BARNCURT. See
Bancord.
BARNES, Augustus (Pvt.) 647
James (Pvt.) 34
John (Pvt.) 313
BARNET(T), David (Pvt.) 265, 292, 296,
313, 643

James (Pvt.) 292, 296
John (Pvt.) 400, 413, 426, 439
Joseph (Pvt.) 162, 281, 293, 297, 313,
  400, 405 (for Matton Hannah), 413,
  427, 432, 642
Moses (Mosey) (Pvt.) 83, 100, 111, 126
Samuel (Pvt.) 56, 247, 252, 475, 486,
  500, 573, 632
Thomas (Pvt.) 345, 352, 459
BARNHART(S), Conrod (Conred) (Pvt.)
  9, 230, 233
Peater (Pvt.) 9
Walter (Pvt.) 391
BARNHILL (Barnhell), John 28, 605
John (Pvt.) 24, 421, 642
Robert 28, 605
Robert (Pvt.) 24, 31, 34, 58, 326, 389,
  396, 444, 490, 559, 571, 574, 579,
  590, 624, 648, 650
Samuel (Pvt.) 461
BARNS, Daniel (Pvt.) 80
John (Pvt.) 296
Teter (Diter) (Pvt.) 79, 101, 107
BARR, Alexander (Alexandrew,
  Allexander) (Pvt.) 135, 285, 315,
  401, 414, 440, 450
David (Pvt.) 331, 558, 567
James (Pvt.) 97, 185, 210, 296, 312,
  504, 573
John (1st Lt.) 369, 377, 382
John (Ens.) 316
John (Lt.) 609
John (Pvt.) 207, 274, 388, 401
Robert (2nd Lt.) 322, 324, 329, 335
Robert (Pvt.) 561
Samuel (Pvt.) 400, 413, 426, 439
William (Pvt.) 17, 136, 150, 396, 422,
  434, 544, 561, 585, 627
BARRAN, Thomas (Pvt.) 413, 439
BARRANGER, Andrew (Pvt.) 282
BARRE, James (Pvt.) 78
John (Pvt.) 294
BARREN, Thomas (Pvt.) 426
William (Pvt.) 31, 34, 64, 145, 147, 392,
  403, 444
BARRENHILL, Robert (Pvt.) 136, 443
BARRETT, Richard (Pvt.) 296
BARREY, James (Pvt.) 97
BARRICKMAN, Christy (Pvt.) 35
BARRINGER, Andrew (Pvt.) 275
Lawrence (Pvt.) 275
BARRIT, Thomas (Pvt.) 497
BARRON, William (Pvt.) 440, 443

BARRY, George (Pvt.) 41
John (Pvt.) 104, 291
BARTHOLOMEW, John (Pvt.) 329
BARTLEY, Hugh (Pvt.) 524
Mathew (Pvt.) 64, 145, 147
BARTON, Daniel (Pvt.) 247, 483, 501
BASCHORE, David (Pvt.) 94
BASEHORE, David (Pvt.) 72
BASEM, Peter (Pvt.) 505
BASEOUR, David (Pvt.) 117
BASH, Andrew (Pvt.), 188
BASHFORD, William (Pvt.) 273, 293,
  307
BASKINS (Baskings), Mitchel (Michael)
  (Pvt.) 360, 461, 612, 622
BASTIAN, Mitchel (Pvt.) 354
BATES, Conrad (Pvt.) 311
BATTERSON, Robert (Pvt.) 624
BATTON, Edward (Pvt.) 151
BAUGH, Leonard (Pvt.) 430
BAUM, Charles (Pvt.) 178
Frederick (Pvt.) 554, 561, 570, 649, 650
Frederick 565
Fredrick (Pvt.) 561
Jacob (Pvt.) 650
Jacub (Pvt.) 561
John (Pvt.) 556, 561, 577, 650
BAUMN, Jonas (Pvt.) 561
BAXTER, James (Pvt.) 362, 454, 466,
  624, 654
John (Pvt.) 82, 110, 125, 548
William (Pvt.) 355, 364, 365
BAYLEY, James (Pvt.) 351
BAYMER, Conrad (Conrod) (1st Lt.) 12,
  44, 588
BEADY, Joseph (Qtr. Master) 641
BEAGLY, Thomas (Pvt.) 207
BEAKAN, Peter (Pvt.) 245
BEAKER, John (Pvt.) 543
BEAKHAM, Robert (Pvt.) 430
BEALE (Beal), David (Pvt.) 490, 500
Robert (Pvt.) 617
Thomas (Capt.) 6
Thomas (Pvt.) 56, 493, 496, 507, 573
Thomas (Qtr. Master) 631
BEALY, Ebenezer (Sgt.) 499
John (Pvt.) 568
BEAMER, Conrad (1st Lt.) 17, 139
Conrad (Lt.) 69, 79, 100
Frederick (Ens.) Resigned 15 April
  1778. 170
BEAR, Alexander (Pvt.) 189
BEARD, Andrew (Pvt.) 290

David (Pvt.) 341, 361
Hugh (Pvt.) 330, 597
Isaac (Pvt.) 306
James (Pvt.) 268, 303, 310
John (Ens.) 261, 279, 289
John (Pvt.) 76, 80, 221 (1 Aug 1780 -
 dead), 267, 302, 312, 611, 651
Jonathan (Pvt.) 119
Jons. (Pvt.) 546
Richard (Pvt.) 300
Thomas (Pvt.) 221, 526, 546, 623
William (Pvt.) 221, 268, 302, 308, 310
BEARFIELD, George (Pvt.) 498
John (Pvt.) 618
BEASSEM, Peter (Pvt.) 501
BEATES, Conrad (Pvt.) 278, 287
Orbun (Pvt.) 288
BEATEY, Thomas (Pvt.) 119
BEATS, Urban (Pvt.) 279
BEATTEY, William (Pvt.) 76
BEATTON, Edward (Pvt.) 648
BEATTY, Andrew (Pvt.) 360, 622
Ebenezer (Pvt.) 122, 638
James (Pvt.) 359, 622
John (Lt.) 339
John (Pvt.) 77, 82, 111, 325, 432, 549,
 624
John (Sgt.) 612
Jonathan (Cpl.) 129
Jonathan (Pvt.) 84, 114
Samuel (Pvt.) 122, 252, 472, 474, 488,
 499, 638
Thomas (Pvt.) 74, 88, 538
Walter (Pvt.) 328
Walter (Pvt.) (substitute for Thomas
 Ritchey apprentice), 124
Will (Pvt.) 612
William (Pvt.) 92, 360, 522, 526, 527,
 530, 576, 583, 601, 622
BEATY, --- (Lt.) 359
Ebenezer (Sgt.) 639
James (Pvt.) 198
John (Pvt.) 366, 490, 563
Samuel (Pvt.) 619
Samuel (Sgt.) 639
Walter (Pvt.) 125
William (Pvt.) 138, 145, 147
BEAVAIRD, William (Pvt.) 181
BEAVER, Anthony (Pvt.) 89, 539
Nicholas (Pvt.) 90, 113, 542
Samuel (Ens.) 551
BEAVIS, Isaachar (Pvt.) 473
BEAVOR, Anthony (Pvt.) 112

BECKY, William (Adj.) 329
BEEL, Andrew (Pvt.) 447
BEELL, Andrew (Cpl.), 410 (for Able
 Machan)
BEEMAR, Conrad (1st Lt.) 21
BEER, Samuel (Pvt.) 178
Solloman (Pvt.) 178
BEESHORE, Daniel (Pvt.) 586
BEIRD, John (Pvt.) 574, 579
BELL, Andrew (Cpl.) 631
Andrew (Androw) (Pvt.) 18, 21, 53, 68,
 139, 151, 445
Andrew (employed a substitue James
 Wooden), 24
Arthur (Pvt.) 507
Arthur (Pvt.) (Scout) 652
Charles (Pvt.) 177, 189, 617
David (Lt. Col.) 22, 50, 201, 210
George (Capt.) 322, 324, 330, 335
Hugh (Pvt.) 354(2), 359
James (Capt.) 215, 222, 223, 232, 234,
 235, 637
James (Pvt.) 142, 398
John (Ens.) 241, 248, 256, 321, 324,
 330, 334, 550, 562, 574, 578, 648
John (Lt.) 551, 564, 629
John (Pvt.) 7, 10, 67, 86, 121, 128, 141,
 176, 183, 325, 384, 393, 399, 413,
 415, 439, 445, 447, 515
Jonathan (Pvt.) 193
Joseph (Pvt.) 276, 629
Josiah (Pvt.) 353
Robert (Pvt.) 183, 193, 269, 282, 304
Samuel (Cpl.) 641
Samuel (Pvt.) 66, 388, 400, 404, 413,
 440
Samuel (Sgt.) 133
Thomas (Pvt.) 566
Thomas (Pvt.) (Scout) 652
William (Pvt.) 247, 257, 290(2), 480,
 494, 508, 590
BENEDICK, John (Pvt.) 89, 112
Peter (Pvt.) 89, 112
BENEDICT, Peter (Pvt.) 542
BENEFIELD (Benifield, Bennefield),
 George (Pvt.) 272, 285, 381
John (Pvt.) 272, 285, 315, 615, 643
BENEY, George (Pvt.) 229
BENIGE, George (Pvt.) 233
BENNETT, John (Pvt.) 313
BENTZ, Nicholas (Pvt.) 248
BERACKMAN, Christopher (Pvt.) 251
BERANGER, Laurence (Pvt.) 304

BERCHFIELD, James (Pvt.) 504
BERGER, Charles (Pvt.) 244, 258
BERICKMAN, Christly (Pvt.) 621
BERKLEY, Hugh (Pvt.) 557
BERNHEART, Peter (Pvt.) 398
BERRAT, Thomas (Pvt.) 505
BERREY, James (Pvt.) 425, 636
BERRIT, Thomas (Pvt.) 481
BERRY, George (Pvt.) 37, 39, 64, 145, 147, 388, 401
  James (Pvt.) 7, 82, 144, 146, 399, 413, 415, 439
  James (Sgt.) 63
  James (substitute?) 657
  John 608
  John (Pvt.) 295, 546, 557
BERRYHILL, William (Capt.) 69, 79, 81, 100, 102
BERY, George (Pvt.) 440
  William (Pvt.) 357
BEST, Samuel (Pvt.) 252, 472, 478, 484, 619
BETTINGER, George (Pvt.) 118
BETTY, William (Pvt.) 188
BEUTTY, William (Pvt.) 104
BEVARD, William (Pvt.) 440
BEVARDE, Robert (Pvt.) 176
  William (Pvt.) 198
BEVEARD, Robert (Pvt.) 161
BEVER, Anthony (Pvt.) 74
  Nicholas (Pvt.) 75
BEVISS, Isachur (Pvt.) 498
BEYERS, John (Pvt.) 356
BEYMOR, Conrad (1st Lt.) 56
BEYS, David (Pvt.) 504
BIDDLE, George (Pvt.) 455, 466
  John (Drummer) 408
  Wilmore (Pvt.) 642
BIDINGER, Frederick 406
BIDLE, John (Pvt.) 62
BIGAM, Robert (Pvt.) 125
BIGARD, Andrew (Pvt.) 371
BIGER, James (Pvt.) 300
BIGGAM, Robert (Pvt.) 81, 109, 110, 547
BIGGER (Biggar), Alexander (Pvt.) 375
  Andrew (Pvt.) 271, 284, 289, 314
  James (Pvt.) 297, 305, 372
  John (Pvt.) 298, 306
BIGGS, Thomas (Pvt.) 650
BIRCHFIELD, Aquila (Pvt.) 491
  James (Pvt.) 476
  Thomas (Pvt.) 490

BISHIP, John (Sgt.) 280
BITNER, William (Pvt.) 357, 363
BIT(T)INGER, Frederick (Pvt.) 399, 431
  George (Pvt.) 123, 538, 546, 586
BITTLE, John (Pvt.) 132
BITTNER, Nicholas (Pvt.) 629
BLACHHART, Andrew (Pvt.) 61
BLACK, George (1st Lt.) 452, 457, 463, 468
  George (Pvt.) 350
  Henry (Cpl.) 410 (for Jacob Thomas), 620, 631
  Henry (Pvt.) 52, 517, 518, 519, 546, 586
  James 607
  James (Cpl.) 618
  James (Pvt.) 244, 344, 347, 349, 475, 500, 621
  James (Pvt.) (received substitute money) 590, 591
  John (Pvt.) 85, 119, 120, 198, 347, 348, 362, 455
  Jonathan (Pvt.) 119
  Peter (Pvt.) 180, 197
  Samuel (Pvt.) 350, 357, 364
  Thomas (Pvt.) 180, 342, 618, 621
  William (Capt.) 340, 349
  William (Pvt.) 247, 475, 500
BLACKBURN, John (Lt.) 604
  John (Pvt.) 160, 168
  Moses (Pvt.) 111, 126, 157
BLACKHART, Andrew (Pvt.) 22, 131, 409, 442, 620
BLACKHEART, Andrew (Pvt.) 423
  Andrew (Sgt.) 27
BLACKLEY, David (Pvt.) 305
BLACKNEY, David (Pvt.) 303
  William (Adj.) 153, 163
BLACKWOOD, John (Pvt.) 167, 184, 190
BLAIN, David (Almoner) 194
  James (1st Lt.) 452
  William (Capt.) 452
  William (Ens.) 364
  William (Pvt.) 345, 353, 629
BLAINE, --- 5
  Alexander (Pvt.), 200(2)
  Ephraim (Col.) 8
  Ephraim (Committee of Observation) 4
  Ephraim (Lt. Col.) 5
  Ephraim (Lt.) 3
  James (1st Lt.) 456, 463, 468
  James (Ens.) 340
  James (Lt.) 349, 356

James (Pvt.) 353
Patrick (Pvt.) 353
Thomas (Pvt.) 353
William (Capt.) 5, 457, 463, 468, 609
William (Pvt.) 357, 459
BLAIR, Alexander (Pvt.) 330, 561, 650
Alexander (Pvt.) (Scout) 652
Charles (Pvt.) 252, 470, 472, 478, 602, 619
George (Pvt.) 246, 257, 478
James (Pvt.) 30, 33, 95, 96, 149, 150, 180, 197, 418, 437
John (Pvt.) 57, 136, 331, 372, 507, 554, 589, 597
Randles (Pvt.) 181, 198
Robert (Pvt.) 587
Thomas (2nd Lt.) 319, 323, 327, 332, 337
Thomas (Pvt.) 561
Thomas (Pvt.) (Scout) 652
William (Lt.) 6
William (Pvt.) 299, 301, 306, 561
William (Pvt.) ("commissary of purchases") 162
BLAKENEY, David (Pvt.) 620
BLAKENY, John (Pvt.) 563
BLAKNEY, John (Pvt.) 323
BLANE, Thomas (Pvt.) 343
BLARE, Charles (Pvt.) 484
George (Pvt.) 504
James (Pvt.), 106, 119, 389 (over age as of Aug 1780)
BLEANY, Jacob (Pvt.) 348
BLEAR, Alexand (Pvt.) 561
John (Pvt.) 556, 561, 577
Thomas (Lt.) 611
BLECKLEY, James (Pvt.) 72, 94, 117
BLITHE, John (Pvt.) 30
BLOCK, Henry (Cpl.) 636
Henry (Pvt.) 62
Henry (Pvt.) (substitute for Peter Houghenberry) 426
BLYTH, Benjamin (Pvt.) 124, 422, 434
Benjamin (Sub. Lt.) 41, 86, 152, 426
Jacob (Pvt.) 589
John (Sgt.) 390, 397, 404, 429, 641
Samuel (Pvt.) 395, 421, 431
BLYTHE, Benjamin (Sub. Lt.), 3(2)
James (Sub. Lt.) 28
John (Pvt.) 143
BOAL, David (Capt.) 476, 509, 614, 651
James (Pvt.) 438
BOANBRAKE. See Bonbreak

BOAR, Michael (Cpl.) 8
BOCHANNAND, Thomas (Pvt.) 196
BOCHANON, John (Pvt.) 483
BOCHAR, Henry (Pvt.) 504
BOCKER, Henry (Pvt.) 476
BOGEL, Andrew (Pvt.) 35, 434
Joseph (Pvt.) 35
BOGGLE, Joseph (Pvt.) 68
Ralph (Pvt.) 177
BOGGS, Aaron (Pvt.) 309
Aaron (Sgt.) 267, 302
Andrew (Sgt.) 472, 619
James (Pvt.) 57, 136, 475, 500, 508, 515
John (Capt.), 5
John (Maj.) 5
John (Pvt.) 106, 503, 508, 585, 587
Robert (Pvt.) 347, 348, 455, 478, 484
Samuel (Pvt.) 87, 119, 548
William (Pvt.) 105, 107
BOGLE, Andrew (Pvt.) 27, 250, 408, 417
James (2nd Lt.) 252
James (Pvt.) 16(2), 67, 243, 259, 445, 447, 628
Joseph (Pvt.) 243, 260, 445, 447
Ralph (Pvt.) 419
BOGS, James (Pvt.) 141
Robert (Pvt.) 466
BOHANNAN (Bohonan), William (Pvt.) 86, 384
BOICE. See Boyce.
BOID, Alexander (Pvt.) 223
BOIL, Daniel (Adj.) 194
BOLAN, Matthew (Pvt.) 246
Thomas (Adj.) 451
BOLAND, Patrick 605
Robert (Pvt.) 110
Robert (Sgt.) 125
BOLD, Adam (Pvt.) 448
Alexander (Pvt.) 226
BOLDRIDG, Thomas (Pvt.) 86
BOLE, --- (Capt.) 490, 609
David (Pvt.) 35
Thomas (Pvt.) 249
BOLF, Dennis (Pvt.) 295
BOLLAN, Robert (Pvt.) 82
BOLTON, John (Pvt.) 33, 68, 443
BONAR, James (Pvt.) 247
BONBRAKE. See Bonbreak.
BONBREAK, Daniel (Cpl.) 545
Daniel (Pvt.) 87, 119, 538
Davalt (Dewalt) (Pvt.) 74, 89, 119, 542
Frederick (Fredreck) (Pvt.) 87, 119, 538, 546

Henry (Pvt.) 74, 89, 119, 542
Peter (Petter) (Pvt.) 87, 118, 545
BONBRICK. See Bonbreak.
BONEBRAKE. See Bonbreak.
BONEBREAK. See Bonbreak.
BONEBRICK. See Bonbreak.
BOND, Hugh (Pvt.) 264, 278, 287, 311, 643
BONE, Andrew (Pvt.) 209
BONER, James (Pvt.) 473
John (Pvt.) 244, 258, 494
BONNER, James (Pvt.) 498
John (Pvt.) 479, 503, 639
BOOK, Anthony (Pvt.) 205, 214
BOOR, Michael (Pvt.) 207
BOORINGER, Leonard (Pvt.) 395
BOOSEHEAD, Phelty (Pvt.) 100
BOOVINGER, Leonard (Pvt.) 421
BORE, Nicholas (Pvt.) 207
William (Pvt.) 206
BORELAND, James (Pvt.) 114, 169, 535, 586
Mathew (Pvt.) 479
Matthew (Pvt.) 494
William (Pvt.) 480, 494, 508
BORLAND, James (Pvt.) 84, 124, 129, 540
Mathew (Pvt.) 506
Patrick (Pvt.) 199
BORNBUCK, Peter (Pvt.) 537
BOROCK, Christopher (Pvt.) 287
BORSEN, David (Pvt.) 307
BOST, Barney (Pvt.) 219
BOUGEL, Andrew (Pvt.) 35
BOULTON, John (Pvt.) 448
BOUTCH, John (Pvt.) 298
BOVARD, Robert (Pvt.) 183, 193
BOWAN, David (Pvt.) 572
Ezekiel (Pvt.) 244
BOWEN, Clifton (Pvt.) 458
David (Pvt.) 294
John (Pvt.) 64
Levy (Pvt.) 252
BOWER, George (Pvt.) 633
Jacob (Pvt.) 351
John (Pvt.) 243, 245, 258, 260
Martin (Pvt.) 178
BOWERS, Martin (Pvt.) 174
BOWL, David (Capt.) 257
BOWLAND, John (Pvt.), 181, 198 (removed)
BOWLEN (Bowlin), Patrick (Pvt.) 142, 397

BOWLS, Thomas (Pvt.), 179
BOWMAN, John (Pvt.) 157 445, 447
BOYCE (Boice), David (Pvt.), 245, 476, 509
John (Lt.) 652
John (Pvt.) 490, 505
Jonathan (Pvt.) 115
William (Pvt.) 271, 285, 314
BOYD(E), Abraham 28
Alexander (Pvt.) 209, 220
Andrew (Pvt.) 589
Daniel (Pvt.) 604
David (Pvt.) 207, 214
James (Pvt.) 65, 133, 267, 302, 309, 373, 399, 413, 415, 439
James (employed a substitute) 425
John (Pvt.) 24, 145, 646
Robert (Clerk) 127
Robert (Pvt.) 83, 100, 111, 290, 457, 548, 561
Simeon (Pvt.) 187
Thomas (Pvt.) 149, 151, 281, 292, 296, 313, 459
William (1st Lt.) 13, 31, 44, 144, 146
William (Pvt.) 68, 91, 103, 114, 130, 297, 300, 325, 336, 402, 419, 544, 569, 646, 650
BOYER, Daniel (Ens.) 112
Samuel (Pvt.) 112
BOYL(E), Andrew (Pvt.) 423
James (2nd Lt.) 252, 255
James (Pvt.) 283
Joseph (Pvt.) 249
Robert (Pvt.) 327, 337, 570
BOYL(E)S, Thomas (Pvt.) 175, 613
BOYS. See Boyce.
BOYSE. See Boyce.
BRACHER, John (Pvt.) 353
BRACKENRIDGE, John (Pvt.) 430
Samuel (Pvt.) 8, 10, 142, 429
BRACKER, John (Pvt.) 358
BRACKINBRIDGED, Samuel (Pvt.) 397
BRACKINRIDGE, John (Pvt.) 143
BRACKRING, John (Pvt.) 398
BRADEY, Hugh (Pvt.) 65, 152
BRADFORD, William (Pvt.) 105
BRADLEY, Fil (Pvt.) 435
Philip (Phillip) (Pvt.) 30, 33, 95, 149, 150, 390
William (Pvt.) 435
BRADLY, Philip (Phillip) (Pvt.) 398, 450
Thomas (Pvt.) 174
BRADY, Car. (Pvt.) 96

Coard (Pvt.) 95
Cord (Pvt.) 30, 145, 147
Ebenezer (Pvt.) 134(2), 404, 642
Hugh (Pvt.) 19, 21, 133, 134, 139
James (Pvt.) 134(2), 404, 642
Joseph (Capt.) 14, 28, 38, 45, 132
Joseph (Wagon Master) 4, 598
Samuel (Pvt.) 411, 631, 647
BRAIDY, James (Pvt.) 232
BRAKENRIDGE, Samuel (Pvt.) 416
BRAKINRIDGE, John (Pvt.) 26
BRALING, James (Pvt.) 563
BRAMEN, John 28
BRAN, Adam (Pvt.) 219
    Isaac 608
    John (Pvt.) 219, 271, 610
    Lawrence (Pvt.) 502
    Loudwick (Pvt.) 219
BRANARD, Barney (Pvt.) 191
    Barry (Pvt.) 184
BRAND, Adam (Pvt.) 225
    Isaac (Pvt.) 572
    John (Pvt.) 225, 314, 602
    Larens (Pvt.) 476
    Ludwick (Pvt.) 225
BRANDON, Carnes (Pvt.) 413
    Christopher (Pvt.) (received payment as
        a substitute) 591
    Karens (Pvt.) 437
    Kearns (Pvt.) 402
BRANEN, Christian 607
BRANK, John (Pvt.) 380
BRANN, John (Pvt.) 285
BRATEN, Samuel (Pvt.) 630
BRATING, James (Pvt.) 556, 577
BRATTAN (Bratten, Brattin, Bratton),
    Adam (Lt.) 446
    Adam (1st Lt.) 7, 10, 12, 23, 43
    Edward (Pvt.) 323, 574, 578
    George (Geoarg) (Pvt.) 326, 448
    James (Pvt.) 325, 329, 332, 552, 553,
        645
    John (Pvt.) 291, 295, 300
    John (Sgt.) 312
    Robert (Pvt.) 39, 41, 448
    Samuel (Pvt.) 33, 448, 566, 587, 645
    William (Pvt.) 332, 645
BRAY, Nicholas 605
BRAYER, Nathaniel (Pvt.) 296
BRAYN, Natt. (Pvt.) 141
BREADY (Breaddy, Breadey), Choard
    (Pvt.) 403, 419
    Cord (Pvt.) 32

Cord. (Pvt.) 391
Ebenezar (Pvt.) 440
Ebenezer (Pvt.) 387, 400, 413
Hugh (Pvt.) 18, 399, 400, 413(2), 415,
    439
James (Capt.) 627
James (Pvt.), 66, 229, 388, 400, 414(2),
    440(2)
Joseph (Pvt.) 66, 401, 414, 440
Joseph (Qtr. Master) 388
Samuel (Pvt.) 188
BREATEN, Frederick (Pvt.) 315
BREATHUNTER, William (Almoner)
    127
BRECK, Geoarg (Pvt.) 448
BREDEY, Ebenezer (Pvt.) 66
BREKENRIDGE, --- 23
BRENOUR, Peter (Pvt.) 273
BRETHERTON, James (Pvt.) 110
BREVEARD, Robert (Pvt.) 640
BREYER, Nathaniel (Pvt.) 292
BRIAM, James (Pvt.) 121
BRIAN, Alexander (Pvt.) 133, 152
    James (Pvt.) 407
    Nathaniel (Pvt.) 392
    Nathinal (Pvt.) 120
BRIAR, Peter (Pvt.) 546
BRICE, Robert (Pvt.) 393, 481, 497, 502
BRICELAN, Thomas (1st Lt.) 159
BRICELAND, Thomas (1st Lt.) 154, 165
    Thomas (Lt.) 172
BRICELIN, Thomas (Pvt.) 157
BRICKER, Jacob (Pvt.) 236, 238
    Peter (Pvt.) 230, 233
BRIDGET, Thomas (Pvt.) 567
    William (Pvt.) 264, 290, 643
BRIDGS, Andrew (1st Lt.) 323
    Thomas (Pvt.) 561
BRIER, Nathaniel (Pvt.) 313
BRIGG, Thomas (Pvt.) 330
BRIGGS (Brigs), Andrew (1st Lt.) 319,
    325, 332, 336
    Benjamin (Pvt.) 21, 37, 52, 62, 131,
        132, 151
    John (Pvt.) 495
    Joseph (Pvt.) 630
    Samuel (Pvt.) 61, 132
BRIGHT, David (Pvt.) 175, 179, 186
BRINDLE (Brindal), John (Pvt.) 219, 225
    Laurance (Pvt.) 142
    Lawrance (Pvt.) 397
    Lawrence (Pvt.) 416, 429
    Marks (Pvt.) 9

Samuel (Pvt.) 142, 152, 398, 430
BRINGHAM (Bringam), John (Pvt.) 27,
  250, 476, 484
BRINSON, William (Pvt.) 32
BRISAN. See Brison.
BRISE, Robert (Pvt.) 417
BRISELAND, Thomas 595
BRISEN. See Brison.
BRISLIN, Thomas (Lt.) 616
BRISON (Brisan, Brisen), James (Pvt.)
  220, 303
John (Pvt.) 27, 214, 250, 481, 486, 497
William (Pvt.) 34, 64, 95, 145, 147, 264,
  616
BRITAIN, Adam (1st Lt.) 444
Adam (Pvt.) 67
George (Pvt.) 68, 446
Robert (Pvt.) 68, 446
Samuel (Pvt.) 68, 446
BRITTAN, Robert (Pvt.) 37
Thomas (Pvt.) 413, 439
BRITTON, Samuel (Pvt.) 31
Thomas (Pvt.) 426
BROADLEY, Thomas (Pvt.) 178
BROATING, Edward (Pvt.) 562
BRODLAY, William (Pvt.) 449
BROKING, George (Pvt.) 562
BROOKS, --- (Ens.) 210, 212
David (Pvt.) 208, 220, 226
Henry (Ens.) 162, 166, 170
Henry (Pvt.) 160
James (Ens.) 217, 616
John (Maj.) 22, 153, 163, 595(2), 596
John (Pvt.) 298, 306
Robert (Pvt.) 117
Samuel (Ens.) 203
Samuel (Pvt.) 229, 233
Thomas (Pvt.) 273, 298, 305
BROOKY, John (Pvt.) 382
BROON, Robert (Pvt.) 35
William (Pvt.) 35
BROTEN, James (Pvt.) 564
BROTHERENTEN (Brotherenton,
  Brotherington) James (Pvt.), 114,
  129, 311
BROTHERINTON, James (1st Lt.) 535
BROTHERTON, James (1st Lt.) 168,
  511, 514, 516, 532, 539
James (Lt.) 580
James (Pvt.) 82, 83, 108, 548
Joseph (1st Lt.) 512
Robert (Pvt.) 82, 267, 302, 309
William (Pvt.) 267, 302, 548, 597

BROWM, James (Pvt.) 123
BROWN, Alexander 645
Alexander (Col.) 555, 557, 559, 560,
  562, 563, 564, 573, 576, 578, 644,
  649
Alexander (Lt. Col.) 30, 319, 323, 332,
  549
Alexander (Pvt.) 298, 300, 306, 323,
  459
Allen (Alan Alen) (Pvt.), 86, 121, 128,
  141, 384, 393, 515
Andrew (Pvt.) 220, 223, 226
Benjamin (Pvt.) 323, 336, 560, 568,
  581, 636
David (Pvt.) 195, 331, 640
Esiah (Pvt.) 415
George (Pvt.) 58, 269, 282, 352, 353,
  358(2), 454, 457, 466
Henry (Pvt.) 265, 292, 296, 313, 643
James 607
James (Pvt.) 52, 78, 97, 101, 126, 149,
  151, 176, 183, 193, 285, 292, 313,
  325, 336, 389, 396, 422, 433, 507,
  562, 569(2), 574, 579, 648
James (substitute?) 657
John 595
John (1st Lt.) 328
John (2nd Lt.) 240, 244, 254, 258
John (Ens.) 154, 160, 164
John (Pvt.) 48, 49, 140, 145, 168, 182,
  199, 251, 292, 296, 313, 325, 330,
  336, 338, 383, 438, 479, 494, 503,
  515, 561, 562, 564, 566, 570, 574,
  576, 579, 583, 597, 649
John (Pvt.) 120, 126 , 128
Jonathan (Pvt.) 84, 193, 573
Joseph (1st Lt.) 321, 324, 334
Joseph (Capt.) 550
Joseph (Pvt.) 332, 558
Joseph (Scout) 626
Joshua (Capt.) 562
Josiah (Pvt.) 57, 135, 395, 420, 432, 589
Michael (Pvt.) 553, 630, 646, 650
Moses (Pvt.) 214
Nathaniel (Pvt.) 563, 581, 635, 648
Nethanel (Pvt.) 574, 579
Oliver (Pvt.) 292, 296
Robert (Pvt.) 27, 35, 56, 250, 480, 487,
  494, 573, 587, 633
Rodger (Pvt.) 347
Samuel (Pvt.) 325, 560
Sims (Pvt.) 299, 301
Sinsey (Pvt.) 281

Thomas (Pvt.) 104, 331, 357 (substitute for Thomas Williams), 489, 560, 621, 624

William (Pvt.) 26, 35, 114, 124, 129, 163, 176, 183, 193, 244, 250, 258, 277, 331, 353, 358, 414, 440, 445, 447, 457, 480, 489, 494, 541, 553, 597, 618, 624, 646

William (Pvt.) (Scout) 487

BROWNE, John (Pvt.) 195

Thomas (Pvt.) 555

BROWNFIELD, John (Pvt.) 16, 17, 133, 135

BROWNJON, Richard (Sgt.) 300

BROWNLEE, John (Pvt.) 208, 219, 267, 302

BROWNSON, Richard (Sgt.) 298, 304

Richard (Surgeon) 367, 375

BRUCE, Robert (Pvt.) 423

BRUMBOUGH, Conrad (Pvt.) 273

BRUMF(I)ELD, John (Pvt.) 65, 400, 413, 426, 439

BRYAN, James (Pvt.) 86, 128

Nathaniel (Pvt.) 86, 128, 515, 620

Stophel (Pvt.) 540

William (Cpl.) 620

William (Pvt.) 30

BRYANS, Nathaniel (Pvt.) 384

BRYCE, Robert (Pvt.) 408, 441

BRYONS, James (Pvt.) 132

BRYSON, James (Pvt.) 209, 223, 226, 278, 287, 311

John (Pvt.) 206

William (Pvt.) 31, 278, 287

BUAGE, Samuel (Pvt.) 478

BUCH, Jacob (Pvt.) 482

BUCHANAN (Buchannan, Buchanon, Buckhanan, Buckhanen, Buckhannan, Buckhanon, Buckhonan), Archibald (Pvt.) In the service of the U.S., 20 Jan - 30 March 1778. 91, 103, 109, 575, 582

Arthur (Sub. Lt.), 3, 555 (Bachanan)

Arthur (Col.) 29, 319, 323, 332, 600, 608

Arthur (Pvt.) 630

Daved (Pvt.) 366

James (Pvt.) 604

John (Capt.) 341, 360, 453, 460, 464, 469

John (Pvt.) 23, 61, 131, 207, 251, 485, 501, 510

John (Sgt.) 27, 651

Robert (Robart) (Pvt.) 331, 554, 556, 561, 577

Samuel (Pvt.) 346, 356, 366

Thomas (Sub. Lt.) 3

Thomas 175, 179, 181, 183, 185, 190, 192, 194, 196, 198

William (Cpl.) 620

William (Pvt.) 141, 393, 515

BUCKHONAN, George (Pvt.) 441

John (Cpl.) 441

BUCK, George (Pvt.) 68, 446

George (Pvt.) (substitute) 657

Jacob (Pvt.) 501, 502, 510, 244

BUCKHOLDER, Adam (Pvt.), 280

Chrisly (Pvt.) 289

Christifer (Pvt.) 279

John (Pvt.) 280, 290

BUCKLEY, William (Pvt.) 87, 597

BUCKS, Anthony (Pvt.) 9

BUDD, David (Pvt.) 243, 260

BUDLEERY, William (Pvt.) 538

BULL, Henry (Pvt.) 344, 347, 349

John (Lt.) (Scout) 652

Thomas (Ens.) 242, 259

William (Pvt.) 347, 349

BURCH, Jacob (Pvt.) 325

BURCHFIELD, Aguil(l)a (Pvt.) 56, 633

Aquar (Pvt.) 251

James (Pvt.) 509, 651

Quilla (Pvt.) 573

Thomas (Pvt.) 476, 505

BURCK, Francis (Pvt.) 163

BURDAY, John (Pvt.) 478

BURG(E), Jacob (Pvt.) 563, 568, 574, 578

John (Pvt.) 563, 567

Samuel (Pvt.) 472, 484, 619

BURGES, Jacob (Pvt.) 648

BURINGOR, Christy (Pvt.) 58

BURK, Edward (Pvt.) 588

Francis (Pvt.) 186

William (Sgt.) 103, 137

BURKDULL, Joseph (Pvt.) 93

BURKE, William (Sgt.) 76, 91

BURKET, Adam (Pvt.) 94, 117

BURKHAMMER, Leonard (Pvt.) 542, 546

Lodewick (Pvt.) 546

Ludwick (Pvt.) 542

BURKHAMNER, Lodowick (Pvt.) 538

BURKHOLDER, Adam (Pvt.), 290(2)

Jacob (Pvt.) 185, 191

BURLEY, James (Pvt.) 361

John (Pvt.) 342, 361
Joshua (Pvt.), 342
BURNET, Adam (Pvt.) 175, 186
John (Pvt.) 448
BURNHET(T)ER, John (Pvt.), 221 (1
Aug 1780 - "run off"), 227
BURNS, Andrew (Pvt.) 612
James 606
James (Pvt.) 31, 58, 136, 366, 389, 396,
421, 433, 565, 590, 656
John (Pvt.) 72, 94, 117, 249, 567, 630,
566
Patrick (Pvt.) 52, 557
William (Pvt.) 561
BURNSIDE(S), William (Pvt.) 344, 365,
622, 607
BURRIS, Ebenezer (Ebonezer) (Pvt.)
470, 602
William (Pvt.) 476
BURST, Burnets (Pvt.) 9
BURTNET(T) (Burtnott),
Adam (Pvt.) 179, 613
Robert (Pvt.) 342, 361
BUSH, Barny (Pvt.) 225
Conrad (Conrod) (Pvt.) 76, 92, 104,
138, 549
Martin (Pvt.) 309
Nic(h)olas (Pvt.) 160, 174, 188, 197
William (Pvt.) 76, 92
BUSTON, Samuel (Pvt.) 96
BUTCHEY, James (Pvt.) 276
BUZ(Z)ARD, Henry (Pvt.) 278, 311
John (Pvt.) 277, 286, 288, 311
BYARD, James (Pvt.) 460
John (Pvt.) 538
BYARS (Byers), David (Ens.) 341, 366
Fred (Pvt.) 130
Frederick (Fred) (Pvt.), 75, 84(2), 114,
115, 130, 540(2)
Jacob (Pvt.) 174, 179
James (Pvt.) 174, 192, 346, 366
Samuel (Pvt.) 456, 466
William (Pvt.) 206
BYRNE, James (Pvt.) 412
BYRNS, Charles (Pvt.) 633
BYRONS, Patrick (Pvt.) 604
BYSON, William (Pvt.) 311, 643

-C-
CAGHEY, John 607
CAIN, John (Pvt.), 540(2)
Martin (Pvt.) 246, 505
Tubal (Pvt.) 651, 653

CAINER, Conrod (Pvt.) 398
CAIRISH, Hamigle (Pvt.) 183
CAIZEY, John (Pvt.) 297, 305
CALAGHIN, William (Pvt.) 298
CALAHAM, Jeremiah (Pvt.) 104, 138
CALAHAN, Jeremiah (Pvt.) 92
Patrick (Pvt.) 225
CALAVEGHON, William (Pvt.) 306
CALBREATH, Andrew (Pvt.) 592
William (Pvt.) 406
CALDWELL, --- (Pvt.) 528
Bratten (Pvt.) 181
David (Pvt.) 278, 287, 311, 372
Hugh (Cpl.) 529
Hugh (Pvt.) 268, 281, 303, 310
Hugh (Sgt.) 537
James 28
James (Ens.) 370, 379, 381
James (Lt.) 260, 301, 309
James (Pvt.) 8, 58, 150, 263, 288, 302,
309, 389 ("took up a deserter"), 396,
421, 433
John (Ens.) 260, 266, 301, 309
John (Pvt.) 82, 110, 318
Joseph (Pvt.) 268, 303, 310, 318, 643
Robert (Pvt.) 263, 268(2), 303(2),
310(2), 318, 374, 643
Samuel (Lt.) 266
CALERY, John (Pvt.) 273
CALHOON, Adam (Pvt.) 208, 224
Hugh (Pvt.) 409, 442
James (Pvt.) 433, 558
James (Scout) 625
John (Committee of Observation) 4
John (Pvt.) 134, 232, 414, 440, 544, 549
John (Pvt.) 125
Samuel (Pvt.) 207
CALHOUN, Adam (Pvt.) 218
George (1st Lt.) 613
George (Pvt.) 328
Hugh (Pvt.) 393
James (Pvt.) 336, 375
John (Pvt.) 39, 210, 229, 405
Samuel (Pvt.) 215
CALHOUNE, James (Pvt.) 570
John (Pvt.) 110
John (Pvt.) (Dr.) 81
John (Pvt.) 82
CALL, William (Pvt.) 327
CALLAHAN, Jeremiah (Pvt.) 76, 576,
583
Patrick (Pvt.) 219
CALLEHON, William (Pvt.) 647

14

CALLENDER, Robert (Col.) 5
Robert (Committee of Observation) 4
CALLER, Adam (Pvt.) 408
James (Pvt.) 408
Samuel (Pvt.) 409
CALLEY, William (Pvt.) 20
CALLY, Joseph (Pvt.), 291
CALNED, James (Pvt.) 267
CALTER Samuel (Pvt.), 61
CALVER, John (Pvt.) 244, 259
CALVERT, Daniel (Pvt.) 52
CALWELL, James (Pvt.) 24, 148
CAMBEL, Francis (Pvt.) 604
James (Pvt.) 183
John (Pvt.) 183, 435
Joseph (Pvt.) 182
Patrick (Pvt.) 195
Robert (Ens.) 182
William (Pvt.) 183
CAMBLE, David (Pvt.) 294
James (Pvt.) 294
John (Pvt.) 460, 538
Robert (Pvt.) 558
CAMBPHEL, Alexander (Pvt.) 611
CAMBRIDGE, Archibald (Pvt.) 143
John (Pvt.) 431
CAMERON, Alexander (Pvt.), 649(2)
Duncan (Pvt.) 325, 559
James (Pvt.), 457
CAMLIN, William (Pvt.) C. makr. 126
CAMOL, Jeremiah (Pvt.) 540
CAMON, John (Pvt.) 328
CAMPBEL, Alexander (Pvt.) 629
Daniel (Pvt.) 632
John (Pvt.) 269
CAMPBELL, --- (Capt.) 62, 141, 490,
509
Alexander (Pvt.), 354(2)
Andrew (Pvt.) 61, 132, 271, 408, 409,
417, 423, 424, 441, 442
Andrew (Sgt.) 285, 314
Archibald 605
Archibald (Pvt.) 160
Daniel (Pvt.) 56, 180, 475, 492, 500,
573
David (Pvt.) 264, 274, 308, 642
Edward (Sgt.) 60
Francis (Pvt.) 273, 307, 625
Hercules (Pvt.) (Scout) 652
James (Pvt.) 27, 176, 193, 250, 271,
272, 284, 285(2), 304, 314
John 608
John (Capt.) 28, 31, 33, 44, 141, 443,

609, 627
John (Ens.) 328, 335
John (Pvt.) 41, 61(3), 82, 131(2: One
listed as Senr. and other "at
McMulen's"), 132 (Senr.), 176, 274,
283, 293, 294, 297, 299, 307, 313,
330, 355, 364, 391, 394, 408, 409,
409, 423, 431, 441, 442(2), 455, 466,
548, 558, 567, 617, 650
John (Scout) 626
John (Sgt.) 18, 60, 131, 408 (miller),
423
Joseph (Pvt.) 61, 132, 389 ("gon"), 396,
409, 427, 432
Patrick (Light Dragoon) 640
Patrick (Pvt.) 81, 109, 110, 125, 265,
270, 283, 547, 615
Robert (Ens.) 171, 192, 194
Robert (Pvt.) 174, 252, 298, 305, 327,
337, 406, 570
Robert (Scout) 625
Rodger (Pvt.) 289, 303
Roger (Cpl.) 277
Roger (Pvt.) 311
Samuel (Pvt.) 141, 515
Ter. (Capt.) 125
Terence (Capt.) 127
Terence (Qtr. Master) 530
Terrence (Pvt.) 528, 548
Terrence (Qtr. Master) 511
Thomas 605
Thomas (Capt.) 613
Thomas (Lt.) 314
Thomas (Pvt.) 61, 131, 208, 271, 284,
289, 393, 409
Torrence (Qtr. Master) 531
William (Capt.) 474, 499
William (Pvt.) 7, 15, 17, 61(2), 88, 98,
131, 142, 151, 185, 194, 252, 271,
373, 408, 417, 423, 427, 430, 441,
480, 487, 494, 507, 618, 621
CAMPBLE, John (Capt.) 13
John (Pvt.) 365, 398
Robert (Pvt.) 179, 398
Samuel (Pvt.) 402, 419
William (Pvt.) 397
CAMREN, James (Pvt.) 350
CANADAY, John (Pvt.) 61
CANADY, James (Pvt.) 631
John (Pvt.) 515
CANAN, James (Pvt.) 621
CANN, William (Pvt.) 434
CANNAN, James (Sgt.) 618

CANNIDY, James (Pvt.) 450
CANNON, James (Pvt.) 487
CANNUN, James (Pvt.) 480, 494
CANNY, Thomas (Pvt.) 621
CANSOLUS, Richard (Pvt.) 552
CAPBELL, James (Pvt.) 314
CAPEHART, Andrew (Pvt.) 94, 116
  Henry (Pvt.) 71, 94, 117
CAPPER, John (Pvt.) 124
  Jonathan (Pvt.) 114, 129
CARBERRY, Joseph (Pvt.) 473
CARBEY, Joseph (Pvt.) 498
CARBRIE, John (Pvt.) 251
CARBURY, Joseph (Pvt.) 257
CARD, Anthony (Pvt.) 538
CARE, Thomas (Pvt.) 137
  William (Pvt.) 570
CARENS, John (Pvt.) 476
CARES, William (Pvt.) 643
CARGILL, David (Pvt.), 247, 476
CARITHERS John (Pvt.), 167
CARLEIL, John (Pvt.) 410
CARLILE, John (Pvt.) 448, 574, 578,
  648
CARLISLE, John 27
  John (Pvt.) 36, 40, 68, 326, 446, 563,
  568, 631
CARLON, James (Pvt.) 103
CARLOW, James (Pvt.) 114, 124, 129,
  540, 575, 583
CARLYLE, John (Pvt.) 191
CARMADAY, James (Pvt.) 121
CARMADY, James (Pvt.) 515
CARMEDAY, James (Pvt.) 412
CARMEDEY, James (Pvt.) 393
CARMICHAEL, John (Pvt.) 111
  Thomas (Pvt.) 207
CARMODY, James (Pvt.) 86, 128, 384
CARMUDY, James (Pvt.) 620
CARN, James (Pvt.) 573
CARNAGHAN, Robert (Pvt.) 478
  William (Pvt.) 491
CARNAHAN, --- (Maj.) 51
  Adam (Pvt.) 30, 32, 64(2), 95(2), 145,
  147, 391, 403(2), 407, 419, 420, 437,
  438
  James (Maj.) 11, 20, 42, 595
  John (Pvt.) 653
  Joseph (Pvt.) 146, 631, 657
  Joseph (Sgt.) 63, 402, 418, 436
  Robert 606
  Robert (Pvt.) 402, 417, 418, 436
  William (Pvt.) 251

CARNAHON, Robert (Pvt.) 425, 636
CARNAUGHAN, Adam (Pvt.) 411
  Joseph (Pvt.) 411
CARNEDAY, James (Pvt.) 141
CARNEGHAN, William (Pvt.), 479
CARNES John (Pvt.) 502
CARNS, William (Pvt.) 456
CAROTHER, John 196
  John (Capt.) 198
CAROTHERS, Andrew (Pvt.) 198
  Armstrong (Pvt.) 181, 198
  Charles (Pvt.) 440
  Ezekiel (Pvt.) 616
  James (Pvt.), 181, 198
  John (1st Lt.) 155, 161, 165
  John (Capt.) 5, 6, 172, 179, 217, 227,
  233
  John (Lt.), 3, 590, 591(2), 592(2),
  593(2), 594, 595(2)
  John (Pvt.) 157, 180, 197
  John 531
  Martin (Pvt.) 181, 198
  Samuel (Pvt.) 225, 616
  Thomas (Pvt.) 215
  William (Pvt.) 180, 197, 209, 225
CARPENTER, Gabl. (Pvt.) 169
  Gabriel (Pvt.) 76, 576, 583, 599
  Gabril (Pvt.) 84
  Thomas (Pvt.) 431
CARPINER, Gabril (Pvt.) 130
CARPINTR, Gabriel (Pvt.) 115
CARR, John (2nd Lt.) 527, 547
  Michael (Pvt.) 143
  William (Scout) 625
CARRALL, William (Pvt.) 408
CARREL, William 605
  William (Pvt.) 620
CARRELL, Jeremiah (Pvt.) 586
  William (Pvt.) 24, 61, 131
CARREN, James (Pvt.) 482, 497
CARROL, Jarad (Pvt.) 114
  Jerry (Pvt.) 291
  John (2nd Lt.) 513
  William (Pvt.) 417, 423
CARROTHERS, John (Pvt.) 635
  Thomas (Pvt.) 178
CARSON, Archibald (Pvt.) 279, 288, 312
  Becraft (Pvt.) 413
  Beeraft (Pvt.) 439
  Benjamin (Pvt.) 437
  David (Pvt.) 455, 624
  Henry (Pvt.) 247, 475, 500
  James (Pvt.) 403, 407, 420, 438, 461

John (Pvt.) 64, 145, 147, 392, 403, 419, 437
Robert (Pvt.) 343, 625, 655
William (Pvt.) 327, 437, 459, 565, 574, 579, 649, 650
CARSWEL, Robert (Pvt.) 556
CARSWELL, Andrew (Pvt.) 579, 649
David (Pvt.) 337, 558
David (Scout) 626
Elidga (Pvt.) 574, 579
Elijah (Pvt.) 338, 569
Elisah (Ens.) 324
Elisha (Ens.) 320
Elisha (Pvt.) 569, 646
Elysha (Pvt.) 574, 579
James (Pvt.) 558
Robert (Pvt.) 125, 611
Robert (Sgt.) 557
CARTER, John (Pvt.) 136, 395, 419, 437
William (Pvt.) 152
CARTEY, William (Pvt.) 21
CARTY, William (Pvt.) 85, 120, 127, 139, 140, 515, 620
CARUTHERS, Benjamin (Pvt.) 278, 311
James (Pvt.) 186
John (Capt.) 176, 181
John (Lt.) 592
John (Pvt.) 187, 248
Martin (Pvt.) 176
Robert (Pvt.) 186
Samuel (Pvt.) 219
William (Pvt.) 219
CARVAN, Thomas (Pvt.) 597
CARVER, John (2nd Lt.) 166
John (Pvt.) 221, 227
CASHNER, Adam (Pvt.) 296, 382
CASKEY, Archibal (Pvt.) 137
Archibald (Pvt.) 124
James (Pvt.) 91
Robert (Pvt.) 391, 398, 431, 656
CASKY, Archebald (Pvt.) 103
James (Pvt.) 103
Robert (Pvt.) 143
CASLEY, John (Pvt.) 85
CASNER, Adam (Pvt.) 91, 313
CASPER, William (Pvt.) 563
CASSADY, John 28
CASWELL, Benjamin (Pvt.) 327
Elijah (Pvt.) 326
Elisha (Ens.) 325
Elisha (Pvt.) 646
James (Pvt.) 326
John 608

Master (Pvt.) 275
CATTER, Samuel (Pvt.) 620
CAUGHEY, John (Pvt.) 191
CAUGHRIN, Hugh (Pvt.) 142
CAUL, John (Pvt.) 329
CAULINS, John (Pvt.) 205
CAUM, John (Pvt.) 329
CAVAN, James (Pvt.) 7, 139, 433, 589
CAVAT, Pattrick (Pvt.) 101
CAVEN, James (Pvt.) 478
William (Pvt.) 152
CAVET, Patrick (Pvt.) 91, 137
CAVIN, James (Pvt.) 10
CAVIT, Patrick (Pvt.) 576, 583
CAWL, Samuel (Pvt.) 329
CEACE, Melcher (Pvt.) 306
CEASE, Balsor (Pvt.) 112
Balsure (Cpl.) 541
Casper (Pvt.) 542, 585
Gasper (Pvt.) 123
Melcar (Pvt.) 89
Welker (Pvt.) 542
CEESE, Casper (Pvt.) 89
Jasper (Pvt.) 112
CEGLE, Jacob (Pvt.) 504
CELLAR, Jacob (Pvt.) 91
CELLON, Adam (Pvt.) 20
CENTRY, Dinas (Pvt.) 413
CEPHART, John (Pvt.) 308
CESNA, James (Fifer) 641
Theo (Ens.) 429
William (2nd Lt.) 377
William (Pvt.) 642, 643
CESNEY, Theophilus (Ens.) 397
Theophilus (Pvt.) 143
CESSNA, James (Pvt.) 96, 396, 422, 433
Stephen (Pvt.) 395, 421
William (2nd Lt.) 369
William (Pvt.) 290
CEVER, John (Pvt.) 566
Samuel (Ens.) 564
CHAIN, John (Pvt.) 35, 247
William (Pvt.) 456
CHALMBERS, William (Col.) 59
CHAMBER, William (Col.) 601
CHAMBERS, Benjamin (Pvt.) 81, 109
   ("took up a deserter"), 110, 125, 297, 305, 360, 437, 455, 622
Charles (Pvt.) 74, 88, 298, 305, 538, 544
Daniel (Pvt.) 354
Ezachael (Pvt.) 119
Ezekial (Pvt.) 546
Ezekiel (Pvt.) 538

Ezikel (Pvt.) 87
George (Pvt.) 82, 110, 126
James (Pvt.) 218, 224
John (Pvt.) 189, 231, 235, 616
John (Sgt.) 633
Joseph (Light Dragoon) 640
Joseph (Pvt.) 82, 111, 126, 548
Joseph (Pvt.) (Light Dragoon) 77
Randal (Pvt.) 507
Randall (Pvt.) 495
Randels (Pvt.) 510
Randle (Pvt.) 651
Ranold (Pvt.) 258
Robert (Pvt.) 330, 422, 433, 590, 567
William (Capt.), 6
William (Col.) 20, 51, 201, 210, 470,
    602, 603, 604, 609
William (Pvt.) 83, 100, 111, 116, 126,
    549
CHANE, John (Pvt.) 35
CHAPMAN, Amos (Pvt.) 574, 578
Amos (Sgt.) 648
John (Pvt.), 200(2)
CHARLES, George (Pvt.) 73, 80
CHEAMBERS, Robart (Pvt.) 561
CHENET, William (Pvt.) 251
CHENO, William (Pvt.) 630
CHERYNY, William (Pvt.) 572
CHESNEY, Thomas (Pvt.) 637
William (Pvt.) 480, 492, 495, 632
CHESNUT, Benjamin (Pvt.) 83, 100
William (Pvt.) 182, 420, 425, 432, 636
CHESSNO, John (Pvt.) 276
CHESTNUT, John (Pvt.) 183
Samuel (Pvt.) 183
Thomas (Pvt.) 277, 288
William (Pvt.) 167, 416
CHESTNUTT, Thomas (Pvt.) 286, 311
CHEW, Robert (Pvt.) 455
CHILDERS, Joseph (Pvt.) 353, 358, 457
CHINA, William (Pvt.) 630
CHISNEY, William (Pvt.), 56
CHRICENSTONES, George (Pvt.) 136
CHRISEY, Jacob (Pvt.) 79
CHRISTEY, Dennis (Pvt.) 492
Dinace (Pvt.) 495
James (Pvt.) 630
CHRISTIE, Denis (Pvt.) 251
CHRISTY, Archibald (Pvt.) 622
Daniel (Pvt.) 84
David (Pvt.) 207
Dennis (Pvt.) 480
James (Pvt.) 563

Robert (Pvt.) 68, 445
William (Pvt.) 496
CHRONKLETON, Joseph (Pvt.) 540
CHUNCK, Simon (Pvt.) 517
CHUNK, Simon (Pvt.) 519, 586
CIELLAND, Adam (Pvt.) 161
CILGORE, Joseph (Pvt.) 85
CINCLAIR, Neal (Pvt.) 571
CIRGILL, David (Pvt.) 35
CISH, Christiphor (Pvt.) 58
CISNA, James (Pvt.) 58, 136, 590
Stephen (Pvt.) 62, 136, 589
Theaphilus (Ens.) 410
Theofles (Ens.) 386
CISNEY, James (Pvt.) 404
CISSNA, Stephen (Pvt.) 51, 57
Thomas (Ens.) 630
CLAIN, Patrick (Pvt.) 359
Thomas (Pvt.) 359
William (Pvt.) 358
CLANCEY, Lawrance (Pvt.) 413
Lawrence (Pvt.) 426
CLANCY, Lawrance (Pvt.) 400, 439
CLANDENNING, John (Pvt.) 218
CLANDININ, John (1st Lt.) 208
CLANDINNEN, James (Pvt.), 484
CLANEY Thomas (Pvt.) 373
CLAPPER, Henry (Cpl.) 93, 116
CLAPSADDLE, George (Pvt.) 266, 299
John (Pvt.) 298
Michael (Pvt.) 297, 300, 305
CLAPSADLE, Daniel (Capt.), 614
George (Pvt.) 301, 306, 643
John (Pvt.) 300, 305
CLAPSADLER, Daniel (Capt.) 92, 94,
    115, 117
Michael (Pvt.) 304
CLAPSIDER, Daniel (Capt.) 69
CLARCK, George (Pvt.) 84, 115, 130
Robert (Pvt.) 130
CLARK, Alexander (Pvt.) 353, 355, 358,
    362, 364, 466
Andrew (Pvt.) 318
Charles 606
Charles (Cpl.) 618
Charles (Pvt.) 56, 252, 480, 487, 494,
    572, 621
Frances (Pvt.) 579
Francis (Pvt.) 330, 561, 574, 597, 630,
    648
George (Cpl.) 180
George (Pvt.) 76, 133, 134, 180, 197,
    297, 300, 415

18

Isaac (Pvt.) 302, 309
James (Pvt.) 18, 21, 81, 109, 110, 139,
  142, 310, 356, 365, 366, 398, 521,
  523, 572
James (Sgt.) 587
John (Pvt.) 18, 19, 21, 82, 110, 133,
  135, 139, 152, 176, 195, 236, 238,
  303, 310, 355, 364, 365(2), 395, 421,
  443, 617
John (Sgt.) 33, 142
Joseph 607
Joseph (Pvt.) 90, 99, 113, 483, 485, 501,
  510, 543
Robert 28, 606
Robert (Pvt.) 23, 26, 73, 80, 102, 133,
  134, 355, 364, 365, 400, 467, 653,
  654
Samuel (Pvt.) 263, 267, 302, 442, 643
Thomas (Capt.) 5, 454, 461, 465
Thomas (Pvt.) 16, 47, 83, 85, 100, 111,
  200, 219, 225, 268, 303, 366, 516,
  561, 626
Thomas (Sgt.) 55, 141, 515
William 605
William (Lt. Col.) 5, 9, 153
William (Pvt.) 47, 48, 55, 61, 131, 180,
  197, 218, 224, 263, 268, 303, 310,
  560, 620
William (Pvt.) 24
CLARKE, Francis (Pvt.) 567
George (Pvt.) 65
James (Pvt.) 152
John (Pvt.) 65
William (Paymaster) 4
CLAWSON, Peter (Pvt.) 342, 361
Richard (Pvt.) 341, 361, 363
CLAY, David (Pvt.) 252, 488, 499
CLAYMENS, David (Pvt.) 653
CLAYTON, David 606
David (Ens.) 479, 494
David (Pvt.) 248
John (Pvt.) 225
Philip (Pvt.) 243, 259
CLE, David (Pvt.) 474
CLEATON, John (Pvt.) 219
CLEAVR, Barney (Pvt.) 219
CLEELAND, Adam (Pvt.) 195
CLELLAND, Adam (Sub.) 140
CLEMANS, David (Pvt.) 504
CLEMENS, Alexander (Pvt.) 176, 183,
  617
CLEMMANS, David (Pvt.) 654
CLEMMONS, David (Pvt.) 478

CLEMONS, David (Pvt.) 490
CLENDENEN, James (Pvt.) 472, 478
CLENDENING, Samuel (Pvt.) 209
CLENDENNIN, John (1st Lt.) 203, 212
John (Pvt.) 622
CLENDININ, James (Pvt.) 243
CLENNING, James (Pvt.) 619
CLERK, Charles (Pvt.) 632
George (Pvt.) 399, 413, 439
James (Pvt.) 125
John (Pvt.) 126, 400, 439
Robert (Pvt.) 66, 413, 439
Samuel (Pvt.) 424
Thomas (Pvt.) 126
William (Lt. Col.) 163
CLERY, John (Pvt.), 294
CLEVER, Barney (Pvt.) 225
John (Pvt.) 645
CLIDE, William (Pvt.) 472, 478, 484,
  619
CLIFFORD, John (Pvt.) 149, 150
CLINCEY, Larance (Pvt.), 405 (for John
  Simrell)
CLINCHY, Lary (Pvt.) 588
CLINCOY, Lawrence (Pvt.) 642
CLINDENNON, John (Pvt.) 224
CLINDIEN, Samuel (Lt.) 216
CLINDNEN, James (Pvt.) 259
CLINE, Andrew (Pvt.) 162
CLITON, Philip (Pvt.) 259
CLIVES, Thomas (Pvt.) 276
CLOID, Soloman (Pvt.) 404
Solomon (Pvt.) 641
CLOUSER, Jacob (Pvt.), 186, 248
CLOVER Philip (Pvt.) (Scout) 652
CLOWZER, Simon (Pvt.) (Drum Maj.),
  178
CLOYD, Solomon (Pvt.) 389, 396, 421,
  433
CLUCAS, John M. (Cpl.) 87
CLUGSTON, John (Pvt.) 83, 108, 114
Jonathan (Pvt.) 129
Robert (Pvt.) 83, 108, 114, 129, 514,
  539
William (Pvt.) 84, 114, 130, 541
COALMAN, William (Pvt.) 414, 440
COAN, James (Pvt.) 619
COARD, John (Pvt.) 366
COARY, Joseph (Pvt.) 586
COATES, Alexander (Pvt.) 186
COATS, Alexander (Pvt.) 181, 198
Richard (Pvt.) 181
COBURN, James (Pvt.) 360, 365, 622

John (Pvt.) 360, 622
William (Pvt.) 344, 360, 374, 622
COCHRAN, Alexander (Pvt.) 249, 484, 559
David 607
David (Pvt.) 209, 591
Jacob (Pvt.) 586
John (Ens.) 170
John (Pvt.) 159, 174, 272, 275, 390, 527, 596
John (Sgt.) 93, 106, 115
Samuel (Pvt.) 72, 78, 106, 523, 527, 544, 585, 623
William (Pvt.) 111, 209, 548
COCHRANE, John (Pvt.) 530
COCHY, John (Pvt.) 382
COCK, John (Pvt.) 308, 375
COCKLEY, John (Pvt.) 229, 232
CODLER, Steven (Pvt.) 75
CODLOR, Stephen (Pvt.), 84
COEN, James (Pvt.) 472
COFFE Robert (Pvt.) 443
COFFEE, Robert (Pvt.) 590
Robert (Sgt.) 57, 420
Thomas (Pvt.) 20, 139, 589
COFFEY, Michael (Pvt.) 302, 309
Robert (Pvt.) 31, 34, 444
Robert (Sgt.) 395, 432
Thomas (Pvt.) 18, 21, 152
COFFMAN, Christn. (Cpl.) 541
Christopher (Pvt.) 112
Frederick (Pvt.) 90, 113
George (Pvt.) 90, 542
Henry (Pvt.) 90, 113
Jacob (Pvt.) 90, 99, 543
COFFY, James (Pvt.) 57
Robert (Sgt.) 135
COFMAN, Frederick (Pvt.) 75
George (Pvt.) 74
Henry (Pvt.) 75
COGHRAN, Alexander (Pvt.) 478
William (Pvt.) 126
COHAN, Charles (Pvt.) 180, 197
John (Pvt.) 635, 647
COIL, Henry (Pvt.) 126
Manes (Pvt.) 273
COIN, Thomas (Pvt.) 56
COINER, Conrad (Ens.) 161, 166
Conrad (Pvt.) 391, 431
George (Pvt.) 159, 248
Yargle (Pvt.) 160
COLBERT, Daniel (Pvt.) 48, 59, 140, 383, 515

Joshua (Pvt.) 233
COLBERTS, Daniel (Pvt.), 603
COLDRIGE, Thoms. (Pvt.) 412
COLDWELL, James (Pvt.) 136
COLE, John 606
John (Pvt.) 114, 540
Jonathan (Pvt.) 84, 129
Joshua (Pvt.) 130, 519, 540
Josiah (Pvt.) 524
Josua (Pvt.) 84
Samuel 606
Samuel (Pvt.) 566
COLEMAN, John (Pvt.) 282, 625
Michael (Pvt.) 625
Nicholas (Pvt.) 76, 92
William (Pvt.) 617
COLERY, Daniel (Pvt.) 274
John (Pvt.) 274, 293
COLETREP, William (Pvt.) 102
COLHOON, Hugh (Pvt.) 424
James (Pvt.) 57, 136, 395, 421, 589
John (Pvt.) 401, 589, 590
COLIVELL, James (Pvt.) 10
COLL, William (Pvt.) 327
COLLENS, John (Pvt.) 251
Patrick (Pvt.) 446
Solomon (Pvt.) 619, 632, 639
thomas (Pvt.) 338
COLLEPTER, Hugh McGill 566
COLLER, James (Pvt.) 441
COLLERS, Samuel (Pvt.) 442
COLLINGS, Solomon (Pvt.) 572
COLLINS, Brice (Pvt.) 249, 475, 500
David (Pvt.) 373
Henry (Pvt.) 24
Moses (Pvt.) 654
Moses (Sgt.) 653
Patrick (Pvt.) 448
Pierce (Pvt.) 486
Robert (Pvt.) 590
Samuel (Pvt.) 472
Solomon (Pvt.) 56, 478, 504, 651
Thomas (Pvt.) 326
COLLONS, Thomas (Pvt.), 644
COLMAN, William (Pvt.) 134 180
COLONS, Solomon (Pvt.) 508
COLTER, Adam (Pvt.) 417
Andrew (Pvt.) 230
Francis (Pvt.) 345
John (Pvt.) 345, 391, 398, 657
Joseph (Pvt.) 337
Samuel (Pvt.) 132, 394
COLTHER, David (Lt.) 649

COLWELL, James (Pvt.) 590
COMB, Frederick (Pvt.) 329
COMBLE, John (Pvt.) 450
COMINS, John (Pvt.) 15
COMMEL, Alexander (Pvt.) 359
COMMINS, John (Pvt.) 136, 315
COMMONS, Charles (Pvt.) 309
COMPBELL, John (Sgt.) 441
CON, Daniel (Pvt.) 293
CONCLE, Paul (Pvt.) 205
CONE, Phelty (Pvt.) 294
CONELY, William (Pvt.) 632
CONER, James (Pvt.) 251
  John (Cpl.) 555, 577
CONERY, James (Pvt.) 200
CONEY, Benjamin (Pvt.) 58, 96, 396,
  406, 422, 433, 590
CONINGHAM, Robert (Pvt.) 615
CONINGTON, George (Sgt.) 309
CONLEY, William (Pvt.) 56
CONN, Joseph (Pvt.) 565
CONNAL, John (Pvt.) 490
  William (Pvt.) 496
CONNALS, John (Pvt.) 475
CONNASS, William (Pvt.) 572
CONNEL, John (Pvt.) 500, 653
  William (Pvt.) 251
CONNELEY, Hugh (Pvt.) 442
CONNELL, John (Pvt.) 654
CONNELY, James (Pvt.) 193, 330
  Joseph (Pvt.) 183
CONNEN, Alexander (Pvt.) 307
CONNER, Darby (Pvt.) 144
  James (Pvt.) 243, 260, 474, 493
  Thomas 607
  Thomas (Cpl.) 180, 197
  Thomas (Pvt.) 591
CONNING, John (Pvt.) 564
CONNLEY, Patrick (Pvt.) 565
CONNOLY, Patrick (Pvt.) 328
CONNON, John (Pvt.) 505
CONNOR, Daniel (Pvt.) 24
  James (Pvt.) 499
  Thomas (Pvt.) 161, 247
CONOLY, John (Pvt.) 185 ("movd.", 191
CONOR, William (Pvt.) 427
COOCKSON, Daniel (Pvt.) 473, 491
  Thomas (Pvt.) 474
  William (Pvt.) 491
COOE, Samuel (Pvt.) 39
COOEN, Benjamin (Pvt.) 258
COOK, Adam (Pvt.) 74, 88, 108, 112,
  119

Alexander (Pvt.) 162
George (Pvt.) 76, 82, 111
Hugh (Pvt.) 236, 238
Jacob (Pvt.) 83, 89, 100, 111, 123
John (Pvt.) 160
Joseph (Pvt.) 138
Martin (Pvt.) 77, 82, 111, 523, 526, 623
Michael (Pvt.) 74, 542
William (Pvt.) 91, 103, 137, 249, 483,
  485, 501, 514, 517, 575, 582
COOKE, Adam (Pvt.) 89, 542
George (Pvt.) 89, 112, 126, 542, 548
Jacob (Pvt.) 112, 126, 548
John (Sgt.) 180, 197
Martin (Pvt.) 126, 548
Michael (Pvt.) 89, 112
COOKSON, Charles (Pvt.) 56, 632
Dan (Pvt.) 35
Daniel (Pvt.) 246, 498, 506
Thomas (Pvt.) 493, 499
William (Pvt.) 473, 498, 506
COOLE, James (Pvt.) 557
COON, James (Pvt.) 249
COOPER, James (Pvt.) 267, 422, 433
John (Pvt.) 325, 569, 648, 650
Richard (Pvt.) 602, 643
Ritchard (Pvt.) 610
Robert (Pvt.) 79, 114, 124, 129, 169,
  575, 583, 599, 600
William (Pvt.) 271, 643
COPELAND, Thomas (Pvt.) 277, 286
COPPER, John (Pvt.) 574, 578
CORBERRY, Joseph (Pvt.) 506
CORBET, Joseph (Pvt.) 645
CORBIT, Joseph (Pvt.) 330
CORD, John (Pvt.) 356, 460
CORDAL, Henry (Pvt.) 75, 90, 542
CORDLE, Henry (Pvt.) 113
COREDERS, Thomas (Pvt.) 147
CORITHERS, Alexander (Pvt.) 206
Andrew (Pvt.) 160
James (Pvt.) 330
John (Pvt.) 205
Rodger (Pvt.), 189 (deaf)
CORMICHAEL, John (Pvt.) 126
CORN, Thomas (Pvt.) 572
CORNAILIS, Jacob (Pvt.) 227
CORNELAS, Joseph (Pvt.) 128
CORNELIOUS, Jacob (Pvt.), 220
COROTHERS, Thomas (Pvt.) 174
CORRAN, James (Pvt.) 487
CORRELL, William (Pvt.) 441
CORREN, John (Pvt.) 403

William (Pvt.) 180, 197
CORSEWELL, John (Pvt.) 556
CORSON, James (Pvt.) 193
CORSWELL, Robert (Pvt.) 577
CORVEN, John (Pvt.) 32
COSLET, James (Pvt.) 86
COSTNET, James (Pvt.) 392
COTTEMAN, George (Pvt.) 632
COTTER, Aaron (Pvt.) 480, 494
COTTERMAN, George (Pvt.) 572
COUGHRAN, John (Pvt.) 285
William (Pvt.) 184, 191
COUGHREN, John (Pvt.) 178
COULTER, Adam (Pvt.) 423
Andrew (Pvt.) 206, 234
David (Lt.) 551, 555, 557, 576
David (Pvt.) 332
Francis (Pvt.) 344, 347, 365
Frank (Pvt.) 352
James (Pvt.) 65, 423
John (Pvt.) 352, 365, 431, 459
Joseph (Pvt.) 558, 611
Joseph (Scout) 626
Richard (1st Lt.) 51, 53
Richard (2nd Lt.) 11, 21, 43, 139
Richard (Capt.) 337
Richard (Pvt.) 569, 644
Samuel (Pvt.) 424
COUNTS, John (Pvt.) 56, 573, 633
COUPER, John (Pvt.) 646
COUSON, Anthony (Pvt.) (Scout) 652
COUTLER, Aaron (Pvt.) 247
COVAN, James (Pvt.) 19
COVER, Andrew (Pvt.) 119
Andrw (Pvt.) 87
George (Pvt.) 231, 235
Jacob (Pvt.) 87, 118, 123
Jedian (Pvt.) 221
Samuel (Ens.) (Scout) 652
Samuel (Pvt.) 337
COVR, Gideon (Pvt.) 227
COW, Henry (Pvt.) 274
Jacob (Pvt.) 273, 293
Paul (Pvt.) 273
Phillipy (Pvt.) 274
COWAN, Benjamin (Pvt.) 244
Daniel (Pvt.) 77, 82, 111, 548
David (Pvt.) 77, 82, 106, 111
David (Sgt.) 543, 584
Henery (Pvt.) 419
Henry (Pvt.) 37, 68, 446
Isaac (Pvt.) 251
James (Pvt.) 271, 484, 633

Robert (Pvt.) 287, 311
Thomas (Pvt.) 73, 78, 106, 530, 544,
  585, 632
Thomas (Pvt.) 484
Will (1st Lt.) 394
William (1st Lt.) 135
William (Pvt.) 58, 287, 311, 449, 590
COWBURN, John (Pvt.) 460
COWDAN, John (Pvt.) 110
COWDEN, Hendry (Pvt.) 189
COWDON, John (Pvt.) 82
COWE, Henry (Pvt.) 307
COWEN, Daniel (Pvt.) 126
Henery (Pvt.) 438
Henry (Pvt.) 39
Patrick 606
Patrick (Pvt.) 548
Thomas (Pvt.) 478, 527
William (Lt.) 385
William (Pvt.) 353, 358
COWHAKE, Patrick (Pvt.) 230
COWHAWK, James (Pvt.) 616
Patrick (Pvt.) 233
COX, Charles (Pvt.) 75, 115, 130, 537
Daniel (Pvt.) 397, 428, 430
Richard (Pvt.) 329
Samuel (Pvt.) 143, 391, 398, 431
COXES, Charles (Pvt.) 84
COY, Philip (Pvt.) 470, 491, 498, 506,
  602, 653, 654
Phillip (Pvt.) 473
COYLE, David (Pvt.) 643
Henry (Pvt.) 77, 82, 111, 548
Manus (Pvt.) 643
COZEY, John (Pvt.) 304
CRADGE, John (Drummer) 556, 577
CRAFART, John (Pvt.) 366
CRAFFORD, Samuel (1st Lt.) 95
CRAFORD, John (Pvt.) 233, 467
Josias (Pvt.) 280
Samuel (Pvt.) 435, 450
William (Pvt.) 223
CRAFT, Abraham (Pvt.) 169, 536, 599
John (Pvt.) 87, 123
Jonathan (Pvt.) 118
CRAGE, John (Pvt.) 410, 442, 645
Robert (Pvt.) 404
CRAGHEAD, Thomas (Pvt.) 184, 190
CRAGUE, Andrew (Pvt.) 149, 151
CRAIG, Andrew (Pvt.) 657
Jesse (Pvt.) 279
John (Pvt.) 104, 332, 407 (a servant),
  620

Robert (Pvt.) 68, 642
CRAIGE, Andrew (Pvt.) 390
John (Pvt.) 306
Robert (Pvt.) 266
CRAIGHEAD, John Rev. (Pvt.) 316
Thomas (Pvt.) 205
CRAIGO, Robert (Pvt.) 300, 643
CRAIN, Benjamin (Pvt.) 485
George (Pvt.) 653
John (Pvt.) 251
CRAMEN, Kern 28
CRAMER, James (Pvt.) 298
CRAMPTON, John (Pvt.) 244
CRANE, George (Pvt.) 206, 247, 654
William (Pvt.) 218
CRANER, James (2nd Lt.) 170
CRANKELTON, Joseph (Pvt.) 80
CRANSON, William (Pvt.) 632
CRAVEN, John (Pvt.) 285, 315
Thomas (Pvt.) 285, 300, 315
CRAVENSTINE, George (Pvt.) 21, 152
CRAVESTON, George (Cpl.) 19
CRAVINE, Jacob (Pvt.) 260
Matthew (Pvt.) 243
CRAW, James (Pvt.) 620
CRAWFORD, David (Pvt.) 538
Edward (Pvt.) 74, 88, 119, 546
George (Capt.) 367, 370, 376, 608
George (Pvt.) 87, 108, 118, 274, 294,
307, 537, 545
James (Capt.) 633
James (Ens.) 216
James (Pvt.) 79, 102, 181, 206, 265,
270, 276, 283, 306, 480, 494, 523,
527, 530, 546
James (Sgt.) 520, 571, 575, 582
John (Pvt.) 229, 455, 633
Joseph (Pvt.) 87, 118 (clerk), 119, 181,
198, 538, 587
Josies (Pvt.) 290
Robert (Pvt.) 180, 185(2), 191, 197,
266, 298, 300, 306, 360, 382, 622,
643
Samuel (1st Lt.) 13, 29, 32, 45, 141
Samuel (Pvt.) 390, 404, 642
William (Pvt.) 73, 80, 102, 220, 226,
507, 616
CRAWLY, Patrick (Pvt.) 356
CRAYNOR, James (Pvt.) 305
CREAG, Andrew (Pvt.) 431
Joshua (Pvt.) 431
CREAMER, Christopher (Pvt.) 73, 80
John (Pvt.) 231

CREAMOR, John (Pvt.) 235
CREAN, William (Pvt.) 224
CREATON, John (Pvt.) 274, 643
CREE, James (Pvt.) 629
John (Pvt.) 348, 349, 354, 461
Patrick (Pvt.) 454
Robb (Pvt.) 612
Robert (Pvt.) 362, 624, 655
William (Pvt.) 459
CREEGER, John (Pvt.) 9
CREEKINSTONE, George (Pvt.) 57
CREER, William (Sgt.) 587
CREIGH, John (Capt.) 155
Robert (Pvt.) 456
CREMER, Christpher (Pvt.) 102
CRENE, Benjamin (Pvt.) 476
George (Pvt.), 480(2), 494(2)
John (Pvt.) 477, 491
CRESWELL, Elisha (Ens.) 333
CRETON, John (Pvt.) 294
CREVENSTINE, George (Pvt.) 589
CREWSELL, John (Pvt.) 648
CRILY, John (Pvt.) 330
CRINDEL, Jacob (Pvt.) 104
CRINDLE, Hendry (Pvt.) 103
John (Pvt.) 103
CRISEY, Jacob (Pvt.) 101
jacob (Pvt.) 107
CRISLIP, Charles (Pvt.) 236
Jacob (Pvt.) 9
CRISLOP, Jacob (Pvt.), 219 ("run
away"), 225 ("run off")
CRISTEY, James (Pvt.) 566
CRISTIE, Robert (Pvt.) 447
CRISTLIP, Charles (Pvt.) 238
CRISTLOP, Jacob (Pvt.) 225
CRISTY, Archibald (Pvt.) 360
Jonathan (Pvt.) 84
CRISWELL, Andrew (Pvt.) 650
Elijah (Pvt.) 650
Elisha (Pvt.) 649
Hugh (Pvt.) 650
John (Pvt.) 562
Robert (Pvt.), 650(2)
Samuel (Pvt.) 650
CRITZER, Adam (Pvt.) 208
Godfrie (Pvt.) 220
Godfry (Pvt.) 227
Jacob (Pvt.) 219, 225
CROBERGER, George (Pvt.) 267, 302,
309
Leonard (Pvt.) 268, 303, 310
Michael (Pvt.) 267, 302, 309

CROCET, John (Pvt.) 653, 654
CROCKET, Alexander (Pvt.) 214
Andrew (Pvt.), 210, 230 (unfit for duty
as of 14 March 1781)
John (Pvt.) 490
Joseph (Ens.) 228
Samuel (Pvt.) 476, 502, 638
William (Pvt.) 247
CROCKETT, Andrew (Pvt.) 233
James (Pvt.), 205
Samuel (Pvt.) 122
CROCKIT, Samuel (Pvt.) 639
CRONKELTON, Joseph (Pvt.) 101
Robert (Pvt.) 101
CRONKHEAD, Mathew (Pvt.) 19
CROOKS, James (Pvt.) 72, 93, 94, 107,
116, 117
John (Pvt.) 94, 97, 117
William (Cpl.) 93, 116, 529, 596
William (Pvt.) 520, 524
CROOKSHANK, John (Pvt.) 232, 633
CROOKSHANKES, John (Pvt.) 435
CROOKSHANKS, Alexandrew (Sgt.)
434
John (Pvt.) 229, 450
CROSAN, William (Pvt.) 56
CROSBEY, James (Pvt.) 476
CROSBY, James (Pvt.) 247
CROSIER, John (Pvt.) 619
Morton (Pvt.) 619
CROSLEY, Thomas (Pvt.) 438
CROSON, William (Pvt.) 484
CROSS, James (Pvt.) 270, 276, 283
Robert (Pvt.) 79, 101, 107
Samuel (Pvt.) 79, 101, 107, 521, 571
CROSSAN, William (Pvt.) 478
CROSSIN, William (Pvt.) 249
CROSSLEY, Adam (Pvt.) 307
CROSSMAN, William (Pvt.) 409, 423,
442
CROSURE, John (Pvt.) 489
CROTHERS, Andrew (Pvt.) 181
John (Lt.) 592
CROTLEY, Thomas (Pvt.) 610
CROTS, Thomas (Pvt.) 476
CROTTE, Thomas 608
CROTTEY, Thomas (Pvt.) 601
CROTTY, James (Sgt.) 547
William (Pvt.) 125
CROUS, Jacob (Pvt.) 217, 222, 223
CROUZER, Morton (Pvt.) 507
CROW, James (Pvt.) 86, 383, 393
Mathias (Pvt.) 274, 294

Matthias (Pvt.) 308
CROWDER, Jonathan (Pvt.), 192 ("gone
into the army")
CROWE, Michial (Pvt.) 308
CROWS, Jacob (Cpl.) 8
John (Pvt.) 9
John (Sgt.) 8
CROWSON, William (Pvt.) 573
CROZER, John (Pvt.) 496
Martin (Pvt.) 496
CROZIER, Martin (Pvt.) 246, 472
CRULL, John (Pvt.) 79
CRUMB, Gilbert (Pvt.) 328
Thomas (Pvt.) 331
CRUMLEIGH, Frederick (Pvt.) 229
Stophel (Pvt.) 223, 226
CRUMLIEGH, Frederick (Pvt.) 233
CRUMMELIGH, Stoffel (Pvt.) 220
CRUNK, Matthew (Pvt.) 68
CRUNKELTON, Joseph (Pvt.) 114, 130
Josh (Pvt.) 84
Robert (Pvt.) 79, 123, 517, 586
CRUNKHEAD, Mathew (Pvt.) 139
CRUNKLETON, Robert (Pvt.) 521
CRUPLEATHER, Adam (Pvt.) 185, 191
CRUSTON, George (Pvt.) 139
CRUTHERS, Benjamin (Pvt.) 287
CUBBERTSON, Alexander (Pvt.) 125
CUCKSTON, Charles (Pvt.) 653
CUE, Robart 592
Robert 607
Robert (Pvt.) 591
CULANS, John (Pvt.) 235
CULBERSON, John (Pvt.) 574, 578
Richard (Pvt.), 199(2)
William (Pvt.) 574, 578
CULBERT, Joshua (Pvt.), 229
CULBERTSON, -- (Capt.) 316
Alexander (Pvt.) 82, 110, 267, 309, 393,
548, 620
Allexander (Pvt.) 86
James (Capt.) 261
James (Cornet) 640
James (Pvt.) 290, 316
John (Lt.) 316
John (Pvt.) 18, 20, 139, 142, 279, 280,
289, 290, 353, 359, 395, 421, 430,
569, 646, 648, 650
Joseph (Capt.) 279, 280, 289, 290, 369,
377
Joseph (Pvt.) 396
Robert (Capt.) 5
Robert (Lt. Col.), 11, 42

Robert (Maj.) 384, 598, 641
Robert (Pvt.) 290, 316, 546
Robert (Wagon Master) 4
Samuel (Capt.) 316
Samuel (Clark) 280
Samuel (Clerk) 290
Samuel (Col.) 268, 271, 273, 274, 277,
   282, 284, 286, 301, 307, 310, 314,
   367, 375, 443, 623
Samuel (Lt. Col.) 260, 266, 279, 291,
   295, 312
Samuel (Lt.) 293
Samuel (Pvt.), 142, 279(2), 289(2)
William (Pvt.) 228, 232, 648
CULLENS, John (Pvt.) 237
CUMINS, Mathaw (Pvt.) 448
Robert (Pvt.) 342, 460
CUMMENS, James (Pvt.) 58
CUMMIN, John (Pvt.) 328
CUMMINGS, Andrew (Pvt.) 24
James (Pvt.) 406
John (Pvt.) 279
CUMMINS, Andrew 605
Charles (Pvt.) 267, 302, 381
James (Pvt.) 136, 396, 422, 434
John (Pvt.) 17, 47, 49, 142, 395, 627
Matthew 605
Matthew (Pvt.) 446
Moses (Pvt.) 540
Robert (Ens.) 340
Thomas (Pvt.) 396, 421, 433
William (Pvt.) 540
CUNE, Petor (Pvt.) 104
CUNING, Alexander (Pvt.) 269
John (Pvt.) 556, 577
CUNINGHAM, Adam (Pvt.) 66, 135, 439
Charles (Pvt.) 488
George (Cpl.) 81, 100, 110
James (Pvt.) 645
John (Pvt.) 120, 506
Roger (Pvt.) 491, 632
William (Pvt.) 487
CUNINHAM, John (Pvt.) 85, 127
CUNKLE, Michael (Pvt.), 235, 237
Paul (Ens.) 215
CUNNING, Alexander (Pvt.) 283, 373
John (Pvt.) 552
CUNNINGHAM, Adam (Pvt.) 23, 133,
   400, 413
Alexander (Pvt.) 78, 521, 523, 584
Arthur (Lt.) 242, 259
Charles (Pvt.) 27, 35, 250, 472, 474,
   498, 619

George (Pvt.) 548
Hugh (Pvt.) 272, 285, 315
James (Pvt.) 285, 315, 478, 484
John (Pvt.) 236, 238, 245, 258, 271,
   274, 284, 294, 308, 314, 329, 379,
   382, 417, 426, 479, 494
Richard 606
Richard (Cpl.) 617
Robert (Pvt.) 207, 214, 272, 281, 286,
   316, 572
Roger (Pvt.) 56, 479
Thomas 605
William (Pvt.) 285, 314, 457, 480, 494,
   618, 621, 637
William (Pvt.) 494
CUNNY, Benjamin (Pvt.) 136
CUPPLES, James 605
CURMICKLE, John (Pvt.) 644
CURRE, James (Pvt.) 35
CURREA, William (Pvt.) 188
CURREN, John (Pvt.), 407 ("gone a
   privateering")
CURREY, John (Pvt.) 235, 507
William (Pvt.) 437
CURRIER, Anthony (Pvt.) 648
CURRIN, John (Sgt.) 63, 146
CURRY, John (Pvt.) 191, 231, 247, 480
John (Pvt.) 494
Thomas (Pvt.) 269
William (2nd Lt.) 154, 158, 165
William (Pvt.) 187, 647
CURSERS, Antoney (Pvt.) 574
Antony (Pvt.) 578
CURSWELL, Andrew (Pvt.) 574
David (Pvt.) 570
James (Pvt.) 570
John (Pvt.) 569, 574, 579
Robert (Pvt.) 124
CURTAIN, Peter 607
Peter (Pvt.) 537
CURTEN, Peter (Pvt.) 647
CURTIN, Peter (Pvt.) 114, 518, 540
CURTON, Peter (Pvt.) 130
CURTS, John (Pvt.) 198
Lowe (Pvt.) 639
Thomas (Pvt.) 505, 653
CURTZ, Thomas (Pvt.) 654
CUSTARD, John (Pvt.) 291, 295, 304,
   313, 647
CUSTS, Thomas (Pvt.) 490
CUTHBERTSON, John (Pvt.) 21, 152
Joseph (Capt.) 381, 609
Robert (Lt. Col.) 46

Samuel (Col.) 30, 608
Samuel (Pvt.) 214
CUTHERBERTSON, Robert (Lt. Col.)
15
CUTTEHAN, Alexander (Pvt.) 381
CYERMOND, Thomas (Pvt.) 565

-D-
D---, John (Pvt.) 619
DABBS, Thomas (Pvt.) 573
DABS, Thomas (Pvt.) 500
DAIL, Josh (Pvt.) 371
DAILY, John (Pvt.) 299, 301, 643
Peter 608
DAIR, Philip (Pvt.) 307
DALLY, John (Pvt.) 266
DALY, Robert (Pvt.) 651
DANIEL, Andrew (Pvt.) 20
DARAS, Frederick (Pvt.) 381
DARBY, John (Pvt.) 306
DARLINGTON, Meridith (Pvt.) 625
Robert (1st Lt.) 587
DARRICK, Richard (Pvt.) 221
DARRSON, James (Pvt.) 509
DATLEY, Joshua (Pvt.) 653
DAUGHARTY, Patrick (Pvt.) 152
DAUGHERTY, Barnabas (Sgt.) 402, 656
Barney (Pvt.) 587
Daniel (Pvt.) 588
Moses (Pvt.) 380
Neal (Pvt.) 52, 142
Patrick (Pvt.) 52
DAVICE, James (Pvt.) 479
Phillip (Pvt.) 294
Samuel (Pvt.) 496
DAVID, John (Pvt.) 130
Samuel (Pvt.) 491
Walter (Pvt.) 397
DAVIDSON, Elias (Capt.) 6
Gorge (Pvt.) 450
James (1st Lt.) 167
James (Pvt.) 178, 270, 283, 326, 570,
651
John (Ens.) 155
John (Pvt.) 160, 176
John (Waggon master) 4, 598
Joseph (Pvt.) 157
Patrick (Pvt.) 208, 417, 515
Pattrick (Pvt.) 179
Robert (Pvt.) 73, 559
Samuel (Ens.) 163, 165
Samuel (Pvt.) 246, 248
Thomas (Pvt.) 589

DAVIES, Joseph (Pvt.) 557
Samuel (Pvt.) 624
DAVIS, Bartholomew 606
Benjamin (Pvt.) 527, 530, 597
David (Pvt.) 199
Elias (Capt.) 513, 533
George (Pvt.) 102, 350, 357
Isaac (Pvt.) 82, 110, 126, 291, 548
James (Pvt.) 200(2), 494, 503
John 606
John (Col.) 15, 153, 163, 626(2), 627,
628(2)
John (Pvt.) 75, 115, 128, 178, 273, 274,
285, 288, 293, 294, 307, 308, 315,
323, 353, 371, 540, 568, 582, 596,
604, 613, 634, 636
Jonathan (Pvt.) 402, 84, 396
Joseph 606
Joseph (Pvt.) 84, 114, 130, 519, 524,
540
Philip (Pvt.), 274(2)
Phillip (Pvt.) 294, 308
Robert (Pvt.) 327
Samuel (Pvt.) 489, 507
Walter (Pvt.) 8, 10, 24, 142, 416, 430
William (Pvt.) 160, 199
DAVISE, John (Pvt.) 336
Samuel (Pvt.) 646
DAVISON, Elias (Pvt.) 80, 101
Frank (Pvt.) 184, 191
George (Pvt.) 390, 149, 151
Gorg (Pvt.) 435
James (1st Lt.) 169
James (Pvt.) 174, 276, 574, 649
John (Pvt.) 85, 120, 121, 127, 198, 625
Joseph (Pvt.) 184, 190, 644
Mathew (Pvt.) 180, 197
Patrick (Pvt.) 7, 85, 120, 127, 383, 426,
637
Patrick 24
Robert (Pvt.) 80, 102
Samuel (Pvt.) 181, 198, 389, 396, 421,
553, 657
William (Pvt.) 276
DAVS, William (Pvt.) 587
DAVY, John (Pvt.) 577
DAWSON, James (Pvt.) 200
Robert (Pvt.) 352, 459
William (Pvt.) 219, 225
DAYLY, Peter (Pvt.) 619
DEALEY, Robert (Pvt.) 495
DEALLEY, Robert (Pvt.) 503
DEALY, Peter (Pvt.) 472

26

Robert (Pvt.) 510
DEAN, Abraham (Pvt.) 91, 103
Samuel (Pvt.) 341, 361
William (Pvt.) 382
DEARMIN, John (Pvt.) 439
DEARVICE, Benjamin (Pvt.) 546
DECOMB, William (Pvt.) 243, 260
DEEDS, John (Pvt.) 278, 287, 311
DEEL, George (Pvt.) 161
DEEN, Abraham (Pvt.) 137
DELAHUNT, Valentine (Pvt.) 588
DELANCY, Francis (Pvt.) 355
Francy (Pvt.) 366
John (Pvt.) 355
DELANEY, John (Pvt.) 365
DELEANY, John (Pvt.) 364
DELINGER, Frederick 28
DELLINGER, Frederick (Pvt.) 31
DELMER, Henry (Pvt.) 515
DELONG, David (Pvt.) 61, 359, 408
Davis (Pvt.) 354
DENEY, David (Pvt.) 187
William (Pvt.) 163
DENISTON, Andrew (Pvt.) 448
DENNEY, David (Pvt.) 182
James (Pvt.) 570, 579
John (Pvt.) 186
DENNISTON, Andrew (Pvt.) 68, 446
DENNY, Daniel (Pvt.) 184, 191
David (Pvt.) 192, 635
James (Pvt.) 558, 574
John (Pvt.) 184
Walter (Capt.) 155, 162, 166, 170, 609
Walter (Pvt.) 196
William (Pvt.) 182, 184, 193
DENY, John (Pvt.) 190
William (Pvt.) (Clerk) 190
DERBIN, William (Pvt.) 328
DERICK, Richard (Pvt.) 227
DEROCH, Abraham (Pvt.) 94
DEROCHE, Abraham (Pvt.) 117
DERVE, Martin (Pvt.) 633
DERWICK, George (Pvt.), 267, 302
(alias Stark)
DEVENEY, Andrew (Pvt.) 104
DEVENY, Andrew (Pvt.) 83
William (Pvt.) 99
DEVER, John 608
John (Pvt.) 248
DEVERS, Tobias (Pvt.) 332
DEVILIHON, Frances (Pvt.) 383
DEVINE, John (Pvt.) 646
DEVINEY, Andrew (Pvt.) 138

William (Pvt.) 138
DEVINNEY, James (Pvt.) 647
DEVINPORT, John (Pvt.) 450
Samuel (Pvt.) 435, 449
DEVINY, William (Pvt.) 85
DEVIOUR, David (Pvt.) 637
DEVISON, James (Pvt.) 561
DEVLIN, John (Pvt.) 457
DEVOAR, John (Pvt.) 424
DEVORE, David (Pvt.) 629
DEWALT, Loudwick (Pvt.) 116
Louwick (Pvt.) 93
DEYARMOND, Henry (Pvt.) 195
DICK, Cornelius (Pvt.) 296
DICKE, Moses (Pvt.) 648
DICKESON, James (Pvt.) 137
DICKEY, Adam (Pvt.) 73, 80
Andrew (Lt.) 262, 284
Andrew (Pvt.) 271, 315
Andrey (Pvt.) 373
David (Pvt.) 206
George (1st Lt.) 211, 215
George (2nd Lt.) 202, 204
James (Pvt.) 247, 284, 289, 314, 371,
478
John (Ens.) 262
John (Ens.) 271, 284, 368, 370, 377, 379
John (Pvt.) 285, 315, 382
Mosas (Pvt.) 556
Moses (Pvt.) 554, 558, 577
Mosey (Pvt.) 574, 579
Nathaniel (Pvt.) 244
Peter (Pvt.) 148
Petter (Pvt.) 150
Robert (Capt.) 284
Robert (Pvt.) 221 (unfit for service),
272, 285, 314, 373, 375, 615
Samuel (Pvt.) 205, 231, 234
William (Pvt.) 272, 286, 315, 554, 556,
558, 577
DICKIE, Robert (Pvt.) 228
DICKSON, Alexander (Pvt.) 418, 436
Andrew (Pvt.) 273, 293, 307
David (Ens.) 211
George (Pvt.) 37, 41, 92, 104, 141, 347,
348, 393, 576, 583
Gorge (Pvt.) 138
James (1st Lt.) 320, 324, 333, 337
James (Ens.) 512, 532, 575, 582
James (Lt.) 550, 644
James (Pvt.) 91, 124, 299, 325, 337,
338, 624
James (Sgt.) 304, 561

John (Pvt.) 185, 191, 476, 490, 505
John (Sgt.) 87, 118
Joseph (Pvt.) 554, 561, 611
William (Pvt.) 78, 97, 195, 325
DIDIER, Henery (Pvt.) 199
DIERFIELD, Henry (Pvt.) 248
DILL, Frederick (Pvt.) 248
Michael (Pvt.) 230, 233
DILLAM, John (Pvt.) 496
DILLEN, Thomas (Pvt.) 244, 258
DILLIN, John (Pvt.) 489
DILLINER, Fredrick (Pvt.) 143
DILLINGER, Frederick (Pvt.) 34, 391, 431
DILLON, John (Pvt.) 508, 618
DILTO, William (Pvt.) 116
DILTS, William (Pvt.) 93, 122
DIMOND, Daniel (Pvt.) 307
DINIS, Henry 593, 594
DINSMORE, Henry (Pvt.) 175, 179
John (Pvt.) 174, 179
Samuel (Pvt.) 174, 179
DINWIDY, Samuel (Pvt.) 643
DISART, Benjamin (Pvt.) 66, 405
James (Pvt.) 66, 405
DISORT, Benjamin (Pvt.) 134
DITCH, Abraham (Pvt.) 71, 94, 117
David (Pvt.) 71, 94, 117
Henry (Pvt.) 94, 116
DITLINGER, Fredrick (Pvt.) 398
DITTY, Peter (Pvt.) 80, 101
DIVEN, James (Pvt.) 361
John (Pvt.) 342
DIVENPART, John (Pvt.) 433
DIVENPORT, Jonas (Pvt.) 450
DIVER, John (Pvt.) 472, 475, 486, 500, 586
DIVIN, James (Pvt.) 342
John (Pvt.) 612
DIXCON, George (Pvt.) 121
DIXKSON, James (Pvt.) 103
DIXON, Alexander (Pvt.) 428
George (Pvt.) 76, 128, 515, 620
James (Pvt.) 654
James (Sgt.) 297
John (Pvt.) 278, 286, 311, 653, 654
William (Pvt.) 106, 279(2), 281 (miller), 287, 288, 312(2: one a miller), 585
DIXSON, George (Pvt.) 86, 384, 456
Hendery (Pvt.) 562
James (1st Lt.) 327
James (Pvt.) 327
John (Pvt.) 246

Josuf (Pvt.) 556, 577
DNOUGHY, William (Pvt.) 301
DOBBS, Thomas (Pvt.) 475, 486
DODD, Andrew (Pvt.) 389
DODDS, Andrew (Pvt.) 134, 136, 396, 421, 433, 657
John (Pvt.) 209
Samuel (Pvt.) 207
Thomas (Pvt.) 421, 433
DODS, Andrew (Pvt.) 58
DOEY, Frederick (Pvt.), 222 ("run off")
Martin (Pvt.) 161, 222
DOFFLE, William (Pvt.) 538
DOHARTY, Charles (Pvt.) 90
DOHERTY, John (Pvt.) 446
Neal (Pvt.) 397
Patrick (Pvt.) 140
DOLL, Frederick (Pvt.), 228 ("run off")
Martin (Pvt.) 228
DON, Richard (Pvt.) 473
DONAL, James (Pvt.) 403
Thomas 27
DONALD, Alexander (Pvt.) 397, 429
Andrew 607
Andrew (Sub.) 140
Barnabas (Pvt.) 214
Francess (Pvt.) 68, 446
Francis (Pvt.) 31, 33, 443, 444
James (Pvt.) 446
Samuel (Clerk) 194
Thomas (Pvt.) 445
William (Pvt.) 36, 40, 446
DONALDSON, Andrew (Pvt.) 159, 189
George (Pvt.) 343
Hugh (Pvt.) 372
Isaac (Pvt.) 78
John (Pvt.) 189
Robert (Pvt.) 161, 189
Thomas (Pvt.) 206, 231
William (Capt.) 159, 165, 173, 177, 595, 609
William (Pvt.) 296, 313
DONALLY, Frederick (Pvt.) 361
John (Pvt.) 99
DONALSON, George (Pvt.) 354, 359
Thomas (Pvt.) 234
DONANDSON, James (Pvt.) 206
DONAVAN, Robert (Pvt.) 395
DONELL, Alexander (Pvt.) 142
DONELY, John (Pvt.) 104
DONJALLY, John (Pvt.) 92
DONLAP, Alexander (Pvt.) 103
DONLEY, Frederick (Pvt.) 341

Thomas (Pvt.) 342
DONLY, John (Pvt.) 313
DONN, Andrew (Pvt.) 298
DONNAL, Francis (Pvt.) 448
  James (Pvt.) 407, 411
  William (Pvt.) 448
DONNALD, Andrew 605
  Francis (Pvt.) 657
  James (Pvt.) 68, 420, 438, 631
  Samuel (Ens.) 160
  Thomas (Pvt.) 68
  William (Pvt.) 68
DONNALIE, John (Pvt.) 312
DONNALL, Alexander (Pvt.) 416
DONNANL, James (Pvt.) 448
DONNEL, Alexander (Pvt.) 425
  Samuel (Ens.) 156, 166
  William (Pvt.) 411, 631
DONNELL, Alexander (Pvt.) 636
DONNELSON, William (Capt.) 154
DONNOLEY, Thomas (Pvt.) 323
DONOLY, Hugh (Pvt.) 191
DONOVAN, Robert (Pvt.) 421, 432
DONWODY, Samuel (2nd Lt.) 370
DONWOODY, James (Pvt.) 615
DOOEY, Frederick (Pvt.) 159
DOOLY, Philip (Pvt.) 190
DORMAN, George 606
  George (Pvt.) 650
  Robert 606
DORMOND, George (Pvt.) 556, 577
DOTHARTY, Patrick (Pvt.) 120
DOUDS, James (Pvt.) 392
DOUGAL, Hugh (Pvt.) 162
DOUGAN, Charles (Pvt.) 207
DOUGHARTY, Daniel (Pvt.) 224
  Neal (Pvt.) 152
  Roger (Pvt.) 115
  William (Pvt.) 152
DOUGHERTY, Barnabas (Sgt.) 391
  Charles (Pvt.) 99, 113
  Daniel 605
  Daniel (Pvt.) 218, 433
  Frederick (Pvt.) 603
  Fredrick (Pvt.) 59
  James (Pvt.) 121, 277, 278, 284, 287,
    311, 638, 639, 647
  John (Ens.) 261, 277
  John (Pvt.) 158, 298, 318
  Moses (Pvt.) 273, 293, 307
  Neal 607
  Neal (Pvt.) 20, 21, 53, 139, 430, 518,
    603

Niel (Pvt.) 18, 80, 101
Patrick (Pvt.) 85, 127, 383, 515
Patt. (Pvt.) 53
Peter (Pvt.) 76, 92, 530, 576, 583
Petor (Pvt.) 104
Roger (Pvt.) 102
Thomas (Pvt.) 554, 558, 630
Thomas (Scout) 626
William (Pvt.) 18, 20, 21, 139
DOUGHORTY, Neal (Pvt.) 59
  Patrick (Pvt.), 59, 603
DOUGLAS, Alexander (Pvt.) 515
  Andrew (Pvt.) 85, 383, 515
  George (Pvt.) 461
  James (1st Lt.) 157
  James (Capt.) 167, 173, 176
  William (Pvt.) 174
DOUGLASS, --- (Capt.) 183
  Andrew (Pvt.) (weaver) 127, 141
  George (Pvt.) 625, 655
  Gray (Pvt.) 302
  James (1st Lt.) 153, 164
  James (Capt.), 169, 171, 175, 179,
    613(2)
  James (Pvt.) 613
  John (Pvt.) 355, 366, 457
  Patrick (Pvt.) 446
DOUGLES, Patrick (Pvt.) 448
DOUGLESS, James (Capt.) 178
  William (Pvt.) 179
DOUGLIS, Andrew (Pvt.) 428
DOUTHWART, Thomas (Pvt.) 199
DOUWGLASS, Andrew (Pvt.) 140
DOVEY, Philip (Pvt.) 186
DOWDS, James (Pvt.) 64, 403, 419, 438,
  657
DOWLAR, Thomas (Pvt.) 576, 583
DOWNEY, David (Pvt.) 79, 101, 107,
  129
  James (Pvt.) 94, 97, 117
  Samuel (Pvt.) 81, 98, 102
  William (Pvt.) 79, 101, 123
DOWOODY, Samuel (Sgt.) 615
DOWTY, Zachariah (Pvt.) 624
DOYL, Barnabas (Pvt.) 424
  Steven (Pvt.) 78
DOYLE, Barnabas (Pvt.) 61, 132, 394,
  409, 412, 442
  Martin (Pvt.) 272, 389 ("gon"), 396
  Stephen (Pvt.) 299, 306
DRAKE, Edward (Pvt.) 323, 562
  Sameal (Pvt.) 577
  Samuel (Pvt.) 553, 645

Somial (Pvt.) 556
DREADEN, Samuel (Pvt.) 82
DREDGE, John (Cpl.) 647
DRENAN, William (Capt.) 234
William (Pvt.) 527
DRENANS, William (Capt.) 236
DRENING, William 644
DRENNAN, Thomas (Pvt.) 527
Thomas (Sgt.) 596
William (Pvt.) 596
DRENNAR, David (Pvt.) 421
DRENNEN, William (Pvt.) 530, 648
DRENNON, Thomas (Pvt.) 518
William (Lt.) 216
William (Pvt.) 578
DRENON, William (Pvt.) 574
DREYDON, Samuel (Pvt.) 290
DRIMER, Anthony (Pvt.) 478
DRINEN, Thomas 607
DRININ, William (Pvt.) 326
DRINNEN, William (Pvt.) 210
DRIVER, Casper (Cpl.) 616
Casper (Pvt.), 226 ("run off")
Gasper (Pvt.), 220 (1 Aug 1780 - "run off")
Samuel (Pvt.) 58, 264, 422, 433, 588
DROMMAN, Alexander (Pvt.) 412
DRUDGE, John (Pvt.) 197
DRUMAN, Alexander (Pvt.) 61
DRUMAND, Alexander (Pvt.) 409
DRUMIN, James (Ens.) 523
DRUMMIN, Samuel (Sgt.) 83
DRUMMON, Alexander (Pvt.) 394
James (Ens.) 511, 525
James (Pvt.) 114, 129
Samuel (Sgt.) 113, 129
DRUMMOND, Alexander (Pvt.) 424
James (Ens.) 520, 532, 539
James (Sgt.) 571
Samuel (Sgt.) 539
DRUMOND, Alexander (Pvt.) 131
DRUNIAN, Samuel (Sgt.) 520
DRYBROUGH, Alexander (Cpl.) 575, 582
Alexander (Pvt.) 91
DRYBRUGH, Alexander (Pvt.) 103
DUCKE, Mark (Pvt.) 633
DUFFEL, William (Pvt.) 372, 565, 574, 87
DUFFIEL, William (Pvt.) 578
DUFFIELD, Pat (Pvt.) 357
Patrick (Pvt.) 345, 350
Samuel (Pvt.) 288, 293

William (Armourer) 273
William (Pvt.) 273, 293, 303, 307, 570, 649
William (Sgt.) 648
DUGAL, Hugh (Pvt.) 189
DUGAN, James (Pvt.) 549
DUGLASS, Andrew (Pvt.) 120
DUKE, Mark (Pvt.) 229, 232
DULL, Joseph (Pvt.) 89, 108, 541
Peter (Pvt.) 89, 112, 123, 542, 585
Stophel (Pvt.) 108, 541
Stophell (Pvt.) 89, 112
DUN, Hezekiah (2nd Lt.) 320
Hezikiah (2nd Lt.) 324
James (Pvt.), 430(2)
John (Pvt.) 431
Michael (Pvt.) 604
Richard (Pvt.) 503
Robert (Pvt.) 391, 398, 431
DUNAVAN, Daniel (Pvt.) 178
DUNAVEN, Robert (Pvt.) 148, 150
DUNBAR, David (Pvt.) 15, 17, 395, 421, 427, 432, 589, 628
David (Sgt.) 57
John (Pvt.) 160, 180, 197, 354, 625, 655
Robert (Pvt.) 629
Samuel (Pvt.) 181, 186, 198
Thomas (Pvt.) 157, 167, 180
William (Pvt.), 167, 180, 197 (gone to Virginia)
DUNCAN, Alexander (Pvt.) 82, 110
Dainal 657
Daniel (Pvt.) 58, 136, 389, 396, 421, 433, 590
David (Pvt.) 625, 655
James (1st Lt.) 248, 255
James (Pvt.) 431
John (Pvt.) 65, 133, 135, 413, 426, 439, 400
Samuel (Pvt.) 30, 33, 42, 134, 658
Stephen (Pvt.) 440
Thomas (Pvt.) 199
William (1st Lt.) 240
William (Pvt.) 401, 405, 414, 440
DUNDORE, George (Pvt.) "Run off," as of 1 Aug 1780. 220, 227
DUNE, Robert (Pvt.) 405
DUNING, William (Pvt.) 209
DUNKEN, Alexander (Pvt.) 125
DUNKLE, Jacob (Pvt.) 281, 299, 301
DUNLAP, Alexander (Pvt.) 124, 137
James (Col.) 9, 10, 19, 56, 60, 67, 96, 131, 138, 150, 408, 412, 422, 429,

432, 434, 441, 449, 608
James (Lt. Col.) 384
James (Pvt.) 8, 10, 24, 142, 269, 275(2),
  289, 297, 299, 305, 371
James (Sgt.) 290
John (Pvt.) 272, 285, 315, 323, 559
Joseph (Pvt.) 297, 300, 305, 372
Samuel (Col.) 47
Thomas (Pvt.) 87, 105, 517, 518, 519,
  575, 583, 586
William (Pvt.) 189
DUNLOP, James (Col.) 42, 132, 394,
  399, 410, 420, 438
James (Lt.) 3
John (Pvt.) 649
DUNN, Hezekah (2nd Lt.) 334
Hezekiah (2nd Lt.) 325
Michael (Pvt.) 616
Richard (Pvt.) 56, 278, 498, 621, 632
Richard (Sgt.) 618
Robert (Pvt.) 642
DUNNING, James (Pvt.) 221
John (Pvt.) 246
Joseph (Pvt.) 227
Robert (Pvt.) 180
Samuel (Pvt.) 181, 186, 198, 206
DUNRAVEL, Robert (Pvt.) 427
DUNSEATH, Robert (Pvt.) 624
DUNUN, James (Pvt.) 649
DUNWOODY, Adam (Pvt.) 281, 299,
  301
James (Pvt.) 266, 299(2), 301, 643
Joseph (Pvt.) 306
Samuel (2nd Lt.) 378
Samuel (Pvt.) 266, 298, 300, 305
Thomas (Pvt.) 298, 300, 305
William (Pvt.) 375
DURBIN, William (Pvt.) 650
DUTCH, Andrew (Pvt.) 91
Cornelius (Pvt.) 87, 538, 597
DYCHE, William (Pvt.) 650
DYSART, Benjamin (Pvt.) 401, 414, 440
James (Pvt.) 401, 414, 440, 631

-E-
EACHORD, Michael (Pvt.) 498
EACISSON, John (Pvt.) 286
EACKMAN, James (Pvt.) 68, 403
John (Pvt.) 402
Thomas (Pvt.) 403
EAGAR, John (Pvt.) 63, 146
EAGELBY, John (Pvt.) 48
EAGLE, Domnick (Pvt.) 9

EAKEN, George (Pvt.) 539
James 28
William (Pvt.) 130
EAKER, George (Pvt.) 83, 108, 114, 129
William (Pvt.) 84, 114, 540, 557
EAKIN, James (Pvt.) 402
Robert (Pvt.) 488
EAKINS, James (Pvt.) 25, 145, 147
EAKLEBARGER, Valintine (Pvt.) 505
EAKLES, Nathaniel (Pvt.) Dead by ca. 1
  Aug 1780. 218
EAKMAN, Alexander 606
John (Pvt.) 416
Thomas (Pvt.) 392
William 28
William (Pvt.) 388 (not to be found),
  401, 414
EARB, Richard (Pvt.) 501
EARHEAR, Nicholas (Fifer) 290
EARL, David (Pvt.) 398
James (Pvt.) 189, 442
Richard (Pvt.) 27, 250, 485
EARLE, David (Pvt.) 143
Richard (Pvt.) 56, 483, 573
EARLEY, Daniel (Pvt.) 81, 109, 110
John (Pvt.) 72, 544
EARLY, Daniel (Pvt.) 125, 371
John (Pvt.) 78, 290
William (Cpl.) 584
EARS, Thomas (Pvt.) 106
EASORD, Jacob (Pvt.) 252
EASTMAN, Thomas 425
EASTON, Richard (Pvt.) 128, 407, 631
EATIN, William (Pvt.) 200
EATING, David (Pvt.) 557
EATMAN, James (Pvt.) 446
John (Pvt.) 425
Thomas (Pvt.) 637
EATON, David (Pvt.) 568, 582, 649
Isaac (Pvt.) 650
John (1st Lt.) 368, 373, 382
John (Pvt.) 278, 287, 311
Joseph (Pvt.) 277, 286, 288, 311
Richard (Pvt.) 86
EATTEN, John (Pvt.) 318
EATTON, John (1st Lt.) 376
EAVENS, Henry (Pvt.) 84
EBERCRUMBY, William (Pvt.) 176
EBERHART, Andw. (Pvt.) 365
ECCLES, Peter (Pvt.) 643
ECHELS, Andrew (Pvt.) 293
ECKELS, Andrew (Pvt.) 297, 313
James (Pvt.) 316

ECKERT, Jacob (Pvt.) 219, 225
ECKLEBERGER, Felty (Pvt.) 246
ECKLES, Daniel (Pvt.) 313
Nathaniel (Pvt.), 224 (Aug 1780 - dead)
William (Pvt.) 278, 311
ECLAS, James (Pvt.) 200
EDENTON, Robert (Pvt.) 574, 578, 648
EDINTON, Edward (Pvt.) 629
EDLER, David (Pvt.) 62, 132
John (Pvt.) 132
EDMESTON, Thomas (Pvt.) 274
EDMISON, Thomas (Pvt.) 294
EDMISTON, Joseph (Pvt.), 197 (mov'd.)
Thomas (Pvt.) 307
EDMONDSTONE, James (Pvt.) 455
EDMONSON, Joseph (Pvt.) 167
EFFINGTON, --- (Capt.) 62
EGNEW, Samuel (Pvt.) 227
William (Pvt.), 227 ("not to be found")
EICHELBERGER, Valentine (Pvt.) 500
EICLERS, Widlliam (Pvt.) 643
EIKELBERGER, Valentine (Pvt.), 475
ELDER Abraham (Pvt.) 140, 408, 423,
429, 441
Abram (Pvt.) 383, 515
David (Pvt.) 34, 141, 132, 309, 323,
384, 394, 409, 409, 413, 424, 442,
443, 444, 515
John (Pvt.) 41, 62, 132, 394, 408, 409,
423, 424, 441, 442, 620
Mathew (Pvt.) 556, 564, 568, 577
Samuel (Pvt.) 36, 42, 121, 128, 141,
384, 407, 515, 658
William 596
William (Ens.) 11, 25, 27, 43, 54, 60,
62, 131, 387, 408, 422, 441
ELIOT, Alexander (Pvt.) 448
Johnston (Pvt.) 380
ELLERY, Daniel (Pvt.) 294
ELLET, George (Maj.) 572
ELLICOTT, John (Maj.) 631
ELLIOT, Alexander (Pvt.) 68, 446
Archibald 596
Archibald (1st Lt.) 50, 140, 383
Archibald (Lt.) 28
Benjamin (Pvt.) 380
David (Pvt.) 232
Frances (Pvt.) 85, 127
Francis (Pvt.) 140, 152, 383
George (Pvt.) 647
John (Capt.) 609
John (Maj.) 483
John (Pvt.) 68, 629

John (Sgt.) 55
Joseph (Pvt.) 224
Robert (Pvt.) 68, 228, 336, 657
William (Pvt.) 128, 141, 384, 466
ELLIOTT, A. Johnston (Pvt.) 276
Abraham (Lt.) 387
Alexander (Pvt.) 31, 33, 443, 444
Archibald (1st Lt.) 12, 22, 25, 43, 54,
62, 515
Benjamin (Pvt.) 297, 300, 305
David (Pvt.) 229
Francis (Pvt.) 18, 21, 139, 515
James (Pvt.) 218, 353, 357
John (Capt.) 240, 245, 254
John (Pvt.) 343, 354, 459
John (Sgt.) 612
Johnson (Pvt.) 282
Johnston (Pvt.) 269, 275, 304
Robert (Pvt.) 221, 323
Thomas (Pvt.) 289, 357, 460
William (1st Lt.) 369, 378, 381
William (Pvt.) 270, 276, 281, 284, 298,
306, 350, 357, 364, 455, 515
ELLIOUT, Archabald (Capt.) 120
Francis (Pvt.) 120
William (Pvt.) 120
ELLIS, Hendery (Pvt.) 562
Richard (Pvt.) 350
ELLISON, Andrew (Pvt.) 371
David (Pvt.) 251
John (Pvt.) 411
Robert (Pvt.) 325
Robert (Scout) 625
ELLOT, Robert (Pvt.) 644
ELLOTE, Thomas (Pvt.) 279
ELLWOOD, William 606
William (Pvt.) 114, 124, 129
ELWOOD, William (Pvt.) 84, 540
EMBLE, John (Pvt.) 78, 543, 584
Paul (Pvt.) 78, 544, 585
EMINGER, Conrod (Pvt.) 217, 222, 223
EMMINGER, Andrew (Pvt.) 207
ENGLE, John (Pvt.) 21, 139, 142, 397
ENGLISH, Charles (Pvt.) 439
David (Pvt.) 119, 348, 349, 522, 526,
538, 546, 601
ENGLISHMAN, James (Pvt.) 546
ENNES, Francis (Pvt.) 472, 619
ENNIS, Francis (Pvt.) 475
ENSLOW, James (Pvt.) 310, 375
Joseph 605
ERI., Richard (Pvt.) 632
ERLIS, Richard (Cpl.) 35

ERNEST, Henry (Pvt.) 93
ERVEN, Jonathan (Pvt.) 84, 115
  Robert (Ens.) 113
  Robert (Sgt.) 599
ERVIN, Alexander (Pvt.) 309
  James (Pvt.), 373
  John (Pvt.) 58
  Robert (Ens.) 83
  Robert (Pvt.) 143
  William (Pvt.) 143, 398
ERVINE, David (Pvt.) 68, 445
  Robert (Sgt.) 539
ERWIN, Andrew (Pvt.) 206, 214, 352
  Christopher (Pvt.) 246
  David (Pvt.) 21, 139
  Edward (Pvt.) 251
  Francis (Pvt.) 356
  James (Pvt.) 247, 258, 289, 371, 510
  John (Pvt.) 40, 136, 162, 411, 631
  Robert 28
  Robert (Pvt.) 31, 42, 350, 357, 510, 527, 535
  Samuel (Col.) 223
  Samuel (Maj.) 47, 608
  Samuel (Pvt.) 375
  Traney (Pvt.) 366
  William (Pvt.) 78, 460
ERWINE, William (Pvt.) 411
ERWING, John (Pvt.) 366
ESLEY, Casper (Pvt.) 131, 438
  Gasper (Pvt.) 62
  Jasper (Cpl.) 408, 423
ESPY, Casper (Pvt.) 61
  George (Pvt.) 183(2), 193, 194
  Thomas (Pvt.) 193
ESTON, Richard (Pvt.) 121, 412
ETENRIDE, Martin (Pvt.) 294
ETKESON, John (Pvt.) 316
ETMAN, William (Pvt.) 64
EVANS, Benjamin (Pvt.) 558, 650
  Daniel (Pvt.) 342, 361
  David (Pvt.) 325
  Evan (Pvt.) 342
  Henry (Pvt.), 75, 540(2)
  Hugh (Pvt.) 454, 466
  James (Pvt.) 92, 99, 104, 138, 576, 583
  John (Pvt.) 91, 103, 124, 251, 269, 275, 282, 362, 474, 493, 499, 624, 655
  Jonathan (Pvt.) 115, 130
EVART, Francis (Pvt.) 342, 655
  Gudlip (Pvt.) 81
  Nicholas (Pvt.) 96
  William (Pvt.) 80, 101

EVER, Jacob (Pvt.) 616
EVERHART, Andrew (Pvt.) 355, 364, 456
EVERT, Cutlip (Pvt.) 98
  Gudlip (Pvt.) 102
  Nicholas (Pvt.) 152, 395, 421, 432, 589
EVEY, Henry (Pvt.) 158
EVINS, David (Pvt.) 560
  John (Pvt.) 178
EWIN, John (Pvt.) 640
  Thomas (Pvt.) 640
EWING, Alexander (Lt.) 340
  Alexander (Pvt.) 267, 302, 342, 361
  Charles (Pvt.) 560
  James (2nd Lt.) 458, 465, 469
  James (Pvt.) 329, 646, 650
  John (2nd Lt.) 161("ordered back", 166
  John (Pvt.) 246, 355, 365, 457
  Joseph (Pvt.) 366
  Samuel (Pvt.) 459
  Thomas (Pvt.) 157, 188, 195
  William (Pvt.) 177, 195
EYEMAN, Christy (Pvt.) 236
EYMEN, Christley (Pvt.) 238

-F-
FADDON, John (Pvt.) 458
FAGON, James (Pvt.) 62, 132
FAIRMAN, James (Pvt.) 56, 573
FALCON, Daniel (Pvt.) 405
FALCUP, Jonas (Pvt.) 200
FALLOON, Danial (Pvt.) 401
  Daniel (Pvt.) 37, 414, 631
  John (Pvt.) 133
FALLS, Thomas (Pvt.) 292
FALOON, Daniel (Pvt.) 66, 411, 440
  John (Pvt.) 65
FARMAN, Jacob (1st Lt.) 599
  Robert (Cpl.) 529
FARMER, George (Pvt.) 140, 515
FARNEY, Jacob (Pvt.) 217, 223
FARQUHAR, Charles (Pvt.) 196
  Hugh (Pvt.) 311
FARREN, Hugh (Pvt.) 546
  John (Pvt.) 272
FARRIER, Andrew (Capt.) 481, 621
FAURNEY, Jacob (Pvt.) 222
FAY, Richard (Pvt.) 655
FEALS, Thomas (Pvt.) 293
FEAR, Samuel (Pvt.) 507
FEARHALLER, John (Pvt.) 298
FEARY, Moses (Pvt.) 218, 224
FEETORS, Abraham (Pvt.), 305

FEGAN, James (Pvt.) 407, 410, 424, 442
FELLOON, John (Pvt.) 8
FELTON, Alexander (Pvt.) 617
FENORTY, James (Pvt.) 404
FENTEN, James (Pvt.) 502
FENTON, James (Pvt.) 244
Samuel (Capt.) 43, 46, 48, 385
FERGISON, Hugh (Pvt.) 73
Joseph (Qtr. Master), 603d
Joseph (Sgt.) 59
Thomas (Pvt.) 567
FERGUE, John (Pvt.) 323
Robert (Pvt.) 332
FERGUISON, Henry (Pvt.) 588
Hugh (Pvt.) 106
FERGULSON, Joseph (Pvt.) 416
FERGUS, James (Ens.) 454
James 469
FERGUSON, Caul (Pvt.) 177, 200
Cawl (Pvt.) 161
Ebenezer (Pvt.) 31, 34, 58, 444
Ebenezer (Sgt.) 443, 590
Hance (Pvt.) 342, 457
Hanse (Pvt.) 361
Henry (Pvt.) 302
Hugh (Pvt.) 78, 544
James (Pvt.) 279, 292, 312
John (Pvt.) 20, 139, 278, 302, 309, 517,
    519, 584
Joseph (Pvt.) 10, 48, 49, 57, 135, 395,
    420, 432, 589, 635
Joshua (Pvt.) 7
Mathew (Pvt.) 287, 311
Matthew (Pvt.) 244
Moses (Pvt.) 650
Thomas (Pvt.) 581, 636
William (Pvt.) 177, 195, 315, 455, 624
FERGUY, Robert (Pvt.) 630
FERRANS, Albert (Pvt.) 73
FERREN, John (Pvt.) 315
FERRIER, --- (Capt.) 490, 509
Andrew (Capt.) 497, 618
Andrew (Pvt.) 247
John (Pvt.) 481, 497
William (Pvt.) 481, 497
FERRON, John (Pvt.) 286
FERRYER, William (Pvt.) 506
FERSTER, James (Pvt.) 556
FIELD, John (Pvt.) 56, 252, 480, 487,
    494, 572, 632
Samuel (1st Lt.) 240
FIELDS, Samuel (1st Lt.) 245, 254
FILEY, Rankin (Pvt.) 284

FILN, Patrick (Pvt.) 404
FILSON, Robert (Pvt.) 278, 538
Robert (Sgt.) 125
FINDLAY, --- (Capt.) 586
John (Qtr. Master) 367
William (Capt.) 534, 596
FINDLEY, James (Pvt.) 457
Joseph (Pvt.) 397
Samuel 607
William (Capt.) 527, 529, 609
William (Pvt.) 140
FINDLY, William (Pvt.) 152
FINDSEY, Fulton (Pvt.) 546
FINEY, Robert (Sgt.) 656
FINGERTY, James (Pvt.) 128
FINLAY, James (Pvt.) 355
Samuel (Qtr. Master) 304
William (Pvt.) 72, 94, 117
FINLEY, James (Pvt.) 290, 316, 365
John (Pvt.) 279, 289
Samuel (Qtr. Master) 298, 375
William (Capt.) 513, 529
FINNEY, Robert (Pvt.) 306
Robert (Sgt.) 397
Thomas (Pvt.) 159
FINNY, Robert (Sgt.) 142
FINSTON, Samuel (Capt.) 444
FINTAN, Samul (Capt.) 446
FINTON, James (Pvt.) 482, 501
Samue (Pvt.) 637
Samuel (Capt.) 67
Samuel (Pvt.) 425, 448
FIRDLY, Christly (Pvt.) 542
FIRESTONE, Nicholas (Pvt.) 285, 291
FISH, Nathaniel (Pvt.) 206
FISHBURN, Conrad (Pvt.) 142
Frederick (Pvt.) 431
FISHER, Abraham 607
Abram (Pvt.) 518
Conrad (Pvt.) 124, 137
Conrod (Pvt.) 91, 103, 576, 583
Frederick (Pvt.) 75, 84, 114, 130, 540
Isaac (Pvt.) 508
James (Capt.) 338, 451, 454, 462, 465,
    609, 624, 654
Lanard (Pvt.) 9
Philip (Pvt.) 290
Phillip (Pvt.) 143, 280
Samuel (Pvt.) 343, 460, 625, 655
Thomas (1st Lt.) 451, 455, 462, 466
Thomas (Pvt.) 229, 233 (over age
    proved - April 1781), 362, 624, 655
William (Pvt.) 270, 276, 283, 355, 364,

365
Zach (Pvt.) 492
Zachariah (Pvt.) 480, 495, 618, 621
FITCHGERRIL, James (Pvt.) 506
FITZGERAL, James (Pvt.) 479
FITZGERALD, James (Pvt.) 494
  John (Pvt.) 298, 300
  John (Sgt.) 604
FITZPATRICK, William (Pvt.) 625, 655
FLACK, Adam (Pvt.) 90, 98, 113
  Jacob (Pvt.) 89
  Robert (Pvt.) 52
  William (Pvt.) 436
FLAKE, Frederick (Pvt.) 546
  Jacob (Pvt.) 75
  James (Pvt.) 589
FLANAGAN, Andrew (Pvt.) 274, 294
  Elias (Pvt.) 264
  John (Pvt.) 274, 294
  William (Ens.) 367, 376, 383
  William (Pvt.) 294
FLANEGAN, Patrick (Pvt.) 205
FLANIGAN, Andrew (Pvt.) 308
  Elias (Pvt.) 294
  William (Pvt.) 307
FLANNAGAN, Elias (Pvt.) 274
  William (Pvt.) 274
FLANNEGIN, William (Ens.) 373
FLANNIGAN, Elias (Pvt.) 308
FLAUGHER, Adam (Sgt.) 93, 115
FLEAK, Frederick (Pvt.) 538
  James (Pvt.) 10
FLEAMING, James (Pvt.) 229
  John (Pvt.) 221
  Richard (Pvt.) 389
FLECK, Adam (Pvt.) 543
  Frederick (Pvt.) 541
  Jacob (Pvt.) 542
  James (Pvt.) 7
FLEMAN, James (Pvt.) 83, 111
  William (Pvt.) 492
FLEMEN, Pattrick (Pvt.) 80
FLEMIN, James (Pvt.) 100
  John (Capt.) 649
  Patrick (Pvt.) 73
FLEMING, Archibald (Pvt.) 395, 421,
    433
  Henry (Pvt.) 329
  Jacob (1st Lt.) 244
  James (2nd Lt.) 204, 209, 213
  James (Pvt.) 268, 548, 633
  John (1st Lt.) 320, 324, 326, 333, 337
  John (Capt.) 550, 645, 646

John (Pvt.) 228, 275, 294
  Mathew (Pvt.) 275
  Richard (Pvt.) 396, 641
  Samuel (Pvt.) 298, 300, 306
  Sarah 623
  William (Pvt.) 56, 206, 328, 482, 489,
    497, 554, 558, 572, 624
  William (Sgt.) 632
FLEMMING, Joseph (Pvt.) 232
FLENEGAN, John (Pvt.) 281
FLICK, Frederick (Pvt.) 362, 624, 655
FLIN, Patrick (Pvt.) 391
FLINN, Patrick (Pvt.) 403, 419, 430, 432,
    641
FLOID, James (Capt.) 214
FLONING, Richard (Pvt.) 404
FLOOD, Fenel Tally O. (Pvt.) 565
  Henry (Pvt.) 116, 586
FLORA, Abraham (Pvt.) 89, 112, 542
FLOYD, --- (Capt.) 604
  James 596
  James (1st Lt.) 202, 207
  James (Capt.) 211, 604
FLUDD, Henry (Pvt.) 122
FLUDE, Henry (Pvt.) 93
FLYN, Patr. (Pvt.) 147
  Patrick (Pvt.) 64
FOERHALLER, John (Pvt.) 300
FOLEY, Favil (Pvt.) 539
FOLK, Moses (Pvt.) 189
  Steven (Pvt.) 184, 191
FOOCE, Nicholas (Pvt.) 300
FOOKES, Peter (Pvt.) 89
FOORHEALER, John (Pvt.) 306
FOOSE, John (Pvt.) 298
  Nicolls (Pvt.) 298
FOOTS, George (Pvt.), 258
FORBES, James (Pvt.) 403, 404, 419,
    641
  John (Pvt.) 181, 197, 200
  Robert (Pvt.) 198
FORBIS, Arthur (Pvt.) 192
  James (Pvt.) 391
  Robert (Pvt.) 160, 176
FORBUS, Robert (Pvt.) 181
FORCE, John (Pvt.) 305
  Nicholas (Pvt.) 305
FORD, John (2nd Lt.) 211, 214
  John (Ens.) 202, 205
FORE, Jacob (Pvt.) 299, 306
FOREMAN, Daniel (Pvt.) 89, 112, 123,
    585
  Fred (Pvt.) 530

Frederick (Pvt.), 74, 75, 89, 90, 113,
542(2)
Jacob (1st Lt.) 511, 531, 535, 541
Jacob (2nd Lt.) 168
Jacob (Pvt.) 89, 112, 124
James (Pvt.) 486, 497, 632
Robert 608
Robert (Pvt.) 528, 537, 548, 557
FOREMEN, James (Pvt.) 481
FORETRILLOR, John (Pvt.) 104
FORGAY, Francis (Pvt.) 402
FORGESON, Ebenezer (Pvt.) 136
FORGEY, Robert (Pvt.) 552, 564
FORKES, Peter (Pvt.) 542
FORMAN, Daniel (Pvt.) 542
Jacob (1st Lt.) 598
FORREST, John (Pvt.) 269, 275, 282
FORSTER, Daniel (Pvt.) 305
John 622, 623
John (Pvt.) 630
William 655
William (Pvt.) 624
FORSYTH, James (Pvt.) 472, 619
Thomas (2nd Lt.) 241
William (Pvt.) 615
FORSYTHE, James (Pvt.) 244, 259, 474,
499
Thomas (2nd Lt.) Deceased by 23 April
1778 when replaced by James Boyle.
252
William (Pvt.) 281, 299, 301, 306
FORTES, Robert (Pvt.) 613
FORTNEY, Christy (Pvt.) 219, 225
FOSBINDER, Abraham (Pvt.) 178
Abram (Pvt.) 174
Adam (Pvt.) 178
FOSTER, Archibald (Pvt.) 298, 305, 643
Charles (Pvt.) 269, 283
Daniel (Pvt.) 298, 300
Hugh (Pvt.) 299, 301, 306
John 623
John (Pvt.) 427, 434, 449, 646
Robert (Pvt.) 289
FOSTHER, John (Pvt.) 657
FOULER, Archibald (Pvt.) 380
FOUTS, George (Pvt.) 504
John (Capt.) 239, 253
Leonard (Pvt.) 485, 621
Michael (Pvt.) 247
FOX, Abraham (Pvt.) 476, 504, 509, 651
Stofil (Pvt.) 307
FRAME, William (Pvt.) 285, 315
FRAMPTON, Arthur (Pvt.) 568, 630

John (Pvt.) 331, 567, 630
John (Pvt.) (Scout) 652
Samuel (Pvt.) 326, 338, 570
Samuel (Pvt.) (Scout) 652
FRAMTON, Arthur (Pvt.) 565
John (Pvt.) 566
Nathaniel (Pvt.) 565
Samuel (Pvt.) 565
William (Pvt.) 565
FRANKS, Daniel (Pvt.) 221, 227
FRAY, Abraham (Pvt.) 488
FRAZER, John (Pvt.) 58, 389, 396, 422,
590
Moses (Pvt.) 215
FRAZIER, John (Pvt.) 136
FRAZOR, Hugh (Pvt.) 629
FREAGHLY, John (Pvt.) 542
FREAGLEY, Andrew (Pvt.) 89
John (Pvt.) 89
FREBY, Christian (Pvt.) 615
FREDERICK, Charles (Pvt.) 625
Jacob (Pvt.) 89, 112, 542, 585
William (Pvt.) 27, 250
FREEBORN, James (Pvt.) 549
FREELAND, Andrew (Pvt.) 200
FREEMAN, Philip (Pvt.) 588
FREER, Samuel (Pvt.) 496
FREESE, John (Pvt.) 535
FREGUSON, Caul (Pvt.) 200
FREIBERGER, Andrew (Pvt.) 307
FREILY, Christian (Pvt.) 272
FREISH, Leonard (Pvt.) 434
Peter (Pvt.) 432
FRENCH, Airs (Pvt.) 371
Alexander (Pvt.) 410, 631
Arthur (Pvt.) 412, 631
Samuel (Pvt.) 149, 151, 394, 409, 424,
442, 620
William (Pvt.) 159, 180, 197, 267, 302
William (Sgt.) 247
FRETS, George (Pvt.) 270
FREY, Abraham (Pvt.) 422, 433
George (Pvt.) 421, 433
Michael (Pvt.) 422, 433
Samuel (Pvt.) 499
FRIDLEY, Andrew (Pvt.) 542
FRIDLY, Andrew (Pvt.) 112
John (Pvt.) 112
FRIEND, George (Pvt.) 272, 275
FROST, Lorace (Pvt.) 237
Lorrace (Pvt.) 238
FRUSH, Jacob (Fifer) 295, 313
Jacob (Pvt.) 74, 89, 112, 292, 406 (2:

one in Lurgin Township), 542, 647
John (Pvt.) 291
Leonard (Pvt.) 406
Peter (Pvt.) 427
FRY, Abraham (Pvt.) 36, 42, 58, 122,
   406, 472, 474, 498, 619, 638, 639
Abram (Pvt.) 396
Conrad (Pvt.) 58, 352
Gabriel (Pvt.) 244, 259, 498
Gabril (Pvt.) 503
Gebral (Pvt.) 473
George 28
George (Pvt.) 23, 25, 57, 395, 589
Jacob (Pvt.) 40, 590
Jesse (Pvt.) 244, 259
John (Pvt.) 89
Michael (Cpl.) 125
Michael (Pvt.) 82, 547, 586
Peter (Pvt.) 88, 98, 119, 528, 537, 539,
   546
Samuel (Pvt.) 474, 488
FRYE, Abraham (Pvt.) 136
Conrod (Pvt.) 136
FRYER, Hugh (Pvt.) 188
William (Pvt.) 286
FRYLE, Christopher (Pvt.) 286
FRYLEY, Christn. (Pvt.) 315
FRYLY, Christian (Pvt.) 374
FULLER, William (Pvt.) 74, 88
FULLERTEN, Humphrey (Pvt.) 104
FULLERTON, Alexander (Pvt.) 355, 456
Alexander (Sgt.) 651
Hemphrey (Pvt.) 76
Humphra. (Pvt.) 138
Humphrey (Pvt.) 92, 522, 526, 576, 583
William (Pvt.) 305
FULLOON, John (Pvt.) 10
FULTON, Alexander (Pvt.) 177, 189, 287
James (Pvt.) 481, 497
Robert (Pvt.) 41
Samuel (Pvt.) 87, 108, 118, 509, 537,
   545, 651
FURGUSON, John (Pvt.) 587
FURSYTHE, James (Pvt.) 488
FUTHEY, Samuel (Pvt.) 406, 411
FUTHY, Samuel (Pvt.) 631
FYOCK, Jacob (Pvt.) 90, 542

-G-
GABRIEL, Abraham (Pvt.) 107, 169,
   517, 535, 580
Abram (Pvt.) 514, 599
GABRIL, Abraham (Pvt.) 79, 101

GADDES, James (Pvt.) 193
GADDIS, William (Pvt.) 214
GAELY, Alexander (Pvt.) 459
GAFF, Hugh (Pvt.) 80, 101, 536
John (Pvt.) 73, 80, 102, 527, 530
GALADY, Jacob (Pvt.) 601
GALAHER, Charles (Pvt.) 586
William (Pvt.) 586
GALAUGHER, Michael (Pvt.) 424
GALBRAITH, Andrew (Pvt.) 248
James (Lt.) 3
William (Pvt.) 187
GALBREAITH, William (Pvt.) 180
GALBREATH, Andrew 607
George (Pvt.) 332, 630
John (Pvt.) 218, 224, 328
Robert (Pvt.) 414, 440, 457
Samuel (Cpl.) 529, 596
Samuel (Pvt.) 359, 456, 622
William (Pvt.) 167, 197, 360, 399, 457,
   622
GALESPY, William (Pvt.) 182
GALEY, John (Pvt.) 345
GALL, John (Pvt.) 252
GALLACHER, Charles (Pvt.) 517, 519
GALLADEY, Jacob (Pvt.) 102
GALLADY, James (Pvt.) 80
Joseph (Pvt.) 73
GALLAGHER, Charles (Pvt.) 110, 547,
   601
James (Pvt.) 249
GALLAHAN, Charles (Pvt.) 599
GALLAHAR, Thomas (Pvt.) 251
GALLAHER, Alexander (Pvt.) 169
Charles (Pvt.) 82, 124, 600
GALLAWAY, James (Pvt.) 564
Joseph (Pvt.) 327, 611, 644
Samuel (Pvt.) 645
GALLEDAY, Jacob (Pvt.) 80
GALLIDAY, Jacob (Pvt.) 522
GALLOHER, Patrick (Pvt.) 425, 636
GALLOWAY, James (Pvt.) 328, 329
John (Pvt.) 559
Joseph (Pvt.) 337, 569
Samuel (Pvt.) 553
William (Pvt.) 332, 560
GALLOWDY, Jacob (Pvt.) 526
GALLOWY, Andrew (Pvt.) 163
GALLY, James (Pvt.) 456
GALOHER, Patrick (Pvt.) 414
GALTEY, Thomas (Pvt.) 635
GAMBLE, Francis (Pvt.) 293
John (Pvt.), 327

Samuel (Pvt.) 393, 424
William (Pvt.) 539
GAMEL, Samuel (Pvt.) 61
GANCE, George (Pvt.) 93, 116
Jacob (Pvt.) 94, 117
John (Pvt.) 94, 116
Joseph (Pvt.) 94, 117
GANE, Gabriel (Pvt.) 647
GANSALUS, Richard (Lt.) 648
GANSINGER, Abraham (Pvt.) 79, 101, 123
GARACHER, Charles (Pvt.) 536
GARDENER, John (Pvt.) 458
GARDNER, Frances (Pvt.) 110
Francis (Ens.) 368, 372, 376, 383
John (Ens.) 458, 465
John (Pvt.), 346, 356, 366(2)
Robert (Pvt.) 331, 489, 554, 558
Robert (Scout) 626
William (Pvt.) 355, 456
GARIVEN, John (Pvt.) 141
GARNELL, Solomon (Pvt.) 442
GARNER, Frances (Pvt.) 82
Francy (Pvt.) 125
John (Ens.) 469
John (Pvt.) 629
Joseph (Pvt.) 446
GARNET, Samuel (Pvt.) 442
GARNEW, Robert (Pvt.) 624
GARREL, John (Pvt.) 47, 447
Robert 608
GARRET, Robert (Clerk) 346
Samuel (Pvt.) 409
GARRON, Robert (Pvt.) 275
Samuel (Pvt.) 277
GARVEN, John (Pvt.) 515
Thomas (Pvt.) 205, 214
GARVIN, James (Pvt.) 207, 625
GARWOOD, Obed (Pvt.) 342, 361
Samuel (Pvt.) 342
GASS, James (Capt.), 340 (nonjurer - 10 May 1780)
James (Pvt.) 342
Samuel (Pvt.) 342, 361
William (Pvt.) 88, 98, 119, 169, 528, 539, 546, 599
GASSHEAD, Philip (Pvt.) 572
GATIS, Samuel (Pvt.) 206
GATLEY, Thomas (Pvt.) 195
GAUDY, James (Pvt.) 455
John (Pvt.) 275
GAULT, John (Pvt.) 268, 303, 310
GAUNCE, Jacob (Pvt.) 71

Joseph (Pvt.) 72
GAY, John (Pvt.) 80, 101
Thomas (Pvt.) 178
GAYLEY, Alexander (Lt.) 340, 351
John (Pvt.) 352
GAYLY, Alexander (Lt.) 364
John (Sgt.) 364
GEARY, George (Pvt.) 510
GELLASPEY, Reuben (Lt.) 261
GELLESPIE, Alexander (Pvt.) 282
Reuben (Lt.) 290
GELVIN, Hugh (Pvt.) 421, 432
James (Pvt.) 279
GELVINS, James (Pvt.) 289
GEORGE, Adam (Pvt.) 87, 517, 519, 538, 546, 572, 586
David (Pvt.) 231, 235
Francis (Pvt.), 27, 250, 490(2)
Frank (Pvt.) 35
John (Pvt.) 191, 252, 472, 477, 485, 619
Mathew (Pvt.) 287, 312, 643
Stofel (Pvt.) 546
Stoffel (Pvt.) 88
Stophel (Pvt.) 74, 119
Thomas (Pvt.) 647
William 28
William (Pvt.) 23, 26, 143, 187, 195
GERHANGER, Henry (Pvt.) 116
GERINGER, Henry (Pvt.) 93
GETTENY, William (Pvt.) 270
GETTES, William (Pvt.) 285
GETTIS, William (Pvt.) 315
GETTYS, William (Pvt.) 272
GIB, David (Pvt.) 406, 450
Hugh (Pvt.) 109
Robert (Pvt.) 41
GIBB, David (Pvt.) 19, 139, 149, 151
Hugh (Pvt.) 81, 110
Robert (Pvt.) 149, 151, 587
GIBBINS, Edward (Pvt.) 289
GIBBONS, Edward (Pvt.) 279
GIBBONY, Edward (Pvt.) 303
GIBBS, Hugh (Pvt.) 125
Robert (Pvt.) 39
GIBE, David (Pvt.) 435
GIBSON, Andrew (Pvt.) 576, 583
Charles (Pvt.) 31, 34, 86, 141, 310, 393, 443, 444, 515
David (Pvt.) 355, 365
George (Lt.) 3
Hugh (Pvt.) 346, 356, 366, 371, 458
James (Capt.) 5, 242, 243, 259, 260
James (Pvt.) 84, 114, 130, 251, 263,

267, 302, 309, 314, 318, 388, 401,
414, 440, 636, 642
James (Pvt.) 425
John (Pvt.) 158, 184, 190, 199, 200,
266, 272, 285, 300, 306, 315, 375,
446, 448, 521, 523, 571, 575, 583,
586(2), 643
Jonathan (Pvt.) 84, 114
Robert (Pvt.) 174, 178, 613
Samuel (Pvt.) 29, 446
Thomas (2nd Lt.) 155
Thomas (Capt.) 161, 609, 614
thomas (Capt.) 166
Thomas (Col.) 46, 173, 188, 598, 608,
613
Thomas (Lt. Col.) 171
Thomas (Pvt.) 76, 92, 276, 576, 583
William (Pvt.) 30, 32, 95, 267, 302, 309,
446, 448, 521, 523, 544, 571, 585
GIDDEN, James (Pvt.) 150
GIDDENS, James (Pvt.) 423
Richard (Pvt.) 423
GIDENS, Edward (Pvt.) 61
James (Pvt.) 61, 409, 442
John (Pvt.) 62, 409
Richard (Pvt.) 61, 131, 409
GIDIENS, James (Pvt.) 393
John (Pvt.) 407
GIETS, Henry (Pvt.) 116
GIFFAN, William (Pvt.) 187
GIFFEN, Andrew (Pvt.) 29, 68, 448
GIFFIN, James (Pvt.) 574, 579, 648
GIFFON, William (Pvt.) 192
GIFIN, William (Pvt.) 182
GIFT, Adam (Pvt.) 106
George (Drummer) 545
George (Pvt.) 119
Mathias (Pvt.) 546
GILBREATH, Andrew 592
George (Pvt.) 552, 564
William (Pvt.) 354
GILCHRIST, Alexander (Pvt.) 270, 276,
284
Robert (Pvt.) 269, 275, 282
GILESPIE, Robert (Pvt.) 448
GILESPY, George (Pvt.) 182
Nathanil (Pvt.) 448
GILFILLEN, James (Pvt.) 477
GILGORE, Patrick (Pvt.) 30
GILGRIST, Alexander (Pvt.) 374
GILKESON, John (Pvt.) 232
GILKEY, John (Pvt.) 292, 296, 313
Thomas (Pvt.) 430, 431

William (Pvt.) 287, 311
GILKISON, John (Pvt.) 210, 229
GILL, John (Pvt.) 472, 619
William (Pvt.) 296
GILLAN, Phillip (Pvt.) 222
GILLASPY, James (Pvt.), 198 (removed)
GILLELAND, William (Pvt.) 613
GILLEN, Phillip (Pvt.) 209, 218
GILLESPIE, Alexander (Pvt.) 269
Henry (Ens.) 244, 254, 258, 482, 501
James (Pvt.) 501
John (Pvt.) 332, 501
Michael (Pvt.) 343, 353, 359
Nathaniel (Pvt.) 68
Robert (Pvt.) 30, 32, 95, 96
Samuel (Pvt.) 273, 293
William 605
William (Pvt.) 157, 167, 184, 617
GILLESPY, George (Pvt.) 193
Henry (Ens.) 240
James (Pvt.) 183, 193
William (Pvt.) 27, 192, 250
GILLFILLEN, James (Pvt.) 485
GILLILAN, Mathew (Pvt.) 292
GILLILAND, Hugh (Pvt.) 273
Mathew (Pvt.) 296
Matthew (Pvt.) 313
GILLILEN, James (Pvt.) 310
GILLIN, Phillip (Pvt.) 116
GILLION, Daniel (Pvt.) 383
GILLIS, John (Pvt.) 273, 293, 307
GILLISPIE, James (Pvt.) 510
Nathaniel (Pvt.) 446
Robert (Pvt.) 68, 446
Samuel (Pvt.) 307
GILLON, Daniel (Pvt.) 127
GILLSPEY, Barney (Pvt.) 93
GILMORE, William (Pvt.) 40, 182, 186,
193, 229, 232, 446, 448, 633, 647
GILSBEY, Barney (Pvt.) 116
GILSON, George (Pvt.) 569, 644
Richard (Pvt.) 207
William (Pvt.) 206
GILSPE, John (Pvt.) 505
GILSTENE, Richard (Pvt.) 214
GILSTONE, George (Pvt.) 325
GINGE, Henery (Pvt.) 183
GINGER, Henery (Pvt.) 657
Henry (Pvt.) 176, 193
Lodawick (Pvt.) 657
GINNEY, John (Pvt.) 136
GIPSON, Thomas (Pvt.) 104, 138
GIRTS, Henry (Pvt.) 94

GIST, Adam (Pvt.) 87
George (Pvt.) 87
GITNER, John (Sub.) 140
GIVEN, Daniel (Pvt.) 518
William (Pvt.) 342
GLADSTON, William (Pvt.) 427, 589
GLADSTONE, William (Pvt.) 16, 57, 395
GLADSTONES, William (Pvt.) 17, 136, 421, 432
GLASES, James (Pvt.) 577
Joseph (Pvt.) (Scout) 652
GLASFORD, Alexander (Pvt.) 244, 258, 510
GLASGO, James (Pvt.) 554
Samuel (Pvt.) 358, 362
GLASGOW, James (Pvt.) 566
Samuel (Pvt.) 352
GLASS, A. 606
Henry (Pvt.) 459
James (Pvt.) 556
Robert (Pvt.) 650
Samuel (Pvt.) 353, 358, 362, 456, 458, 466
William (Lt.) 63
William (Pvt.) 30, 32, 95, 96, 145, 147, 391 ("took up a deserter"), 403, 419, 437
GLASSCE, Joseph (Pvt.) 371
GLASSD, James (Pvt.) 577
GLASSFORD, Alexander (Pvt.) 495, 503, 651
GLBREATH, Andrew 592
GLEN, David (Sgt.) 180, 197
Gabriel (Pvt.) 187
James (Pvt.) 430, 482, 497
John (Pvt.) 185(2), 199
William (Pvt.) 199
GLENDINNING, Alexander (Pvt.) 300
GLENN, Andrew (Pvt.) 650
Gabriel (Pvt.), 158, 195 (2: one called "Little")
James (Pvt.) 58, 136, 249, 388, 396, 421, 486, 538, 617
John (Pvt.) 192
Matthew (Pvt.) 157
Mosses (Pvt.) 195
Thomas (Pvt.) 184
GLENNIN, Charles (Pvt.) 353
GLENNON, Charles (Pvt.) 359
GLENNOND, Charles (Pvt.) 343
GLIFILLEN, James (Pvt.) 248
GLINGAN, Edward (Pvt.) 292

GOARD, Joseph (Pvt.) 302
GOLD, James (Pvt.) 16, 17, 63, 146, 323, 336, 627
GOLDIN, John (Pvt.) 305
GOLDING, John (Pvt.) 298, 300, 373
GONDEY, William (Pvt.) 221
GONDY, Samuel (Capt.) 5
GONSALUS, Benjamin (Pvt.) 581, 635
GONSLOW, Emanuel (Pvt.) 330
GONSOUL, Benjamin (Pvt.) 314
GOOD, Henry (Pvt.) 527
Jacob (Pvt.) 85, 99, 541
GOOLD, James (Pvt.) 144
GOOSE, John Christy (Pvt.) 246
GOOSEHEAD, Peter (Pvt.) 77, 82
Phelty (Pvt.) 83
Philip (Pvt.) 82, 111
Phillip (Pvt.) 548
Philop (Pvt.) 126
GOOSEHORN, George (Pvt.) 470, 602
GOOSHARN, Jacob (Pvt.) 497
GOOSHEAD, Phelty (Pvt.) 111
Philip (Pvt.) 523
Phillip (Pvt.) 527
Philop (Pvt.) 126
GOOSHORN, Jacob (Pvt.) 481
Nicholas (1st Lt.) 481
Nicholas (Pvt.) 27, 250
GOOSMAN, George (Pvt.) 23
GORD, Joseph (Pvt.) 157
GORDAN, Mathew (Pvt.) 529
GORDEN, Andrew (Pvt.) 64, 147
GORDIN, David (Pvt.) 556, 577
GORDLEY, John (Pvt.), 176
GORDON, Alexander 606
Alexander (Pvt.), 130, 541, 586
Alexander (Pvt.) 99
Amos (Pvt.) 178
Andrew (Pvt.) 401, 405
David (Pvt.) 330
David 645
Gabriel (Pvt.) 8, 10, 148, 150
Gabriel (Pvt.) (Light Dragoon) 105
Gabriel 24
Gabril (Pvt.) (Light Dragoon) 122
George (Cpl.) 129
George (Pvt.) 84, 143, 169, 293, 422, 433, 535, 540, 599, 600
Henry (Pvt.) 99, 541
James (Pvt.) 298, 300, 306, 382
John 605
John (1st Lt.) 154, 155, 156, 164
John (Pvt.) 24, 32, 58, 182, 186, 589

Jonathan (Clar.) 192
Joseph (Pvt.) 252
Joseph 24
Mathew (Pvt.) 102, 537, 541
Robert (Pvt.) 91, 104, 138, 292, 373
Thomas (Ens.) 171, 174, 178
Thomas (Pvt.) 159
William (Pvt.) 104, 138, 210, 291, 352, 358
GORE, Stofel (Pvt.) 538
GORGE, Frank (Pvt.) 35
GORGIS, Samuel (Pvt.) 199
GORL, John (Pvt.) 445
GORLY, John (Pvt.) 180, 197
GORMELY, Joseph (Pvt.) 459
GORMLEY, Jol. (Sgt.) 346
Joseph (Sgt.) 348
GORMLY, Hugh (Pvt.) 457
GORRAL, John (Pvt.) 48
GORREL, John (Pvt.) 55, 67
GOSLET, James (Pvt.), 384
GOSMAN, George 28
George (Pvt.) 145
GOUDAY, James (Ens.) 339
GOUDEY, William (Pvt.), 228
GOUDY, James (Pvt.) 466
GOURLEY, Thomas (Pvt.) 160
GOWAN, William (Pvt.) 150
GOWDY, William (Pvt.) 365
GOWLEY, John (Pvt.) 195
GRABLE, John (Pvt.) 72, 94
GRADY, Elisha (Pvt.) 196
GRAHAM, Alexander (Pvt.) 482, 501, 505
Charles (Pvt.) 121, 638
Christopher (Pvt.) 495, 503, 639
Daniel (Pvt.) 342, 361, 458
David (Pvt.) 186, 193, 392
Edward (Capt.) 6, 340, 351, 364, 453, 609
Edward (Ens.) 612
Edward (Pvt.) 177
Enes (Pvt.) 411
Frances (Pvt.) 436
Francis (Pvt.) 200, 406, 411
George (Pvt.) 245
Gilbert (Pvt.) 391
Hugh (Pvt.) 17, 114, 129, 411, 427, 430, 540, 586, 636
Hugh (Pvt.) 425
James (Pvt.) 162, 206, 269
Jarret (Pvt.) 196
John 596

John (2nd Lt.) 202, 206, 211
John (Pvt.) 20, 327, 384, 435, 450, 646
John (Sub.) 140
Joseph (Pvt.) 64, 323, 392, 567, 581
Leonard (Pvt.) 113
Robert (Pvt.) 328, 349, 460, 553, 581, 634, 636
Samuel (Pvt.) 345, 352, 365
Thomas (Pvt.) 195
William (1st Lt.) 244, 253
William (2nd Lt.) 239
William (Pvt.), 184, 187, 190, 193, 244, 285, 292, 296, 302, 348, 365, 568, 582, 634, 636, 646
GRAHAME, William (Pvt.), 347
GRAHAMES, Joseph (Pvt.) 419
Robert (Pvt.) 344
GRAHAMS, David (Pvt.) 403
Emas (Pvt.) 631
Hugh (Pvt.) 631
Joseph (Pvt.) 403, 437
Robert (Pvt.) 347
William (Pvt.) 272
GRAHMS, Enos (Pvt.) 391
James (Pvt.) 313
William (Pvt.) 313
GRAME, Hugh (Pvt.) 397
GRAMES, Enes (Pvt.) 398
Gilbert (Pvt.) 398
GRANT, Pattrick (Pvt.) 458
GRASS, Samuel (Pvt.) 523
GRAVENSTINE, George (Pvt.) 18
GRAVENWALT, Michael (Pvt.) 523
GRAY, George (Pvt.) 193, 251, 483, 492, 501, 651
Hugh (Pvt.) 56, 475, 492, 500, 573, 632
John (Pvt.) 27, 158, 188, 250, 280, 475, 482, 486(2), 497, 500, 587
John (Sgt.) 290
Joseph (Pvt.) 366
Moses (Pvt.) 174, 625
Robert (Lt.) 499
Robert (Pvt.) 179, 249, 286, 288, 311, 379
Thomas (Pvt.) 343, 625(2), 655
William (Pvt.) 162, 193, 588
GRAYES, Robert (Pvt.) 277
GREASING, George (Pvt.), 548
GREASINGER, George (Pvt.) 126
GREASON William (Pvt.) 229, 232
GREASSEY, George (Pvt.) 82, 110
GREEN, Christopher (Pvt.) 96, 136, 421, 589

Christy (Pvt.) 57
David (Pvt.) 198
George (Pvt.) 27, 35, 250
James (Pvt.) 540, 599
John (Pvt.) 540, 599
Nathaniel (Pvt.) 300
Nathn. (Pvt.) 285, 315
Thomas (Pvt.) 191
William (Pvt.) 48, 476, 490, 505
GREENLEE, James (Pvt.) 653
GREENWALT, Michael (Pvt.) 77, 82, 111, 526, 548, 623
GREER, Christopher (Pvt.) 395
James (Pvt.) 304, 374, 536, 600
John (Pvt.) 91, 124, 205, 219 (smith), 229, 232, 536, 600, 633
Samuel (Pvt.) 168, 564, 597
Thomas (Pvt.) 185, 186, 371, 397, 428
William (Pvt.) 248
GREGARY, John (Pvt.) 219
GREGG, John (Pvt.) 175
Mathew (Pvt.) 187
Matt (Pvt.) 178
Matthew (Capt.) 153, 156, 164, 608
Matthew (Pvt.) 174
GREGORY, David 595
David (Pvt.) 162, 176, 183, 193
James, 324, 594, 595(2)
James (Sub. Lt.) 3, 590
John (Pvt.) 225, 433
Mark (Pvt.) 285, 315
William (Pvt.) 617
GREHAM, Hugh (Pvt.) 84
GREIER, James (Cpl.) 101
GREIR, James (Cpl.) 79
John (Pvt.) 586
GREY, John (Pvt.) 35
GREYOR, John (Pvt.) 137
GRHAM, Hugh (Pvt.) 91, 124
GRIDLEY, Daniel (Pvt.) 578, 648
Daniel 644
GRIER, Isaac (Pvt.) 431
James (Pvt.) 169, 314, 586
John (Pvt.) 103, 169
Samuel (Pvt.), 330(2)
Thomas (Pvt.) 199, 430
William (Pvt.) 160
GRIFEN, Josia (Pvt.) 411
GRIFFEN, Andrew (Pvt.) 446
Josiah (Pvt.) 58, 136
GRIFFEY, Benjamin (Pvt.) 538
GRIFFIN, Andrew (Pvt.) 31
Josiah (Pvt.) 396, 406, 422, 433, 590

GRIFFITH, Joseph (Sgt.) 350, 357
GRIFFY, William (Pvt.) 309
GRIM, Jacob (Pvt.) 481, 486, 497
John (Pvt.) 359
GRIMES, Arthur (Pvt.) 150
David (Pvt.) 645
Edward (Capt.) 459, 464
Edward (Cpl.) 617
Francis (Pvt.) 450
George (Pvt.) 258
Gilbert (Pvt.) 312
Hugh (Pvt.) 15, 148, 150
John (Pvt.) 588
Joseph (Pvt.) 644
Robert (Pvt.) 556, 577, 645
William (Capt.) 609
William (Pvt.) 310
GRINDAL, Jacob (Pvt.) 169, 522
GRINDALS, Henry (Pvt.) 137
GRINDEL, Henry (Pvt.) 586
Jacob (Pvt.) 138, 599
GRINDLE, Henry (Pvt.) 124, 575, 583
Jacob (Pvt.) 76, 92, 526, 576, 583
John (Pvt.) 91, 137, 576, 583
GRINDLED, Henry (Pvt.) 91
GRISLEY, Daniel (Pvt.) 574
GRODON, George (Pvt.) 114
Hedry (Pvt.) 85
GROVE, Abraham (Pvt.) 290
Christepher (Pvt.) 280
Christian (Pvt.) 107
Christipher (Pvt.) 101
Christopher (Pvt.) 290
Jacob (Pvt.) 102
GROVES, Abraham (Pvt.) 366
Abram (Pvt.) 356
GUDTNER, John 607
GUFFIN, Josiah (Pvt.) 631
GUILL, John (Pvt.) 484
GUIN, Charles (Pvt.) 87, 119
William (Pvt.) 47, 55, 390
GUINN, John (Pvt.) 353
GUINNEY, John (Pvt.) 58
GULLESPEY, Reuben (Lt.) 279
GUMBER, Chrisley (Pvt.) 625
Christopher (Pvt.) 655
GUNSAID, Richard (Lt.) 573
GUNSAILS, Daniel (Pvt.) 564
GUNSALUS, Richard (Pvt.) 564
GUNSARIL, Richard (Lt.) 578
GUNSAULY, Richard (Sgt.) 555, 577
GUNSOLO, Richard (Pvt.) 328
GUREL, Robert (Pvt.) 639

GURELL, Robert (Pvt.), 122, 638
GURLSY John (Pvt.) 617
GUSTIAN, William (Pvt.) 475
GUSTINE, Leml. (Pvt.) 199
GUSTON, William (Pvt.) 486, 500
GUTERY, James (Pvt.) 209
GUTHREY, John (Pvt.) 73, 106
GUTHRIE, George (Pvt.) 184
  James (Pvt.) 373
  John (Pvt.) 160, 199, 585
  Thomas (Pvt.) 205
GUTHRY, John (Pvt.) 78
GUTNER, John (Sgt.) 617
GUTTEN, John (Pvt.) 104
GUTTERY, George (Pvt.) 198
  James (Pvt.) 548
GUTTREY, James (Pvt.) 379
GUY, Thomas 595
  Thomas (2nd Lt.) 153, 159, 164
  Thomas (Pvt.) 174
GYLL, John (Pvt.) 478

-H-
H---, Nathan (Pvt.) 199
HACENERY, Casper (Pvt.) 620
HACK, John (Pvt.) 450
HACKENBERRY, James (Pvt.) 429
HACKENBERY, Casper (Pvt.) 409, 441
  Henry (Pvt.) 61, 132
  James (Pvt.) 61, 131, 408, 441
  John (Pvt.) 61, 132
  Peeter (Pvt.) 408
  Peter (Pvt.) 131
  Petter (Pvt.) 61, 441
HACKENBURY, Henrey (Pvt.) 409
  John (Pvt.) 409
HACKET, George (Pvt.) 206
  John (Clerk) 293
HACKETT, George (Pvt.) 199
HADDAN, John (Pvt.) 130
  Jonathan (Pvt.) 114
HADELSAM, William (Pvt.), 654
HADGE William (Pvt.), 404
HADSOUGH George (Pvt.), 87
HAFT John (Pvt.), 189
HAGER John (Pvt.) 80, 102, 290
HAGERTY, Robert (Pvt.) 351
  William (Pvt.), 637
HAGGINS, John (Pvt.) 360
HAGIN, John (Pvt.) 326
HAINEY, John (Pvt.) 57
HAIR, Michael (Pvt.), 604
HAIS, James (Pvt.) 41, 134

HAKE, Frederick (Pvt.) 177
HALADAY, Samuel (Pvt.) 285
  William (Pvt.) 365
HALFORDY, Edward (Pvt.) 267, 301, 309
HALFT, John (Pvt.) 177
HALL, Benjamin (Pvt.) 330, 560, 567, 630
  James (Pvt.) 236, 238
  John (Pvt.) 157, 167, 650
  Samuel (Pvt.) 481
HALLIDAY, Sameul (Capt.) 321
  Samuel (Capt.) 324
HALTE, Thomas (Pvt.) 556
HALTREE, Joseph 607
HAMAL, Robert (Pvt.) 152
HAMALTON, James (Pvt.) 151
  William (Pvt.) 151
HAMAN, John (Pvt.) 181, 182
  Jonathan (Sgt.) 192
  William (Pvt.) 181, 440
HAMBELTON, Jonathan (Pvt.) 574, 579
HAMBLE, Robert (Pvt.) 57, 540
HAMBLETON, Hugh (Pvt.) 24
  James (Pvt.) 139
  James 24
  William (Pvt.) 127
HAMEL, John (Pvt.) 134
  Robert (Pvt.) 21, 139
HAMELTON, Alexander (Pvt.) 645
  David (Pvt.), 225 (Aug 1780 - over age)
  Geoarg (Pvt.) 447
  Hugh (Pvt.) 447
  James (Pvt.) 146, 447
  John (Pvt.), 61, 131, 409
  Jonathan (Pvt.) 115
  Robert (Pvt.) 280
  Thomas (Pvt.) 191
  William (Pvt.) 61, 131, 408, 447
HAMER, Jacob (Pvt.) 267
HAMILTON, Aaron (Ens.) 563
  Alexander (Pvt.) 206, 553
  David (Pvt.) Over age ca. 1 Aug 1780. 219
  George (Pvt.) 48, 49, 67, 362, 445, 466, 624, 655
  George (Sgt.) 587
  Hugh (Pvt.) 7, 67, 192, 229, 232, 402, 425, 445, 636
  James (Pvt.) 7, 10, 18, 19, 21, 52, 53, 63, 68, 353, 359, 402, 445, 460
  James (Sgt.), 59, 603d
  John (Capt.) 26, 34, 240, 249, 255

John (Pvt.) 15, 16, 76, 91, 92, 103, 264,
    278, 287, 312, 382, 394, 424, 442,
    473, 479, 494, 498, 506(2), 626, 643,
    620
John (Sgt.) 242, 259
Jonathan (Pvt.) 569, 644
Jonathn (Pvt.) 648
Robert (Pvt.) 111, 291, 625, 655
Thomas (Pvt.) 457
William (Pvt.) 7, 10, 68, 191, 268, 270,
    294, 308, 350, 357, 392, 403, 417,
    419, 426, 438, 445, 587, 637
William 24
HAMMAN, William (Pvt.) 419
HAMMEL, Robert (Pvt.) 589
HAMMELTON, James (Pvt.) 144
John (Pvt.), 137
Jonathan (Pvt.) 130
Jonethan (Pvt.) 556
HAMMER, Jacob (Pvt.) 302
HAMMIL, Robert (Pvt.) 18
HAMMILTON, Jonathan (Pvt.) 577
HAMMON, John (Pvt.) 178
Thomas (Pvt.) 450
HAMMOND, Thomas (Pvt.) 390, 435
HAMON, William (Pvt.) 186, 198
HANAH, Matthew (Pvt.) 413
HANARD, Thomas (Pvt.) 574
HANAWALT, Henry (Pvt.) 574, 578,
    648
HANDEY, William (Pvt.) 494
HANDY, Hugh (Pvt.) 494
William (Pvt.) 518
HANEWALK, George (Pvt.) 556
HANIWAIT, George (Pvt.) 552
HANIWALTE, George (Pvt.) 577
HANKE, Elijah (Pvt.) 144
HANLEN, Cornelious (Pvt.) 94
HANLIN, Tobias (Pvt.) 116
HANLINE, Cornelious (Pvt.) 71, 117
Samuel (Pvt.) 122, 586
Tobias (Pvt.) 93
HANNA, Archibald (Pvt.) 133
David (Pvt.) 133
John (Pvt.) 133, 411, 414, 588
Mathew (Pvt.) 41, 134
Robert (Pvt.) 139, 301
Samuel (Pvt.), 133(2)
HANNAH, Archibald (Pvt.) 435
David (Pvt.) 8, 10
James (Pvt.) 343
John 28
John (Pvt.) 23, 26, 401, 405, 440, 631

Mathew (Pvt.) 66, 400
Mathias (Pvt.) 33
Matthew (Pvt.) 30
Matton 405
Robert (Pvt.) 19, 21, 142, 152
Samuel (Pvt.), 10, 23, 26, 65, 66, 399,
    400, 413(2), 415, 439(2)
Thomas (Pvt.) 359
William (Pvt.) 80, 382, 589
HANNAK, David (Pvt.) 587
HANNAN, James (Pvt.) 353
John (Pvt.) 406
HANNON, Mathew (Pvt.) 387
HANSPARIER, Henry (Pvt.) 230
HANSPEAN, Henry (Pvt.) 233
HANWALK, George (Pvt.) 564
HAPPER, Alexander (Pvt.) 40
HARBESON, John (Pvt.) 579, 649
HARBISON, John (Pvt.) 325, 574, 558
HARDAY, James (Pvt.) 151
HARDE, William 607
HARDEN, Charles (Pvt.) 316, 374
Ez. (Pvt.) 372
John (Pvt.) 285
Samuel (Pvt.) 615
Samuel (Sgt.) 286, 314, 647
HARDEY, David (Pvt.) 487
Hugh (Pvt.) 479, 503
William (Pvt.) 93, 116, 487
HARDING, Samuel (Pvt.) 271, 371
HARDMAN, Jacob (Pvt.) 647
HARDSOCK, George (Pvt.) 537
HARDY, David (Pvt.) 480, 494, 508, 618
Hugh (Pvt.) 244, 258, 573
James (Pvt.) 18, 21, 68, 421, 432, 445,
    447
William (Pvt.) 56, 480, 572, 632
HAREN, Andrew (Pvt.) 195
HARGER, Peter (Pvt.) 79, 130
Petter (Pvt.) 114
HARKIN, Daniel (Pvt.) 629
HARKNESS, David (Pvt.) 353
James (Pvt.) 353
William 596
William (Ens.) 202, 211
HARMAN, Adam (Lt.) 59
Lemuel (Pvt.) 482, 497
Marten (Pvt.) 9
Martin (Pvt.) 205
HARMON, Adam (Lt.) 603
John (Pvt.) 237
John (Pvt.) 23
John (Sgt.) 423

Martin (Pvt.) 230
Philip (Pvt.) 87
HARMONY (HARMONE,
   HARMONEY), Adam (1st Lt.) 512,
   520, 523, 525, 533, 536, 537, 544,
   581
Adam (Capt.) 537
Adam (Lt.) 571
Adam (Pvt.) 87
John 605
John (Sgt.) 7, 631
Peter (Pvt.) 87
Philip (Pvt.) 123, 538
Phillip (Pvt.) 546
HARON, John (Pvt.) 565
William (Pvt.) 31
HARPER, Alexander (Pvt.) 42, 141, 407,
   631
James (Pvt.) 158, 160, 179, 195, 431
William (Pvt.) 195, 327
HARREL, James (Capt.) 495
James (Pvt.) 35
John (Pvt.) 496
HARRELL, James (Pvt.) 26
HARREN, James (Pvt.) 391
HARRIE, --- (Capt.) 491
HARRIN, David (Pvt.) 407
James (Pvt.) 31, 398
John (Pvt.) 98, 398, 406, 416
William (Pvt.) 553
HARRING, John (Pvt.) 88
HARRIS, James (Pvt.) 27, 35, 243, 250,
   259, 478, 483, 618
John (Committee of Observation) 4
John (Pvt.) 244, 495, 503
John (Sub. Lt.) 3
Richard (Pvt.) 272, 286, 315
Roland (Pvt.) 285
Rolland (Pvt.), 315
Rowland (Pvt.) 272
Thomas (Pvt.) 102, 621
William (Pvt.) 244, 258, 477, 502, 639
HARRON, John (Pvt.) 425
Thomas (Pvt.) 175
William (Pvt.) 435, 636
HARSBARGER, Christopher (Pvt.) 89
Jacob (Pvt.) 89
Samuel (Pvt.) 89
HARSHA, Andrew (Pvt.) 184, 190
William (Pvt.) 191
HARSHAW, Andrew (Pvt.) 186
HARSHBERGER, Samuel (Pvt.) 123
HARSHEY, Andrew (Pvt.) 647

Thomas (Pvt.) 390
HARSOH, George (Pvt.) 119
HART, Charles (Pvt.) 269, 275, 283, 520,
   524, 601
Daniel (1st Lt.) 459, 464
Daniel (Pvt.) 344, 365, 612, 622
Epenetus (Lt.) 477, 508
Epenetus (Pvt.) 27, 250
Epenetus (Sgt.) 35
Epinetus (Lt.) 651
James (Pvt.) Moved to York County by
   14 March 1781. 94, 97, 528, 537
John (1st Lt.) 521
John (2nd Lt.) 513, 525, 534, 600
John (Pvt.) 71, 94, 157, 220 (1 Aug
   1780 - dead), 227, 304, 314, 344,
   360, 365, 601, 610, 612, 622
Jonathan (Pvt.) 114, 130
Ludwick (Pvt.) 79, 101, 107
William (Pvt.) 94, 97, 117
HARTER, Frederick (Pvt.) 477, 485
HARTFIELD, George (Pvt.) 184, 190
HARTLE, Peter (Pvt.) 93, 107, 116
HARTMAN, Adam (Pvt.) 298, 306
Henry (Pvt.) 184, 191
HARTNESS, Daniel (Pvt.) 361
David (Pvt.) 358
James (Pvt.) 358
HARTNIS, David (Pvt.) 456
William (Ens.) 207
HARTS, Daniel (1st Lt.) 453
HARTSHOCK, George (Pvt.) 580
HARTSOCK, George (Pvt.) 545
HARVARD, Thomas (Pvt.) 478
HARVEY, Andrew (Pvt.) 159
Charles (Pvt.) 515
Henderson (Pvt.) 121, 141, 393, 516
James (Pvt.) 7, 10, 16, 17, 131, 140, 428
James (Sgt.) 19
John (Pvt.) 481, 502, 497
William (Pvt.) 29, 161, 176, 516
HARVY, Alexander (Pvt.) 68
Henderson (Pvt.) 128
James (Pvt.) 120, 127, 128
William (Pvt.) 193
HARWICK, Anthony (Pvt.) 161, 177
Jacob (Pvt.) 157
HASBARGER, Jacob (Pvt.) 233, 541
Samuel (Pvt.) 542, 585
HASFETTER, Henry (Pvt.) 158
HASHBARGER, Chrisy. (Pvt.) 112
Jacob (Pvt.) 112, 229
Samuel (Pvt.) 112

HASHER, Andrew (Pvt.) 167
HASLET, James (Pvt.) 558
Joseph (Pvt.) 558, 567
HASLIT, James (Pvt.) 554
HASLOT, James (Pvt.) 328
HASON, Hugh (Pvt.) 336, 559
HASSEN, Hugh (Pvt.) 325
HASTON, William (Pvt.) 559
HATHORN, Adam (Pvt.) 57
HAUCK, John (Pvt.) 309
HAUGENBURGER, James (Pvt.) 423
HAUGHENBERRY, John (Pvt.) 95
HAUK, Archibald (Pvt.) 21
Mical (Pvt.) 222
Michael (Pvt.) 223
HAVARD, Thomas (Pvt.) 644
HAVERLING, Geoarge (Pvt.) 9
HAWES, John (Pvt.) 380
Peter (Pvt.) 382
HAWK, Archabald (Pvt.) 418
Archable (Pvt.) 145
Archibald (Pvt.) 63, 146, 152, 402, 437
John (Pvt.) 80
Michal (Pvt.) 9
HAWKE, Archibald (Pvt.) 18
HAWKINGBURY, Henry (Pvt.) 394
HAWN, Edward (Pvt.) 409
HAWS, John (Pvt.) 271, 643
Peter (Pvt.) 265, 272
HAWTHORN, Adam (Pvt.) 10, 133, 135
HAY, Adam (Pvt.) 474
George (Pvt.) 618
Henry (Ens.) 180, 197
Henry (Pvt.) 158
John (Pvt.) 624
Joseph (Pvt.) 181, 198
Nathan (Pvt.) 161
Samuel (Pvt.) 574
HAYES, George (Capt.) 614, 652
James (Pvt.) 37
Moses (Pvt.) 345, 352
HAYNING, Jacob (1st Lt.) 258
HAYS, --- (Capt.) 653
Aaron (Pvt.) 499
Adam (Pvt.) 502
George (Capt.) 653
George (Ens.) 239, 245, 254
George (Pvt.) 654
Henry (Ens.) 172, 634
Henry (Pvt.) 248
James (Pvt.) 39, 390, 404, 450, 641
John (Pvt.) 655
Mathew (Pvt.) 588

Moses (Pvt.) 459
Robert (Pvt.) 300, 538
William (Pvt.) 270, 276, 283, 382
HAZLET, Robert (Pvt.) 179
HAZY, Thomas (Pvt.) 588
HEADBAUGER, George (Pvt.) 635
HEALT, John (Pvt.) 574
HEANFLIN, William (Pvt.) 563
HEANY, John (Sgt.) 135
HEAP, John (Pvt.) 199, 200
HEARN, John (Pvt.) 144
William (Pvt.) 145
HEARON, John (Pvt.) 63, 146
William (Pvt.) 64, 147
HEASLET, James (Scout) 626
HEATLEY, Valentine (Pvt.) 126
HEATLY, Henry (Pvt.) 459
Robert (Pvt.) 347, 348, 455
HEAY, George (Capt.) 490
HEDDLESTON, James (Pvt.) 573
HEDDLESTONE, William (Pvt.) 573
HEDELAND, James (Pvt.) 654
HEDELSTON, James (Pvt.) 653
William (Pvt.) 653
HEDGERTY, William (Sgt.) 633
HEDLESTON, James (Pvt.) 632
William (Pvt.) 493, 496
HEDSKINS, James (Pvt.) 344
HEER, James (Pvt.) 613
HEFNAR, David (Pvt.) 117
Jacob (Pvt.) 117
HEFNER, David (Pvt.) 94
Felty (Pvt.) 107
Jacob (Pvt.) 72, 94
HEFNOR, David (Pvt.) 72
HEHMAN, Frederick (Pvt.) 89
George (Pvt.) 542
HEHNS, Michael (Pvt.) 116
HELDIBRAN, Steven (Pvt.) 231
HELHAH, Edward (Pvt.) 409
HELLAM, Jacob (Pvt.) 590
HELLAMS, Jacob (Pvt.) 590
HELLAR, Gasper (Pvt.) 188
HELLMAN, George (Cpl.) 541
George (Pvt.) 119
HELLUMS, Jacob (Pvt.), 58(2)
HELM, Jacob (Pvt.), 396
John (Pvt.) 299
HELMAN, Daniel (Pvt.) 89, 108, 112
George (Pvt.) 87, 89
Michael (Pvt.) 74, 89, 112
HELMS (Helmns), Jacob (Pvt.) 71, 94,
117, 136, 406, 422, 433

John (Ens.) 299
Michael (Pvt.) 94
HEMING, Jacob (Pvt.) 504
HEMPHILL, Andrew (Pvt.) 30, 41, 141,
   149, 150, 384, 435, 515
James (Capt.) 212
HENDERNAN, James (Pvt.) 56
HENDERSON, Daniel (Pvt.) 205, 236,
   237
Hugh (Pvt.) 251
James 405
James (Pvt.) 16, 17, 65, 66, 133, 134,
   246, 257, 280, 290, 353, 388(2),
   400(2), 401, 413, 414, 426, 439, 440,
   478, 504, 627
John (Ens.) 26, 35, 242, 249, 256
John (Pvt.) 247, 280, 281, 291, 374, 478
Joseph (Pvt.) 279, 287, 312
Mathew (Pvt.) 136
Matthew (Pvt.) 57, 395, 421, 432
Robert (Pvt.) 144, 397
Samuel (Cpl.) 641
Samuel (Pvt.) 205, 214, 267, 302, 309,
   404, 414, 440, 643
Thomas (Ens.) 216
Thomas (Pvt.) 134, 139, 206, 214, 218,
   224, 226, 230, 234
Thomas (Sgt.) 19
Valentine (Pvt.) 105, 517, 518, 519,
   543, 587
Valintine (Pvt.) 122
Vallentine (Pvt.) 78, 584
William (Pvt.) 96, 247, 257, 303, 310,
   395, 413, 415, 425, 439, 478, 480,
   494, 587, 636
HENDRICKS, George (Pvt.) 220, 226
Tobias (Pvt.) 236, 238
HENDRY, John (Pvt.) 427
HENERY, Ebenezer (Pvt.) 78
John (Pvt.) 200
Robert (Pvt.) 419, 436
Samuel (Pvt.) 585
Samuel (Pvt.) (Light Dragoon) 78
HENEY, John (Pvt.) 421, 432, 589
HENING, Jacob (1st Lt.) 253
John (Pvt.) 209
HENLINE, Samuel (Pvt.) 93, 116
HENNAN, John (Pvt.) 130
Jonathan (Pvt.) 114
HENNEN, James (Pvt.) 193
HENNERY, John (Pvt.) 449
HENNEY, John (Pvt.) 434
HENNING, Jacob (1st Lt.) 239

John 591
HENREY, John (Pvt.) 427
HENRY, Alexander (Pvt.) 622
Ebeneger (Pvt.) 287
Ebenezer (Pvt.) 311
Edward (Pvt.) 290
Francis (Pvt.) 276
James (Pvt.) 279, 281, 288, 312
James (Sgt.) 139
John (Pvt.), 163, 285, 316 (unfit for
   service)
Robert (Pvt.) 161, 177, 184, 198, 374,
   406, 440
Samuel (Pvt.) 527, 530, 544, 597
Samuel (Pvt.) (Light Dragoon) 73
Samuel (Pvt.) (Light Horse) 106
William (Pvt.) 163, 186, 196, 209, 221,
   227, 616
HEPHNER, Phelty (Pvt.) 116
HERMAN, John (Pvt.) 235
John (Sgt.) 60
Lemuel (Pvt.) 486
Martin (Pvt.) 214, 234
HERMANN, John (Sgt.) 410
HERMANY, Peter (Pvt.) 108
HERMON, John (Sgt.) 131
HERMONY, Adam (Pvt.) 119
Peter (Pvt.) 118
Philip (Pvt.) 118, 586
HERO, William (Pvt.) 331
HERON, James (Pvt.) 34
John (Pvt.) 50
William (Pvt.) 25, 34, 563
William (Sgt.) 597
HERR, Thomas 606
HERRAN, Devid (Pvt.) 411
HERRIN, James (Pvt.) 143
John (Pvt.) 143
William (Pvt.) 143
HERRISE, Thomas (Pvt.) 80
HERRON, Andrew (Pvt.) 134, 185
David (Pvt.) 403, 419, 420, 438, 631
James (Pvt.) 402, 419, 431, 443, 657
John (Pvt.) 52, 402, 411, 418, 431, 436,
   539
Jonathan (Pvt.) 119
Samuel (Pvt.) 437
William 28
William (Pvt.) 23, 402, 419, 437, 444
HERSHBARGER, Jacob (Pvt.) 108
HERVEY, James (Pvt.) 626
William (Pvt.) 42, 141, 658
HERVY, Henderson (Pvt.) 86, 384

James (Pvt.) 85(2), 383
William (Pvt.) 183
HERWICK, Anthony (Pvt.) 200
Jacob (Pvt.) 199
HESIER, John (Pvt.) 56
HESLER, John (Pvt.) 632
HESS, Jacob (Pvt.) 90, 98, 113, 543
Peter (Pvt.) 80
HESSEN, John (Sgt.) 555
HESTON, William (Pvt.) 571
HEWEY, Robert (Pvt.) 342
HEWS, John (Pvt.) 366
Patt (Pvt.) 178
Robert (Pvt.) 178
HEYNE, James (Pvt.) 183
HICKEY, James (Pvt.) 633
John (Pvt.) 308
HICKMAN, Albright (Pvt.) 77, 82, 111,
126, 548
Richard (Pvt.) 542
HICKS, Jacob (Pvt.) 74, 87, 88, 538, 546,
586
HIDE, Abraham (Pvt.) 9
Abram (Pvt.) 208
HIDEBOUGH, George (Pvt.) 184, 190
HIGGANS, John (Pvt.) 200
HIGGINS, John (Pvt.) 199, 622
Patrick 606
HIGHLANDS, William (Pvt.) 396, 406,
422, 433
HIGHMAN, Thomas (Pvt.) 119, 538, 546
HIGHT, John (Cpl.) 79, 101
HILANDS, Anthony (Pvt.) 354
William (Pvt.) 58
HILDEBAUGH, John (Pvt.) 187
HILDERBRAND, Steph (Pvt.) 234
HILHOUSE, Benjamin (Pvt.) 341
HILL, Alexander (Pvt.) 287, 311, 318
Asa (Capt.) 168, 170, 199
Asa (Pvt.) 167
Asia (Capt.) 172
Isa (Capt.) 177
Isaiah (Capt.) 172
James (Pvt.) 78, 87, 118, 123, 408, 423,
429, 441
James (Sgt.) 517, 545
John (Pvt.) 278, 427, 434, 449
Robert (Pvt.) 221, 227, 401, 405, 440
Samuel (Pvt.) 92, 99, 576, 583
HILLANDS, William (Pvt.) 590
HILLDOY, Thomas (Pvt.) 79
HILLHOUSE, Benjamin (Pvt.) 456, 467
HILLSEN, John (Pvt.) 554

HILTEBRAN, Philip (Pvt.) 273
HILTERBRAND, Jacob (Pvt.) 174
HILTIBRAND, Isaac (Pvt.) 179
HIMPHILL, Andrew (Pvt.) 128
HINDMAN, James (Pvt.) 264, 279, 287,
312, 318, 643
John (Pvt.) 288, 312
Thomas (Pvt.) 74, 88
HINENG, Jacob (Pvt.) 476
HINEY, John (Pvt.) 395
HINLES, --- (Capt.) 510
HIRRON, William McAll (Pvt.) 450
HISER, Andrew (Pvt.) 546
HISNER, John (Pvt.) 485
HOCKENBERRY, Henry (Pvt.) 33, 55,
443
James (Pvt.) 16, 48
John (Pvt.) 32
Peter (Pvt.) 7
HOCKENBRY, Herney (Pvt.) 442
HOCKENBURG, Henry (Pvt.) 31
HOCKENBURY, Peter (Pvt.) 10
HOCKINBURY, John (Pvt.) 29
HODGE, David (Pvt.) 232
John (Capt.) 386, 401, 403, 418, 420,
436, 438, 614, 656, 657
John (Lt.) 63
John (Pvt.) 147
William (Pvt.) 30, 32, 64, 95, 96, 145,
147, 391, 403, 419, 437, 642
HODGKINS, James (Pvt.) 347, 349
HODKINS, James (Pvt.) 460
HOEY, Samuel (Pvt.) 325
HOFFMAN, Adam (Pvt.) 18
HOFMAN, Adam (Pvt.) 152, 397
John (Pvt.) 404, 641
HOG, David (Pvt.) 218, 228, 269
John (Pvt.) 265, 270
HOGANBERY, Peter 24
HOGE, David (Pvt.) 209, 224, 282, 373
James (Pvt.) 207, 215
John (Ens.) 6
John (Pvt.) 215
Jonathan (Committee of Observation) 4
Michael (Pvt.) 373
Samuel (Pvt.) 207
HOGG, John (Pvt.) 306, 615
Thomas (Pvt.) 299
HOGGE, John (Pvt.) 643
Thomas (Pvt.) 375
HOGGIN, James (Pvt.) 316
HOGHENBERRY, Henry (Pvt.) 24
HOGHMAN, Abraham (Pvt.) 84

HOGMAN, Abraham (Pvt.) 75, 130
HOHENBERRY, Henry (Pvt.) 443
HOHNS, John (Pvt.) 445, 447
HOKINGBERRY, John (Pvt.) 393
HOLADAY, John (Pvt.) 285
HOLADY, Adam (Pvt.) 285
HOLDEN, Thomas (Pvt.) 246
HOLDIN, Thomas (Pvt.) 35
HOLETREE, Joseph (Drummer/Fifer)
 139
HOLIDAY, Adam (Pvt.) 272
 James (Sgt.) 297
 John (Pvt.) 297, 308
 Joseph (unfit for service) 316
 Robert (Pvt.) 351
 Samuel (Capt.) 334, 549
 Samuel (Pvt.) 272, 315
 William (Pvt.) 350
HOLLIDAY, Adam (Pvt.) 315
 James (Pvt.) 299
 James (Sgt.) 304
 John (Lt.) 314
 John (Pvt.) 274, 289, 294, 299, 305,
 576, 583
 Robert (Pvt.) 461
 Samuel (Capt.) 328, 563, 581, 635
 Samuel (Light Dragoon) 640
 Samuel (Pvt.) 265, 323, 615
HOLLMAN, Henry (Pvt.) 56, 573
HOLMAN, Henry (Pvt.) 632
HOLMBS, Jonathan (Pvt.) 341
HOLMES, Andrew (Pvt.) 186, 190
 Francis (Pvt.) 413
 John (Ens.) 263
 John (Pvt.), 10, 24, 200(2)
 Robert (Pvt.) 224
 Thomas (Pvt.) 310
 William 595
 William (Pvt.) 157, 199
HOLMS, Francis (Pvt.) 400, 439
 John (Pvt.) 67, 218, 224
 Robert (Pvt.) 218
HOLSINGER, George (Pvt.) 71, 94, 117
 Jacob (Pvt.) 93, 94, 107, 116, 117
HOLT, John (Ens.) 319, 323, 326, 332
 John (Pvt.) 561, 570, 649, 650
 William (Lt.) 649
HOLTE, Thomas (Pvt.) 577
HOLTT, John (Ens.) 338
 William (Lt.) 560
 William (Pvt.) 338
HOLTZ, William (Lt.) 551
HOMEL, Philip (Pvt.) 267

HONALTON, William (Pvt.) 120
HOOD, John (Pvt.) 265, 270, 298, 306,
 615, 643
 Moses (Pvt.) 613
 Robert (Pvt.) 272, 285, 315
HOOFMAN, Adam (Pvt.) 431
 John (Pvt.) 430
HOON, Philip (Pvt.) 185, 191
HOOPER, Alexander (Pvt.) 36
HOOPES, Alexander (Pvt.) 658
HOOVER, Jacob (Pvt.) 306
 Philip (Pvt.) 431
HOPE, James (Pvt.) 72, 78, 106, 543
 Thomas (Pvt.) 78, 105, 107
HOPER, Alexander (Pvt.) 412
HOPKENS, John (Pvt.) 104, 138
HOPKINS, John (Sgt.) 575, 582
 Mathew (Pvt.) 119, 538, 548
 Matthew (Pvt.) 74, 88
 Richard (Pvt.) 91, 576, 583
HOPPER, Alexander (Pvt.) 121, 516
 Allexander (Pvt.) 128, 384
HORLEY, Daniel (Pvt.) 478, 490, 504
HORMONY, John (Sgt.) 441
HORN, Desard (Pvt.) 412
 Edward (Pvt.) 61, 132, 394, 424, 631
 James (Pvt.) 456
 John (Pvt.) 93, 586
 Joseph (Sgt.) 348
 Samuel (Pvt.) 612
HORNER, Abraham (Pvt.) 89, 108, 112,
 541
 Daniel (Pvt.) 75, 90, 113
 Elias (Pvt.) 116, 122
 Frederick (Pvt.) 112
 John (Pvt.) 72, 89, 94, 117, 542, 585
 Mathew (Pvt.) 25
 Mathew (Sgt.) 139
 Matthew (Pvt.) 23, 589
 Sollomon (Pvt.) 119
 Solomon (Cpl.) 541
 Solomon (Pvt.) 88, 98
HORREL, James (Capt.) 495
HORRELL, James (Capt.) 55, 507, 572,
 632
 John (Capt.) 631
 John (Pvt.) 507
HORSINGER, Daniel (Pvt.) 653, 654
 Jacob (Pvt.) 653, 654
HOTLER, Samuel (Sgt.) 169
HOUGHENBERRY, John (Pvt.) 96
 Peter 426
HOUGHMAN, Abram (Pvt.) 540

49

HOUSEHOLDER, Frederick (Pvt.) 298, 300
HOUSER, John (Pvt.) 95
HOUSHOLDER, Fredrick (Pvt.) 138
HOUSTON, John (Pvt.) 619
Samuel (2nd Lt.) 203, 212
William (Capt.) 378, 614
HOVER, John (Pvt.) 280, 290
Peter (Pvt.) 106
Petter (Pvt.) 280
HOW, Abram (Pvt.) 331
James (Pvt.) 120, 128, 384
HOWARD, Gordon (Pvt.) 327, 563
Samuel 28
Samuel (Pvt.) 279, 288, 289, 601, 610
Thomas (Pvt.) 252, 280, 290, 380, 504, 508, 579, 648, 651
HOWART, Frederick (Pvt.) 71, 94
Fredrick (Pvt.) 117
Thomas (Pvt.) 569
HOWE, Abraham (Pvt.) 597
James (Pvt.) 141, 515
Robert (Pvt.) 475, 500
Thomas (Pvt.) 269
HOWEL, James (Pvt.) 249
HOWELL, James (Pvt.) 26
HOWK, Adam (Pvt.) 189
HOY, Samuel (Pvt.) 559, 571, 578
Thomas (Pvt.) 199
HUCHISON, George (Pvt.) 585
HUCK, Michael (Pvt.) 217
HUDD, Moses (Pvt.) 178
HUDSISON, Thomas (Pvt.) 179
HUDSON, George (Pvt.) 160
Joseph (Pvt.) 193
Thomas (Pvt.) 298
HUEY, Robert (Pvt.) 361, 458
HUFFE, Richard (Pvt.) 520
HUFFER, Rudolph (Pvt.) 102
HUFFMAN, Adam (Pvt.) 20, 21, 139, 142
HUGANBERGER, Peter (Pvt.) 417
HUGAND, John (Pvt.) 565
HUGANS, John (Pvt.) 338
HUGENBURGER, Casper (Pvt.) 423
John (Pvt.) 423
Peter (Pvt.) 423
HUGH, Patrick (Pvt.) 489
HUGHES, John (Pvt.) 297, 300
Patrick (Pvt.) 624
HUGHS, John (Pvt.) 180
HULING, James (Pvt.) 501, 505
Samuel (2nd Lt.) 240, 257

Samuel (Lt.) 482, 500
Thomas (Pvt.) 501
HULINGS, Samuel (2nd Lt.) 245, 254
HULL, Abraham (Pvt.) 104, 138, 549
Samuel (Pvt.) 258, 475, 486, 500, 618, 621
HUMBARGER, Heny. (Pvt.) 224
HUMBRY, Adam (Pvt.) 141
HUMBURG, Adam (Pvt.) 516
HUMBURGHER, Henry (Pvt.) 218
HUMBURY, Mical (Pvt.) 128
HUMES, James (Pvt.) 205, 236, 237
John (Pvt.) 556, 577
HUMMEL, Philip (Pvt.) 302, 309
HUMPHREY, William (Pvt.) 283
HUMPHREYS, David (Pvt.) 269, 275, 282
John (Pvt.) 372
William (Pvt.) 276
HUMPHRIES, David (Pvt.) 304
HUNSINGER, Joseph (Pvt.) 94, 97, 117
Nicholas (Pvt.) 93
HUNT, John (Pvt.) 185, 284
William (Pvt.) 160, 191
HUNTER, Alexander (Pvt.) 269, 276
Alexander (Sgt.) 283
David (Pvt.) 276, 421, 433
Edward (Pvt.) 589
George (Pvt.) 285, 382, 601, 610
James (Pvt.) 121, 128, 265, 270, 283, 643
John (Ens.) 420, 432
John (Pvt.) 7, 10, 24, 56, 57, 135, 199, 353, 395, 455, 572, 589, 632
Joseph (Pvt.) 508
Robert (Pvt.) 353, 358
William 405
William (2nd Lt.) 454
William (Pvt.) 30, 32, 61, 64, 68, 86, 95, 96, 121, 128, 145, 147, 149, 150(2), 356, 366, 389, 392, 393(2), 403, 409, 419, 424, 430, 437, 442, 446, 448, 620, 656
HURELEY, Daniel (Pvt.) 653
HURLEY, Daniel (Pvt.) 257, 654
HURLY, Daniel (Pvt.) 246
HUSAW, Henry (Pvt.) 73
HUSE, John (Pvt.) 304, 305
Robert (Pvt.) 174
HUSKINS, James (Pvt.) 365
HUSTON, Allexander (Pvt.) 189
Arnold (Pvt.) 195
Christopher (Pvt.) 208

Christy (Pvt.) 218, 224
Daniel (Pvt.) 293
David (Pvt.) 269, 275, 282, 373
James (Pvt.) 180, 197, 219, 225, 269,
   275, 282, 288, 289, 291, 295, 313,
   558, 567, 616
John (Pvt.) 208, 215, 218, 224, 328,
   472, 553, 562, 616, 630
Paul (Pvt.) 307
Robert (Pvt.) 472, 480, 487, 494
Samuel (2nd Lt.) 210
Samuel (Pvt.) 229, 232
Thomas (Pvt.) 306
William (Capt.) 262, 268, 282, 369, 609,
   642
William (Pvt.) 160, 189, 219, 225, 249,
   269, 275, 282, 292, 296, 313, 330,
   374(2), 566, 581, 597, 616, 635, 646,
   650
HUSTONE, James (Pvt.) 371
   William (Pvt.) 206
HUTCHESON, Carnelus (Pvt.) 442
   Cornelius (Pvt.) 423
   Robert (Pvt.) 292, 337
   Samuel (Pvt.) 104, 138
HUTCHINSON, John (Pvt.) 296
   Robert (Pvt.) 296, 327
   Samuel (Pvt.) 300, 455, 612
HUTCHISON, Curnelus (Pvt.) 409
   George (Pvt.) 88, 98, 119, 539, 544
   John (Pvt.) 313
   Robert (Sgt.) 611
   Samuel (Pvt.) 92, 297, 359, 621
   Thomas (Pvt.) 185
HUTCHSON, Robert (Pvt.) 562
HUTICHOSON, Samuel (Pvt.) 76
HUTMAN, --- (Pvt.) 89
HUTON, John (Pvt.) 357
HUTSON, William (Capt.) 5
HUTTON, John (Pvt.) 351
   Jonathan (Pvt.) 249
HUZAN, Henry (Pvt.) 80, 102
HYLANDS, Willams (Pvt.) 136

-I-
ILROY, James (Pvt.) 26
ILWOOD, William (Pvt.) 586
IMBLE, John (Pvt.) 105
   Pawl (Pvt.) 105
INGLE, John (Pvt.) 18, 20, 152, 430
INNES, Francis (Pvt.) 508
   James (Pvt.) 251, 289, 299, 475, 490,
   500, 505

Nathaniel (Pvt.) 505
INNIS, Francis (Pvt.) 486, 500
   James (Pvt.) 297, 305
   Nathaniel (Pvt.) 500
IRELAND, John (Pvt.) 64, 145, 147, 403,
   407, 420, 438, 587
   Samuel (Pvt.) 272, 285, 315
   William (Pvt.) 271, 284, 314
IREMBEL, James (Pvt.) 449
IRICH, Conrode (Pvt.) 112
IRVEN, Jonathan (Pvt.) 130
   Robert (Ens.) 129
IRVIN, David (Pvt.) 151, 447
   Edward (Pvt.) 508
   James (Capt.) 194, 616
   John (Pvt.) 490, 617, 508
IRVINE, David (Pvt.) 18
   James (Pvt.), 282, 379(2)
   John (Pvt.) 36, 590
   Robert (Pvt.) 34
   Robert (Sgt.) 517
   Samuel (Lt. Col.) 215
   William (Committee of Observation) 4
IRWIN, Andrew (Pvt.) 458
   Archibald (Pvt.) 266, 298, 300
   Christopher (Pvt.) 496, 507
   David (Pvt.) 19
   James (1st Lt.) 204, 209 ("ordered not to
   march"), 213, 378
   James (Capt.) 172, 176, 196, 640
   James (Lt.) 615
   James (Pvt.) 157, 219, 245, 269, 275,
   297, 298, 299, 300, 305(2), 495, 507,
   615, 651
   John (2nd Lt.) 156
   John (Pvt.) 75, 94, 97, 177, 257, 346,
   356, 388, 396, 400, 404, 406, 422,
   433, 641, 654
   John (Pvt.) 653
   Joseph (1st Lt.) 369
   Joseph (Pvt.) 225, 299, 301, 305, 306
   Robert (Ens.) 70
   Robert (Pvt.) 72, 94, 345, 458, 472, 495,
   507, 619, 651
   Samuel (Capt.) 5
   Samuel (Col.) 234, 235
   Samuel (Maj.) 9, 201, 210
   Samuel (Pvt.) 298, 301, 306
   Thomas (Pvt.) 316
   William (Pvt.) 72, 219, 225, 406, 431
IRWINE, Joseph (1st Lt.) 374
   Robert (Sgt.) 599
IRWON, Robert (Sgt.) 169

ISH, John (Pvt.) 505
ISHMAEL, Benjamin (Pvt.) Moved to
  Bedford County by 14 March 1781.
  94, 97
ISK, John (Pvt.) 476
ISSLEY, Casper (Pvt.) 25
IVERT, Nicoles (Pvt.) 136
IVIRT, Nicholas (Pvt.) 57

-J-
JACK, --- (Capt.) 62, 586, 627
  Andrew (Pvt.) 75, 84, 115, 130
  James (Pvt.) 37, 41, 64, 145, 147, 392,
    403, 404, 419, 437, 641
  James (Sgt.) 83
  John (Capt.) 6, 511, 517, 518(2), 532,
    535, 539, 598, 599, 609
  John (Maj.) 69
  John (Pvt.) 82, 110, 125, 292, 296, 313,
    548
  Jonny (Pvt.) 126
  Patrick (Capt.) 13, 28, 29, 31, 44, 63,
    95, 144, 146, 262, 291, 295, 312,
    367, 371, 376, 379, 609
  William (Pvt.) 85, 120, 127, 169, 417,
    535, 539, 580, 599
JACKSON, John Dr. (Pvt.) 307
  Samuel (Pvt.) 149
JACOB, George (Pvt.) 116
  Jarmin (Pvt.) 195
  Thomas (Pvt.) 402
JACOBS, Alexander (Pvt.) 328, 331, 645
  George (Pvt.) 94
  German (Pvt.) 248
  Jeremiah (Pvt.) 158
  Martin (Pvt.) 72, 94
  William (Pvt.) 185 (moved), 191
JAMEL, Samuel (Pvt.) 132
JAMES, Enoch (Pvt.) 264, 274, 294, 308,
  643
  Henry (Pvt.) 285, 299, 315
  Isaac (Pvt.) 351
  Jess (Pvt.) 314
  Jesse (Pvt.) 271, 284, 304
  William (Pvt.) 573
JAMESON, Francis (Pvt.) 200
  John (Pvt.) 384
  Willem 593
  William 593, 607
  William (Pvt.) 448
JAMISON, George (Pvt.) 193, 243, 248,
  259
  John (Pvt.) 342, 361, 393, 459

John (Sgt.) 620
Samuel (Pvt.) 655
William (Pvt.) 446
William (Pvt.) 592
JARDON, John (Capt.) 199
JAYS, John (Pvt.) 617
JEFFERIES, Benjamin (Pvt.) 374
JEFFERY, Benjamin (Pvt.) 292
  John (Pvt.) 219, 291, 295
JEFFERYS, Benjamin (Pvt.) 281, 296
  Thomas (Pvt.) 244
JEFFREY, John (Pvt.) 225
JEFFRY, Benjamin (Pvt.) 313
  John (Pvt.) 313
JEFFRYS, John (Pvt.) 289
JEFREY, John (Pvt.) 133
JEMESON, John (Pvt.) 86
JEMISON, John (Pvt.) 128
  Samuel (Pvt.), 625
JEMMISON, John (Pvt.) 344
  Samuel (Pvt.) 354
JEMOSON, John (Pvt.) 121
JENGER, Henry (Pvt.) 162
JENKINGS, Benjamin (Pvt.) 271
JENKINS, Anthony (Pvt.) 327
  Benjamin (Pvt.) 284, 314, 344, 372
  David 606
  David (Pvt.) 37, 39, 41, 446
  Ervin (Pvt.) 272
  Evan (Pvt.) 265, 283, 615, 643
  Thomas (Pvt.) 283
  William (Pvt.) 323
JINGER, Lodowic (Pvt.) 157
JININGS, John (Pvt.) 588
JIPPER, Charles (Pvt.) 381
JOANS, William (Pvt.) 234
JOB, James (Pvt.) 190
  Thomas (Pvt.) 192, 633
JOHN, the miller 300
JOHN, George (Pvt.) 473, 498, 506
  Gideon (Pvt.) 292, 296, 380
JOHNS, Dennis (Pvt.) 117
JOHNSON, Abram (Pvt.) 622
  Adam (Pvt.) 7
  Anrchd. (Pvt.) 449
  Archabald (Pvt.) 133
  Archibald (Ens.) 14, 32, 45, 95
  Archibald (Pvt.) 434
  Benjamin (Pvt.) 397, 430
  George (Pvt.) 397, 430
  Hugh (Pvt.) 648
  James (Col.) 125, 129
  James (Lt. Col.) 69, 531

James (Pvt.) 435, 563(2), 648
John (Ens.) 7, 10, 44
John (Maj.) 531
John (Pvt.) 17, 435, 516, 648
Lanty (Pvt.) 574, 648
Richard (Ens.) 327, 333
Richard (Pvt.) 650
Robert (Pvt.) 40, 397, 430
Thomas (Adj.) 531
Thomas (Pvt.) 590, 623
William (Pvt.) 175, 398, 431(2), 434,
    449, 563
William McCune (Pvt.) 275
JOHNSTON, Abraham (Pvt.) 363
Abram (Pvt.) 359, 365, 457
Adam (Pvt.) 67, 445, 447
Andrew (Pvt.) 326
Archibald (Ens.) 29, 148
Archibald (Pvt.) 65, 150, 427
Benjamin (Pvt.) 62, 149, 150, 428
David (Pvt.) 328
George (Pvt.) 428
Hugh (Pvt.) 569, 579, 646
Hugh (Pvt.) 574
James (Col.) 77, 83, 86, 92, 103, 105,
    109, 113, 137, 581
James (Commissary) 3
James (Lt. Col.) 38, 81, 90, 100, 118,
    510
James (Pvt.) 120, 162, 182, 183, 305,
    318, 330, 390, 392, 402, 418, 428,
    436, 446, 450, 562, 568, 569, 574,
    578, 620
John (Capt.) 614, 640, 656
John (Ens.) 13, 23, 589
John (Maj.) 30, 511
John (Pvt.) 48, 120, 134, 140, 149, 150,
    200, 208, 327, 389, 428, 450, 486,
    497, 562, 569, 574, 626
Lanty (Pvt.) 579
Richard (Ens.) 320, 324
Richard (Lt.) 611
Richard (Pvt.) 331, 553, 645
Robert (Pvt.) 36, 76, 92, 104, 142, 149,
    151, 199, 351, 363, 427, 576, 583
Robord (Sgt.) 137
Thomas (Adj.) 511, 530
Thomas (Capt.) 70, 85, 115, 130
Thomas (Pvt.) 58, 75, 84, 136, 389, 396,
    422, 433, 522, 526, 540
William (Pvt.) 85, 99, 115, 138, 143,
    331, 391, 427, 541, 553, 577
JOHNSTONE, John (Pvt.) 16, 27, 250,
    325
Robert (Pvt.) 456
William (Pvt.) 179
JOICE, William (Pvt.) 374
JOLLE, Robert (Pvt.) 35
JONES, Benjamin (Pvt.) 219, 225
James (Pvt.) 347
John (Pvt.) 30, 32, 64, 95(2), 145, 147,
    151, 347, 391, 403, 404, 419, 437,
    641
Morgan (Pvt.) 344
Nathaniel (Pvt.) 475
Samuel (Pvt.) 347, 473, 498, 506
William 606
William (Pvt.) 27, 35, 231, 250, 561,
    562, 633
JONS, James (Pvt.) 348
John (Pvt.) 348(2), 447
Morgan (Pvt.) 347, 349
Samuel (Pvt.) 348
JONSON, John (Pvt.) 481
Lanty (Pvt.) 562
JONSTON, James (Pvt.), 86, 128, 193(2)
John (Pvt.) 85, 127, 383
Thomas (Pvt.) 128
William (Pvt.) 556
JORDAN, Andrea (Pvt.) 491
Andrew (Pvt.) 473, 498, 653
David (Pvt.) 302
E--- (Pvt.) 267
John (Capt.) 173
Matthew (Pvt.) 528
Thomas (Pvt.) 245, 473, 498
JORDON, Andrew (Pvt.) 506
David (Pvt.) 309
John (Capt.) 170
Thomas (Pvt.) 506
JOYCE, William (Pvt.) 272, 315
JUDGE, Neal (Pvt.) 40, 384
Neal (Sgt.) 55
Neil (Pvt.) 141
JUMPER, Conrad (Pvt.) 158
Conrod (Pvt.) 167, 174, 178
Jacob (Pvt.) 157, 167, 174, 178, 187
JUNCHAN, John (Pvt.) 564
JUNELY, James (Pvt.) 642
JUNKEN, Landy (Pvt.) 331
Santy (Pvt.) 645
JUNKIN, Adam 605
Benjamin (Ens.) 459, 465, 469
Benjamin (Pvt.) 222, 342, 361
John (Pvt.) 218, 222
Joseph (1st Lt.) 202, 204, 211

Joseph (Lt.) 609
Joshua (1st Lt.) 213
JUNKINS, Benjamin (Pvt.) 217, 223
John (Pvt.) 224
William (Pvt.) 563, 567, 630
JURDIN, John (Capt.) 177
JUSTICE, James 605
James (Pvt.) 24

-K-
KAIN, Edward (Pvt.) 168
Patrick (Pvt.) 460
Richard (Pvt.) 524, 540
William (Pvt.) 643
KANADY, Robert (Pvt.) 439
KANE, Dinnass (Pvt.) 439
John (Pvt.) 75
Richard (Pvt.) 519
KARD, William (Pvt.) 558
KARNS, James (Pvt.) 444
KARSON, William (Pvt.) 570
KASKEY, Archibald (Pvt.) 575, 583
KEAR, John 531
KEASY, John (Pvt.) 643
KECKLER, Christo. (Pvt.) 143
Jacob (Pvt.) 430, 657
Peter (Pvt.) 431
KEEFER, Rudulph (Pvt.) 80
KEELAR, Andrew (Pvt.) 587
KEENE, Jonathan (Pvt.) 84, 115, 130
Richard (Pvt.) 84
KEEPER, William (Pvt.) 356
KEER, Archibald (Pvt.), 232 (April 1781
- "run off")
James (Pvt.) 496
Thomas (Pvt.) 589
KEEVER, Jacob (Pvt.) 421
John (Pvt.) 331, 554
KEIR, Archibald (Pvt.), 229 ("run off")
Mathew (Pvt.) 345
KEIS, John (Pvt.) 488
KEISER, Jacob (Pvt.) 433
John (Pvt.) 421, 433
KEITH, Andrew (Pvt.) 111
KEKLER, Jacob (Pvt.) 397, 416
KELLAH, Edward (Sgt.) 441
KELLAR, Martain (Pvt.) 84
Martin (Pvt.) 75
KELLARS, David (Pvt.) 87
KELLEM, John (Pvt.) 459
KELLER, Frederick (Pvt.), 117
KELLERS Jacob (Pvt.), 87
KELLEY, Abraham (Pvt.) 508

Alexander (Pvt.) 342, 345, 361
Daniel (Pvt.) 392, 403, 419, 437
Edward (Pvt.) 423
Edward (Sgt.) 27
Henry (Pvt.) 342, 345, 361
James (Pvt.) 302
John (Pvt.) 475, 486, 618, 621
Joseph (Pvt.) 32, 61, 95, 96, 132, 393,
409, 424, 442, 620
Matthew (Pvt.) 330
Samuel (Pvt.) 288, 342
William (Pvt.) 62, 132, 271, 407, 409
(b. smith), 410, 424, 428, 442, 620,
631
KELLIAH, Edward (Sgt.) 60, 131
KELLRY, Henry (Pvt.) 460
KELLY, Abraham (Pvt.) 566
Abraham (Pvt.) (Scout) 652
Alexander (Pvt.), 460, 612(2)
Daniel (Pvt.) 64, 145, 147
James (Pvt.) 267, 296, 309, 312, 373,
431
John (Pvt.) 249, 295, 431, 500, 566
John (Pvt.) (Scout) 652
Joseph (Pvt.) 29
Samuel (Pvt.) 267, 302, 309
William 605
William (Pvt.) 24, 36, 40, 142, 285, 315,
330, 412, 424, 576, 583
KELOUGH, Francis (Pvt.) 293
KEN, Thomas (Pvt.) 103
KENADY, James (Pvt.) 409
John (Pvt.) 409
Robert (Pvt.) 337, 438
Thomas (Pvt.) 193
William (Pvt.) 193
KENE, John (Pvt.) 496
Marten (Pvt.) 490
KENEDAY, James (Pvt.) 442
John (Pvt.) 442
KENEDY, Hames (Pvt.) 620
Hugh (Pvt.) 168
James (Pvt.) 104, 283
James (Sgt.) 404
John (Pvt.) 51, 54, 80, 496
Robert (Pvt.) 64
Thomas (Capt.) 609
Thomas (Pvt.) 182, 270
KENNADY, James (Pvt.) 92, 136, 435
Jonathan (Pvt.) 193
KENNEDAY, John (Pvt.) 366
KENNEDY, David (Pvt.) 273, 293, 305,
307

Hugh (Pvt.) 159, 199
James (Pvt.) 62, 76, 143, 210, 270, 276, 389, 394, 396, 424, 576, 583, 586
James (Sgt.) 641
John (Pvt.) 73, 102, 176, 183, 289, 297, 299, 305, 356, 371, 391, 398, 423, 491, 507, 617
Matthew (Pvt.) 208
Robert (Pvt.) 177, 196, 327, 426, 562, 617
Thomas 594
Thomas (1st Lt.) 166
Thomas (Capt.) 154, 157, 164, 593
Thomas (Lt.) 173, 199
Thomas (Pvt.) 101, 107, 157, 276, 281, 284, 374
William (Pvt.) 182, 301
KENNEY, Alexander (Pvt.) 359
James (Pvt.) 66, 400, 414
John (Pvt.) 431, 657
Thomas (Pvt.) 618
William (Pvt.) 168
KENNY, James (Pvt.) 134(2), 388, 440
John (Pvt.) 143
Mathew (Sgt.) 557
KEPLAR, John (Pvt.) 122, 638, 639
KEPNER, Benjamin (Pvt.) 480, 494
John (Pvt.) 477
KER, John (Pvt.) 185, 191
Thomas (Pvt.) 91
KERN, John (Pvt.) 191
KERNAHAN, William (Pvt.) 56, 572, 632
KERNEY, Ritchard (Pvt.) 151
KERNS, --- (Pvt.) 363
William (Pvt.) 359, 622
KERR, Archibald (Pvt.) 210
James (Pvt.) 247(2), 292, 296, 313, 459, 613
John (2nd Lt.) 529, 530, 533, 596
John (Pvt.) 157, 167, 184
Mathew (Pvt.) 350, 357
Matthew (Pvt.) 460
Michael (Pvt.) 430
Mikel (Pvt.) 398
Paul (Pvt.) 371
Robert (Pvt.) 381
Thomas (Pvt.) 58, 422, 433
William (Capt.) 356
William (Pvt.) 326, 461
KERREL, William 426
KERRY, Peter (Pvt.) 278, 287
KESHLER, Jacob (Pvt.) 560

KESNOR, Peter (Pvt.) 440
KEVER, Samuel (Pvt.) 327, 611
KEYLER, Andrew (Pvt.) 543, 584
KEYSER, Jack (Pvt.) 396
John (Pvt.) 395
KIDLINGER, Andrew (Cpl.) 242, 259
Andrew (Pvt.) 244, 258, 473, 498
KIERBY, William (Pvt.) 126
KIGLY, Jacob (Pvt.) 162, 163
KILE, James (Pvt.) 632
John (Pvt.) 574, 579, 646
KILERCRESE, Charls (Pvt.) 280
KILGEES, Hans (Pvt.) 458
KILGORE, Jess (Pvt.) 437
Jonathan (Pvt.) 402
Joseph (Pvt.) 120, 127, 140, 417, 516
Neamiah (Pvt.) 121
Nehemiah (Pvt.), 128(2)
Oliver (Pvt.) 342, 361
Patr. (Pvt.) 147
Patric (Pvt.) 145
Patrick (Pvt.) 32, 64, 95, 96
Samuel (Pvt.) 160
William (Pvt.) 146, 402, 418, 425, 436
KILGOUR, Patrick (Pvt.) 588
KILLEN, Daniel (Pvt.) 429
John 607
Patrick 606
KILLGORE, Samuel (Pvt.) 180, 197
William (Pvt.) 63, 416, 636
KILLHAM, Patrick (Pvt.) 467
KILLIAN, Patrick (Pvt.) 456
KILLION, Daniel (Pvt.) 127
KILLPATRICK, Joseph (Sgt.) 364
KILLWEED, Charles (Pvt.) 290
KILOUGH, Francis (Pvt.) 273, 307
KILPATRICK, Isaac (Pvt.) 345
Joseph (Pvt.) 352, 355, 461
Moses (Pvt.) 345
Robert (Pvt.) 611
Robert (Sgt.) 630
William (Pvt.) 273, 293, 445, 537, 545
William (Sgt.) 629
KIMBLE, Phillip (Pvt.) 207
KIMMINS, Thomas (Pvt.) 143
KINAIRD, William (Pvt.) 311
KINARD, William (Pvt.) 278, 287
KINCADE, Andrew (Pvt.) 356
Archibald (Pvt.) 364, 467
John (Pvt.) 356
KINCAID, Andw. (Pvt.) 366
Archabald (Pvt.) 355, 365
James (Pvt.) 197

John (Pvt.) 366
John (Sgt.) 286, 311, 601, 609
Thomas (Sgt.) 277, 286, 311
KINCART, John (Pvt.) 105
KINCEAD, John (Sgt.) 288
KINDEMAN, James (Pvt.) 632
KINDER, George (Pvt.) 184, 191
Yerkle (Pvt.) 184, 191
KINDSAY, Robert (Pvt.) 331
KING, Adam (Pvt.) 181, 186, 198
Christopher (Pvt.) 80
David (Pvt.) 189
Francis (Sgt.) 350, 357
John (Pvt.) 79, 101, 123, 181, 198
Robert (Pvt.) 180, 198
Thomas (Pvt.) 278, 287, 311
William (Pvt.) 566
KINGRIGHT, John (Pvt.) 27, 250
KINKAAR, James (Pvt.) 635
KINKADE, Andrew (Pvt.) 346
James (Pvt.) 187
John (Pvt.) 287, 346
KINKAID, James (Pvt.) 180
KINKEAD, Andrew (Pvt.) 160, 174, 458,
460
Archibald (Pvt.) 456
James (Pvt.) 157
John (Pvt.) 460
Thomas (Pvt.) 380
KINNEY, William (Pvt.) 246
KINSAUL, Emanuel (Pvt.) 597
KINSLEY, Michael (Pvt.) 624
Patrick (Pvt.) 42
Samuel (Pvt.) 229
KINSLOE, Thomas (Pvt.) 361
KINSLOW, Michael (Pvt.) 654
Patrick (Pvt.) 31, 34, 134
KIPLAR, Abraham (Pvt.) 35
KIPLER, Abram (Pvt.) 27, 250
Benjamin (Pvt.) 247
Jack (Pvt.) 244
Jacob (Pvt.) 510
John (Pvt.) 244, 621
Matthias (Pvt.) 244
Samuel (Pvt.) 56, 573
KIRBEY, William (Pvt.) 83, 111
KIRBY, Peter (Pvt.) 291, 295
Thomas (Clerk) 313
Thomas (Pvt.) 292, 296
William (Pvt.) 100, 548
KIRK, John (Pvt.) 379
John (Sgt.) 79, 101
Joseph 605

Thomas (Pvt.) 273, 380
KIRKPATRICK, Benjamin (Pvt.) 270,
276, 284
Isaac (Pvt.) 352, 612
James (Pvt.) 31, 34, 143, 443, 444
John (Ens.) 452, 456, 463, 468
John (Pvt.) 268, 276, 278, 284, 374
Joseph (Pvt.) 264, 287, 311, 460, 612,
643
Michael (Pvt.) 456
Moses (Pvt.) 161, 275, 323, 352, 460
Samuel (Pvt.) 293
William (Pvt.) 268, 275, 288, 302, 310,
318, 447
KISER, Jacob (Pvt.) 181
KISH, Christopher (Pvt.) 96, 396, 406,
434
Christy (Pvt.) 136, 590
Cristn. (Pvt.) 422
George (Pvt.) 421, 432
John (Pvt.) 433
KISHNER, Frederick (Pvt.) 139
Peter (Pvt.) 95
KISHTATER, George (Cpl.) 311
KISHVATER, Yerrack (Cpl.) 286
KISLER, Jacob (Pvt.) 328
KISLOW, Thomas (Pvt.) 341
KISSH, George (Pvt.) 427
KISSLER, Jacob (Pvt.) 259
Mathias (Pvt.) 258
KITCH, George (Pvt.) 219, 225
KITE, John (Pvt.) 326
KITIRING, Jacob (Pvt.) 152
KITTERN, Jacob (Pvt.) 145
KIZER, Jacob (Pvt.), 198 (removed)
KLINDENON, James (Pvt.) 572
KNISLEY, Samuel (Pvt.) 232
KNOP, Jacob (Pvt.) 227
KNOWLES, John (Pvt.) 420
KNOX, James (Pvt.) 266, 298, 300, 306,
382
John (Pvt.) 252, 475, 486, 500, 618, 621
Robert (Pvt.) 435, 450
Thomas (Pvt.) 18, 53, 59, 68, 318, 445,
603
KOCH, Maurice (Pvt.) 596
KOINER, Conrad (Ens.) 156
KOLT, John (Pvt.) 579
KOOLY, Henry (Pvt.) 576, 583
KOON, Peter (Pvt.) 576, 583
KOONE, Peter (Pvt.) 92, 99
KORK, Nath. (Pvt.) 571
KRUNK, Matthew (Pvt.) 445

KYLE, David (Pvt.) 264, 287
James (Pvt.) 269, 275, 282, 288, 573
John (Pvt.) 569, 649, 650
Joseph (Ens.) 275
Joseph (Sgt.) 265, 270
Josiah (Sgt.) 283
Robert (Ens.) 369, 378
Robert (Pvt.) 270, 276, 283
Samuel (Pvt.) 269, 275, 282, 288
Thomas (Pvt.) 243, 259, 276, 283
William (Pvt.), 275(2)
KYLER, Andrew (Pvt.) 78
KYLES, David (Pvt.) 278
KYNER, Frederick (Pvt.) 19

-L-
LAAGE, John (Cpl.) 408
LACEY, Isaac (Pvt.) 21, 139
LACK, Thomas (Pvt.) 35
LACKEY, Hans 606
LACY, Isaac (Pvt.) 18
LADEY, Daniel (Pvt.) 93
Henry (Pvt.) 71, 94
LADY, Henry (Pvt.) 117
LAFAVOUR, George (Pvt.) 195
LAFERTY, Patrick (Pvt.) 633
Patrick (Pvt.) 593
William (Pvt.) 115
LAFERY, Christian (Pvt.) 248
LAFEVER. See Lefavour.
LAFFERTY, Barnabas (Pvt.) 616
LAIN, Daniel (Pvt.) 301
LAIRD, Alaxander (Pvt.) 136
Allexander (Pvt.) 58
Arthur (Pvt.) 223, 226
Jacob (Pvt.) 637
Jacob (Pvt.) 426
James 596
James (Capt.) 202, 206, 596, 609
James (Pvt.) 189, 191, 207, 214
John (Pvt.) 190, 298, 305, 382
Mathew (Lt.) 173
Mathew (Pvt.) 189, 191
Matthew (1st Lt.) 158, 165
Matthew (Lt.) 247, 595
Matthew (Pvt.) 235
Samuel (Pvt.) 159, 168, 272
Thomas (Capt.) 216, 223, 226, 233, 234, 236, 615
LAKE, Nicholas (Pvt.) 545
LAM, George (Pvt.) 601
Gorge (Pvt.) 610
LAMAN, William (Pvt.) 293

LAMB, David (Pvt.) 179
George (Pvt.) 87, 119, 536, 546, 581
James (Pvt.) 342, 361
James (Sgt.) 87, 108, 118, 545
John 596
John (Capt.) 203, 207, 212, 216, 225, 232, 234, 236, 609
Joseph (Pvt.) 42
Michael (Pvt.) 94, 97, 117
Moscis (Pvt.) 119
Samuel (Lt.) 228
William (Capt.) 551, 560, 561, 649
LAMBERIC, John (Pvt.) 207
LAMBERTON, James (Pvt.) 230, 234
LAMBRIC, James (Pvt.) 206
LAMBRICK, Simon (Pvt.) 218, 224
LAMCEN, John (Sgt.) 194
LAMEN, James (Pvt.) 196
John (Pvt.), 195
LAMON, Alexander (Pvt.) 300
John (Pvt.) 176, 273
Joseph (Pvt.) 300
Robert (Pvt.) 300
William (Pvt.) 285, 307, 417
LAMOND, Alexander (Pvt.) 305
James (Pvt.) 306
John (Pvt.) 305
Robert (Pvt.) 305
LANCASTER, John (Pvt.) 116
John 122
LANCY, John (Pvt.) 647
LANDES, Abraham (Pvt.), 233 ("gone off")
Henry (Pvt.) 233
Jacob (Pvt.) 226
LANDIS, Abraham (Pvt.), 229 (as of 14 March 1781 - "run off")
Jacob (Pvt.) 220, 223
LANDRUM, Robert (Pvt.) 328
LANEY, Daniel (Pvt.) 295, 304
Hugh (Pvt.) 296
LANG, Alexander (Pvt.) 439
Alexander 657
Allexander (Pvt.) 400, 413
James (Pvt.) 535
John (Pvt.) 528
LANGINGOKRE, Peter (Pvt.) 107
LANGWELL, James (Pvt.) 629
LANTHER, Joseph (Lt.) 441
LANTHERS, William (Pvt.) 33
LANTNER, Peter (Pvt.) 252
LANY, John (Pvt.) 104
LAPPING, William (Pvt.) 270

LARD, James (Pvt.) 406
  John (Pvt.) 177
LARDE, Arthur (Pvt.) 220
LARIMER, Ebenezer (Pvt.) 474, 638
LARIMORE, Ebenezer (Pvt.) 499
  Joseph (Pvt.) (Scout) 652
  Robert (Pvt.) (Scout) 652
LARKET, Elijah (Pvt.) 620
LARRANCE, Jonathan (Clarck) 83
LARRETT, Peter (Pvt.) 200
LARRIMER, Ebenezer (Pvt.) 121
LARRIMORE, Ebenezer (Pvt.) 243, 260
LATEMORE, Ebenezer (Pvt.) 639
LATHER, James (Pvt.) 40
  Robert (Pvt.) 39, 394, 426, 636

  William (Pvt.) 31
LATIMER, Ebenezer (Sgt.) 472
  Samuel (Pvt.) 32
LATIMORE, Ebenezer (Sgt.) 619
  Samuel (Pvt.) 128, 141
  Samuel (Pvt.) 24
LATTA, Ephraim (Pvt.) 517
  William (Pvt.) 306
LAUCHLAND, Adam (Pvt.) 329
  John (Ens.) 40
LAUCHLIS, John (Ens.) 658
LAUDERSLAGLE, George (Pvt.) 650
LAUFERRY, Christ (Pvt.) 157
LAUGHLAN, John (Pvt.) 411
  Jonathan (Pvt.) 84
LAUGHLEN, John (Ens.) 146
LAUGHLIN, Adam (Pvt.) 561
  Alexander 592
  Alexander (Pvt.) 18, 19, 139, 145, 146,
    402
  Hugh (Pvt.) 64, 145, 147, 402, 419, 437
  James 28
  James (Pvt.) 23, 62, 64, 145, 147, 207
  John (Ens.) 44, 63, 144
  John (Pvt.) 403, 407, 420, 438, 631
  Rannels (Pvt.) 75
  Robert (Pvt.) 402, 418, 428, 436
  Thomas (Pvt.) 91
  William (Pvt.) 160, 195, 437
LAUGHREY, Joseph (Pvt.) 596
LAUGHURY, John (Pvt.) 647
LAUGLAND, Alexander (Pvt.) 21
LAUGLIN, Alexander (Pvt.) 63
  John (Ens.) 13
LAURY, Joseph (Pvt.) 597
LAUTHER, James (2nd Lt.) 60, 131
  James (Lt.) 387, 408, 422, 620

  James (Pvt.) 36, 41, 658
  Robert (Pvt.) 37, 41, 62, 132, 424, 442
  William (Pvt.) 41, 61, 132, 658
LAVEREY, Daniel (Pvt.) 446
LAVERTY, Barnabas (Pvt.) 210
  Patrick 605, 607
LAVERY, Daniel 606
  Daniel (Pvt.) 39, 55, 68, 425, 636
  Henry (Pvt.) 300, 306
LAVREY, Daniel (Pvt.), 59, 603d
LAW, Hugh (Pvt.) 353, 459
LAWMAN, Jacob (Pvt.) 535
LAWRANCE, Jonathan (Clarck) 130
  Jonathan (Pvt.) 114
LAWRENCE, John (Sgt.) 539
LAWSON, Anthony (Pvt.) 300
  Ralph (Pvt.) 163
LAY, Casper (Pvt.) 143
  Isaac (Cpl.) 19
LAYCOCK, John (Pvt.) 300
LAYMAR, Jacob (Pvt.) 179
LAYSON, John (Pvt.) 133, 134
  Robert (Pvt.), 31, 34, 134(2)
LEACOCK, John (Pvt.) 269, 283, 306,
  642
LEACY, Isaac (Pvt.) 131
  Isac (Pvt.) 151
  Thomas (Pvt.) 132
LEAF, Henry (Pvt.) 504
LEAKINS, David (Sgt.) 91
LEAMAN, Jacob (Pvt.) 175
LEAMOND, William (Pvt.) 402, 418,
  436
LEAMY, Hugh (Pvt.) 292
LEANEY, John (Pvt.) 76, 92, 576, 583
LEANY, Daniel (Pvt.) 313
  Hugh (Pvt.) 313
  John (Pvt.) 138
LEAP, Daniel (Pvt.) 108, 112
LEAR, Jacob (Pvt.) 308
LEARD, James (Pvt.) 399
  Matthew (1st Lt.) 154
  Samuel (Pvt.) 285
LEAS, Hugh (Pvt.) 152
LEASEY, John (Pvt.) 66
LEATH, John (Pvt.) 248
LEATHERN, Moses (Pvt.) 402
LEE, Casper (Pvt.) 398
  Edward (Pvt.) 200
  Gaspar (Pvt.) 411
  Gasper (Pvt.) 406, 431
  John Brown (Pvt.) 225
  Lewis (Cpl.) 410, 631

58

Lewis (Pvt.) 411, 431
Timmothy (Lt.) 216
Timothy 596
Timothy (1st Lt.) 203, 206, 212
Timothy (Lt.) 8
LEECK, Nicholas (Pvt.) 580
LEEF, Henry (Pvt.) 478
LEEK, Nicholas (Pvt.) 169, 535, 599
LEEKY, Alexander (Pvt.) 182, 193
LEEPER, Alen (Pvt.) 248
Allen (Pvt.) 159, 195
Charles (Capt.) 5, 156, 162, 166, 609
Charles (Pvt.) 195, 422, 434
Robert (Pvt.) 291, 295, 304, 313, 372
William (Pvt.) 195
LEETH, John (Pvt.), 184 ("movd.")
LEFAVER, Campbell (Sgt.) 59, 603
LEFAVOUR (Lafever), Cristy (Pvt.) 228
Jacob (Pvt.) 230, 233
LEFERRY, George (Pvt.) 179
LEFEVER, Christy (Pvt.), 222
LEFFERY, Christin (Pvt.) 185
LEGATE William (Pvt.) 10
LEGGAT, Robert (Ens.) 310
LEGGETT, Robert (Pvt.) 286
LEIGHLAP, Soloman (Pvt.) 411
LEIPER, James 196
LEKANS, David (Pvt.) 76
LEMAN, Adam (Pvt.) 197
William (Pvt.) 144
LEMBAR, Richard (Pvt.) 556
LEMMON, Alexander (Pvt.) 298
James (Pvt.) 298
John (Pvt.) 298, 353
Joseph (Pvt.) 297
Robert (Pvt.) 298, 615
Samuel (Capt.) 352
William (Pvt.) 314
LEMON, James (Pvt.) 163
John (Pvt.), 162
Samuel (Capt.) 339, 358
William (Pvt.) 157, 372
LEMONS, John (Pvt.) 358
LENDIS, Henry (Pvt.) 229
LENEHART, Christ (Pvt.) 200
LENERHART, Christopher (Pvt.) 200
LENTNER, Peter (Pvt.) 484
LEONARD, Andrew (Pvt.) 274
George (Pvt.) 347, 349
James (Pvt.) 269, 371, 379
Nathaniel (Pvt.) 357
Samuel (Pvt.) 474, 488, 499, 621
Samuel (Sgt.) 618

Thomas (Lt.) 340
Thomas (Pvt.) 357
LERD, Matthew (Pvt.) 231
LEREU, Jacob (Pvt.) 233
LEREW, Jacob (Pvt.) 230
LESLEY, William (Pvt.) 395
LESSMAN, George (Pvt.) 590
LESSON, Robert (Pvt.), 443, 444
LETHEREN Moses (Pvt.), 467
LEVINGSTON William (Pvt.) 176
LEWEES, Elisha (Pvt.) 308
Joshua (Pvt.) 308
LEWES, John (Pvt.) 308
LEWIS, Abraham (Pvt.) 616
Elisha (Pvt.) 274, 294
Evan (Pvt.) 123, 586
George (Pvt.) 431
Henry (Pvt.) 122, 472, 619, 638, 639
Isaac (Pvt.) 244, 259
Jacob (Pvt.) 300
John (Pvt.) 265, 292, 313, 643
Michael (Pvt.) 351
Robert (Sgt.) 470, 602
Samuel (Pvt.) 613, 635
Samuel (Sgt.) 178
William (Pvt.) 459
William (Sgt.) 346
LIENWIS, John (Pvt.) 296
LIETH, Henry (Pvt.) 246
LIFERRIE, Christopher (Pvt.) 178
LIGAT, Patrick (Pvt.) 189
Robert (Pvt.) 288
LIGGET, Robert (Pvt.) 277
LIGGIT, William (Pvt.) 8
LIGHTCAP, Levi (Pvt.) 437
Samuel (Pvt.) 174, 437
Soloman (Pvt.) 438
Solomon (Pvt.) 631
LIGOT, William (Pvt.) 133
LIMBAR, Richard (Pvt.) 577
LIMBER, James (Pvt.) 562
LIMBO, James (Pvt.) 326
Richard (Pvt.) 552, 562
LIMBS, Richard (Pvt.) 329
LINCH, Andrew (Pvt.) 347, 349, 458
David 606
David (Cpl.) 539
David (Pvt.) 84, 114, 129
George (Pvt.) 223, 226
LINDEMAN, Henry (Pvt.) 264, 294, 308
LINDERMAN, Henry (Pvt.) 274, 642
LINDSAL, William (Pvt.) 18
LINDSAY, David (Pvt.) 569

Fulton (Pvt.) 88, 98, 119, 539
James (Pvt.) 74, 88, 119, 176, 546
James (Waggon master) 598
John (Ens.) 105
John (Pvt.) 72, 74, 78, 522(2), 544, 585
Jonathan (Pvt.) 88
Jonathan (Sgt.) 192
Joseph (Pvt.) 185, 191
Thomas (Pvt.) 78, 105, 107, 543, 584
William (Lt.) 634
William (Pvt.) 163
LINDSEY, David (Pvt.) 342, 648
James (Pvt.) 183, 193, 538, 617
James (Wagon Master) 4
John (Pvt.) 526, 546, 597
William (Lt.) 182, 192
William (Pvt.) 21, 133, 152
LINDSY, David (Pvt.) 630
John (Pvt.) 538
LINE, Henry (Pvt.) 237
LINEARD, Nathaniel (Pvt.) 350
LING, David (Ens.) 534
LINING, Jacob (Pvt.) 509
LINN, James (Pvt.) 404 (for William
    Linn), 416, 425, 434, 449, 636, 642
John (Pvt.) 270, 276, 281, 284, 308,
    390, 404, 642
Robert (Pvt.) 142, 427, 434, 449, 540
Robert (Sgt.) 83, 113, 129
William 404
William (Pvt.) 37, 149, 151, 390, 404
    (James Linn was substitute), 435, 450
LINSEY, David (Pvt.) 361
William (Lt.) 171
William (Pvt.) 19, 139
LINSY, David (Pvt.) 646
LINTNER, Peter (Pvt.) 478
Peter (Sgt.) 472, 619
LINTON, Thomas (Pvt.) 482, 501, 505
LINZEY, David (Pvt.) 574, 578
LIONS, John (Sgt.) 611
LIPECAP, Samuel (Pvt.) 182
LIPER, William (Pvt.) 133
LIPLY, Anthony (Pvt.) 329
LISLE, John (Pvt.) 558, 567
Peter (Pvt.) 360
William (Pvt.) 611
LITAL, Alexander (2nd Lt.) 159
George (Pvt.) 159
James (Pvt.) 161
LITALE, Samuel (Pvt.) 205
LITLE, Alexander (Pvt.) 199
George (Pvt.) 248

LITLED, Alexander (Lt.) 247
LITTEL, George (Pvt.) 193
LITTLE, Alexander (2nd Lt.) 154
Alexander (Lt.) 595
Batt. (Pvt.) 409
George (Pvt.) 182
James (Pvt.) 61, 408, 423, 429, 441
John (Pvt.) 247, 325
Robert (Pvt.) 61, 131, 151, 252, 423,
    441, 472, 480, 487, 494
Samuel (Pvt.) 231, 234
William (Pvt.) 128, 291, 295, 329, 649
LIVESEY, Daniel (Pvt.) 122
LIVESTON, William (Pvt.) 175
LIVESY, Daniel (Pvt.) 638
LIVINGSON, David (Pvt.) 630
LIVINGSTON, Daniel (Pvt.) 650
David (Pvt.) 650
LIVINGSTONE, William (Pvt.) 179
LIWES, Evan (Pvt.) 79, 101
LLOYD, Martin (Pvt.) 285
LOCKENS, Daved (Pvt.) 104
LOCKERT, James (Pvt.) 406
LOCKETT, Joseph (Pvt.) 132
LOCKHART, James (Pvt.) 398, 431
LODIMORE, Robert (Pvt.) 565
LOGAN, Alexander (Pvt.) 182, 193
Daved (Lt.) 366
David (Lt.) 341
George (Pvt.) 346, 356, 366, 460
James (Pvt.) 207, 270, 283, 323, 355,
    356, 366, 496, 557, 568, 581, 629,
    636, 650
John (Pvt.) 182, 265, 270, 283
Jonathan (Pvt.) 193
Samuel (Pvt.) 346, 356, 366, 629
Thomas (Pvt.) 586
William (Pvt.) 355, 356, 366, 461, 629
LOGHAN, John (Pvt.) 643
LOGUE, George (Pvt.) 200
John (Cpl.) 423
John (Pvt.) 433
LOIDSENHOISER, Henry (Pvt.) 125
LONG, --- (Capt.) 586
Adam (Pvt.) 73, 80, 102
Alexander (Pvt.) 120, 127, 140, 383,
    516
Alexandor (Pvt.) 152
Allexander (Pvt.) 85
Andrew (2nd Lt.) 204, 213
Andrew (Pvt.) 89, 90, 112, 274
Benjamin (Cpl.) 647
Charles (Pvt.) 72, 94, 117

Conrad (Pvt.) 288, 293, 307
Conrod (Pvt.) 273
Daniel (Pvt.) 490, 650
David (Ens.) 513
David (Pvt.) 80, 85, 101, 120, 127(2),
    380, 428, 521, 523
Frederick (Pvt.), 221, 231, 235 ("servd.
    by hawl'g waggon")
Frederick (Sgt.) 227
George (Pvt.) 274, 294
James (Pvt.) 79, 101, 123, 169, 517,
    519, 586, 599, 600, 647
John (Cpl.) 93, 106, 116
John (Pvt.) 79, 101, 123, 169, 178, 269,
    275, 282, 288, 430, 476, 484, 599,
    616
Jonathan (Pvt.) 102
Lodovick (Pvt.) 19
Lodowick (Pvt.) 21
Lodwick (Pvt.) 148, 449
Loudin (Pvt.) 435
Ludwick (Pvt.) 20, 139, 150, 152
Michael (Pvt.) 650
Patrick (Pvt.) 276
Pence (Pvt.) 159, 248
Peter (Pvt.) 428, 430
Samuel (Ens.) 203, 205, 212, 214
Samuel (Pvt.) 184, 187, 190
William (Capt.) 512, 519, 524, 525, 533,
    544, 556
William (Pvt.) 74, 77, 82, 87, 88, 111,
    119, 126, 231, 234, 273, 527, 530(2),
    538, 546, 548
William (Pvt.) 119
LONGINARE, Peter (Pvt.) 517
LONGINGACRE, Peter (Pvt.) 93, 116
LONGNECKER, Abraham (Pvt.) 235
Abram (Pvt.) 231
LONGSTAFF, Martin 596
Martin (Ens.) 8, 202, 206, 211
Philip (Pvt.) 228
Phillip (Pvt.) 232
LONGSTAVE, Philip (Pvt.) 210
LONGWELL, James (Pvt.) 68, 366
LONGWILL, James (Pvt.) 346, 356, 446,
    448
LORD, John (Cpl.) 582
John (Cpl.) 575
LORIMORE, David (Pvt.) 73, 80, 102
Ebenezer (Pvt.) 493
John (Pvt.) 73, 80
LORMER, Ebenezer (Pvt.) 251
LOTTERD, Herman (Pvt.) 219

LOTTERT, Herman (Pvt.) 225
LOUDEMORE, Robart (Pvt.) 556
Robert 566
Thomas 566
LOUDEN, Archibald (Ens.) 463
Archibald (Pvt.) 364
George (Pvt.) 623
John (Pvt.) 539
LOUDERMELCH, George (Pvt.) 160
LOUDIMORE, Robert (Pvt.) 577
LOUDON, Archibald (Ens.) 455, 466
Archibald (Pvt.), 230 (proved not of
    age), 357
George (Pvt.) 540
Matthew (2nd Lt.) 215
LOUDWICK, Conrod (Pvt.) 108
LOUDZERHISER, Henry (Pvt.) 546
LOUGE, John (Pvt.) 637
John (Pvt.) 426
LOUGH, John (Pvt.) 298, 300, 305
LOUGHBRIDGE, Abraham (Pvt.) 187
LOUGHERY, John (Pvt.) 637
LOUGHLAND, Randls. (Pvt.) 84
LOUGHLEN, Alexander (Pvt.) 152
LOUGHRIDGE, Abram (Pvt.) 158
LOUGLAND, Randls. (Pvt.), 114
LOURY Joseph (Pvt.), 104
LOUSENHISER, Henry (Pvt.) 110
LOUSINGHISER, Henry (Pvt.) 82
LOUTHERMICK, George (Pvt.) 189
LOVE, Belly 593
David (Pvt.), 198 ("belongs to the
    Army")
Hugh (Pvt.) 351
James (Pvt.) 159, 180, 197
John (2nd Lt.) 155, 162, 165
John (Lt.) 172, 179, 196, 198
John (Pvt.) 185, 192, 198 (remov'd.),
    210, 230, 233, 248, 271
Thomas (Pvt.) 181, 198
William 607
William (Pvt.) 52, 53, 59, 68, 163, 186,
    198, 593, 603
LOVEBERRY, John Wade (Pvt.) 549
Jonathan (Pvt.) 548
LOVEN, Balsor (Pvt.) 290
LOW, Henney (Pvt.) 409
Henry (Pvt.) 294, 423
LOWARDS, Andrew (Pvt.) 294
LOWARY, James (Pvt.) 450
LOWDON (Lowden), Archibald (Ens.)
    452
Archibald (Pvt.) 234, 350

George 606, 608
George (Pvt.) 557
William (Pvt.) 501
LOWE, John (Pvt.) 431
LOWER, Balser (Pvt.) 280
LOWERY, William (Pvt.) 601, 610
LOWMAN, George (Pvt.) 73, 80, 102
Jacob (Pvt.) 79, 101, 107, 169, 580, 599
Michael (Pvt.) 79, 101, 123
Micheal (Pvt.) 586
LOWRE, William (Pvt.), 380
LOWREY, Benjamin (Pvt.) 265, 270, 276, 283
Charles (Pvt.) 297, 300, 305
James (Pvt.) 305
Joseph (Pvt.) 91, 315, 520, 576, 583
Robert (Pvt.) 298, 305, 306
Samuel (Pvt.) 305
Thomas (Pvt.) 300
William (Pvt.) 299, 301, 305, 306, 636
LOWRIE, William (Pvt.) 66, 400, 413, 439
LOWRY, Benjamin (Pvt.) 643
George (Pvt.) 527
James (Pvt.) 298, 430
John Campbell (Pvt.) 424
Joseph (Pvt.) 524
Robert (Pvt.) 300
William (Pvt.) 298, 411, 425, 631
LOY, Martin (Pvt.) 294
LOYD, James (Capt.) 228
LOYDIMED, Robert (Pvt.) 630
LUCAS, Benet (Pvt.) 86, 121
Bennet (Pvt.) 128, 393
Joseph (Pvt.) 127, 429
Thomas (Pvt.) 269, 275, 276, 282, 284, 288, 297, 300, 576, 583
LUCE, Benjamin (Pvt.) 653, 654
LUCKEY, Andrew (Pvt.) 134
Robert (Pvt.) 66, 134, 388, 401, 404, 414, 440, 642
Seath (Pvt.) 434
Thomas (Pvt.) 504
LUDEMORE, Robert (Pvt.) 554
LUDWICK, Conrade (Pvt.) 112
LUFERRY, Christian (Pvt.) 174
George (Pvt.) 174
LUGHLIN, Atchison (Pvt.), 195
LUKE Jacob (Pvt.) 246, 482, 501, 505
Thomas (Pvt.) 476, 509, 651
LUKENS, Abraham (Pvt.) 473, 498
LUKES, Joseph (Pvt.) 620
LUPHER, Jasper (Pvt.) 348, 363

John (Pvt.) 347, 348, 363
LUSK, David (Pvt.) 162, 177, 189
LUTHER, Jasper (Pvt.) 347
Patr. (Pvt.) 409
LUTZS, Godfrey (Pvt.) 200
LYLE, John (Pvt.) 630, 650
LYNCH, Andrew (Pvt.) 344
George (Pvt.) 220, 633
LYNE, Abraham (Ens.) 171, 184
Abram (Ens.) 190
Henry (Pvt.) 238
William (Pvt.) 175, 184, 191
LYNN, William (Pvt.) 579
LYON, Benjamin (Pvt.) 479, 494, 503
James (Pvt.) 323
John (Pvt.) 247, 257, 327, 337, 480, 494
John (Qtr. Master) 253
Joseph (Pvt.) 643
Samuel (Col.) 22, 239, 253
Samuel (Pvt.) 179
William (Pvt.) 168, 200, 574
LYONS, John (Pvt.) 561
LYTLE, Alexander (2nd Lt.) 164
John (Pvt.) 601, 610

-M-
MCADOE, John (Pvt.) 109
MCADOO, John (Pvt.) 91, 575, 582
MCADOS, John (Pvt.) 103, 137
MCAFEE, Henry (Pvt.) 269, 275, 282
John (Pvt.) 270, 276, 283
Robert (Pvt.) 272, 276
MCAFFEE, James (Pvt.) 196
MCALEASE, Daniel (Pvt.) 124
MCALIECE, Daniel (Pvt.) 129
MCALISTER, --- (Capt.) 490
--- (Capt.) 638
Hugh (Capt.) 121, 477, 638
Hugh (Sgt.) 242
James (Pvt.) 350, 357
John (Pvt.), 345, 350(2), 357(2)
Randle (Pvt.) 205
William (Pvt.) 243, 472, 478, 484
MCALLEICE, Daniel (Pvt.) 114
MCALLEN, George (Pvt.) 275, 283
MCALLISTER, Hugh (Capt.) 508
MCALROY, Thomas (Pvt.) 504
MCALWAIN, George (Pvt.) 133
MACALY, Nathaniel (Pvt.) 85
MCANALL, John (Pvt.) 175
MCANANY, John (Pvt.) 365
MCANLEE, Thomas (Pvt.) 347
MCANULTY, James (Pvt.) 72, 94

John (Pvt.) 80, 102, 520
Robert (Pvt.) 129
MCARICKER, Daniel (Pvt.) 347
MCARROL, John (Pvt.) 276
MCARTNEY, William (Pvt.) 245
MCATEER, John (Capt.) 211
MCAVOIE, Hugh (Pvt.) 64
MCAVORE, Hugh (Pvt.) 147
MCBEATH, Andrew (Pvt.) 218
MCBEETH, Andrew (Pvt.) 224
MCBRAYER, David (Pvt.) 292, 296, 313
MCBRIAR, David (Pvt.) 373
MCBRID, Alixandrew (Pvt.), 189 (lame)
MCBRIDE, Caleb (Pvt.) 136, 396, 406,
    422
  James (Pvt.) 323, 557, 568, 581, 634,
    636, 650
  John (Pvt.) 31, 351, 457
  John (Sgt.) 33, 65, 133, 443
  Mathew (Pvt.) 348, 349
  Matthew (Pvt.) 461
  Robert (Pvt.) 177, 189, 617
  Robert (Sgt.) 316
MCBROOM, William (Pvt.) 276, 284
MCCABE, James (Lt.) 341, 360
  John (Pvt.) 294, 357
  Robert (Pvt.) 342, 361, 456, 470, 602
  William (Pvt.) 342, 354, 361
MCCACHLEN, William 639
MCCAFFAGE, John (Pvt.) 588
MCCAFFOGUE, Joshua (Pvt.) 17
MCCAHAY, Philip (Pvt.) 178
MCCAHRAN, Archibald (Pvt.) 292
MCCAIN, Joseph (Pvt.) 435
  Rober (Pvt.) 450
  Robert (Pvt.) 435
  William (Pvt.) 442
MCCAL, Alexander (Pvt.) 648
MCCALE, John (Pvt.) 308
MCCALEB, James (Pvt.) 540
MCCALESTER, James (Pvt.) 467
MCCALEY, Samuel (Pvt.) 120, 152
MCCALISTER, Alexander (Pvt.) 180
  Andrew (Pvt.) 197
  Hugh (Sgt.) 259
  William (Pvt.) 259
MCCALL, Call. (Pvt.) 312
  James (Pvt.) 421, 433
  John (Pvt.) 271, 315
  Natt. (Pvt.) 55
  Samuel (Pvt.), 315
  William (Ens.) 386
  William (Pvt.) 195, 416, 434, 449

MCCALLAGH, Samuel (Pvt.) 205
MCCALLAH, Nathaniel (Pvt.) 15
  Natt (Pvt.) 140
  Samuel (Pvt.) 140
MCCALLASTER, John (Pvt.) 457
  William (Pvt.) 249
MCCALLE, John (Pvt.) 285
MCCALLESTER, Hugh (Capt.) 614, 638
  John (Pvt.) 467, 629
  Tole (Pvt.) 616
  William (Pvt.) 619
MCCALLEY, John (Pvt.) 81, 98
  Nathaniel (Pvt.) 428
MCCALLISTER, Hugh (Pvt.) 27, 250
MCCALLMONT, Alexander (Pvt.) 66
MCCALLY, Samuel (Pvt.) 127
MCCALMANT, Robert (Pvt.) 251
MCCALMASH, James (Pvt.) 372
MCCALMONT, James (Maj.) 5, 260
  John (Pvt.) 651
MCCALVEY, John (Pvt.) 371
MCCALY, Nathanal (Pvt.) 120
  Samuel (Pvt.) 85, 383
MCCAMANT, John (Scout) 626
  William (Pvt.) 314
MCCAMEY, John (Pvt.) 316
MCCAMIN, John (Pvt.) 554
MCCAMMON, John (Pvt.) 478, 504
  Robert (Cpl.) 242
  William (Pvt.) 284
MCCAMMOND, Alexander (Pvt.) 134
MCCAMMONT, Alexander (Pvt.) 388
  James (Maj.) 367
  Thomas (Pvt.) 432
MCCAMON, Alexander (Pvt.) 440
  Allexander (Pvt.) 401, 414
  James (Maj.) 39, 375, 608
  John (Pvt.) 508
  Thomas (Sgt.) 178
  William (Pvt.) 371
MCCAMONT, James (Pvt.) 310
  William (Pvt.) 271
MCCAN, Daniel (Pvt.) 75
MCCANAL, Robert (Ens.) 620
MCCANDLASS, Robert (Pvt.) 430
MCCANDLES, Gorge (Pvt.) 404
  James (Pvt.) 571
MCCANDLESS, George (Cpl.) 641
  George (Pvt.) 58, 388, 589
  Robert (Pvt.) 99, 428
MCCANDLIS, Robert (Pvt.) 115
MCCANDLISS, George (Pvt.) 421, 433
MCCANE, Samuel (Pvt.) 66

MCCANLESS, George (Pvt.) 136
James (Pvt.) 521, 540
Robert (Pvt.) 541
MCCANLEY, James (Pvt.) 523
MCCANLINE, Robert (Pvt.) 529
MCCANLIS, George (Pvt.) 396
Robert (Pvt.) 85, 130
MCCANN, Daniel (Pvt.) 84, 518
MCCANNEY, Joseph (Pvt.) 288
MCCARMICK, John (Capt.) 232
Robert (Pvt.) 121
MCCARNEY, Joseph (Pvt.) 311
MCCARREL, James (Pvt.) 148
John (Pvt.) 31, 149
MCCARRELL, James (Pvt.) 150
John (Pvt.) 34, 151, 444
MCCARREY, Joseph (Pvt.) 277
MCCARROLL, John (Pvt.) 270, 283, 443
MCCARTER, John (Pvt.) 57, 589
MCCARTNEY, Bart. (Pvt.) 495
Bartholomeu (Pvt.) 492
Bartholomew (Pvt.) 56
George (Pvt.) 552, 564, 630
Henry (Pvt.) 315, 373
John (Pvt.) 243, 260
Joseph (Pvt.) 80
Robert (Ens.) 550, 581, 634, 635
Robert (Lt.) 649
MCCARTNY, Bartholomw (Pvt.) 632
MCCARTY, Bartholomew (Pvt.) 480,
573
Charles (Pvt.) 350, 360, 457, 622
Henry (Pvt.) 272
John (Pvt.) 563, 630
Michael (Pvt.) 308
Thomas (Lt.) 572
William (Pvt.) 18
MCCASHAN, James (Pvt.), 66, 388
("served in Westmoreland County" -
1 Aug 1780)
John (Pvt.) 388 ("not warned"), 421
MCCASHEN, John (Pvt.) 433
MCCASHIN, James (Pvt.) 400, 414
John (Pvt.) 66, 400
MCCASHLAND, James (Pvt.) 272
William (Pvt.) 272, 285
MCCASHLEN, William (Pvt.) 643
MCCASHLIN, Andrew (Pvt.) 366
John (Pvt.) 15, 16, 381, 445
William (Pvt.) 382
MCCASHON, James (Pvt.) 405 (for
James McKee), 642
MCCASKEY, Alexander (Pvt.) 457

MCCASKIN, James (Pvt.) 440
MCCASLAN, Andrew (Pvt.) 356
MCCASLAND, William (Pvt.) 315, 615
MCCASLIN, James (Pvt.) 447
John (Pvt.) 447
MCCASLING, William (Pvt.) 265
MCCASTLIN, Andrew (Pvt.) 346
MCCATCHAR, Alexander (Pvt.) 296
MCCAUGHEY, Archibald (Pvt.) 296
MCCAUGHRAN, Archibald (Pvt.) 313
MCCAUL, Nathan (Pvt.) 626
MCCAULES, Robert (Pvt.) 184
MCCAULEY, Nathan (Pvt.) 48
Nathaniel (Pvt.) 17
Samuel (Pvt.) 516
MCCAVEN, Charles (Pvt.) 330
MCCAY, Alexander (Capt.) 319, 323
Alexander (Pvt.) 289, 295, 344, 361,
560, 568
Charles (Capt.) 28
Charles (Pvt.) 435, 625
Gilbert (Capt.) 612
Hugh (Pvt.) 576, 583
James (Pvt.) 68, 75, 270, 289, 298, 305,
570
John (Pvt.) 128, 351, 437, 612, 650
Joseph (Pvt.) 496
Matthew (2nd Lt.) 460
Neal (Pvt.) 507
Thomas (Sgt.) 364
William (Pvt.) 359
MCCEAN, John (Sgt.) 135
MCCELLEN, Robert (Ens.) 70
MCCELLEY, Robert (Pvt.) 323
MCCELLY, G. (Pvt.) 127
MCCEVER, Alexander (Pvt.) 119
MCCIBBEN, Jeremiah (Pvt.), 388 ("not
warned")
MCCIBBINS, William (Pvt.) 127
MCCIBIN, Joseph (Lt.) 449
MCCIM, James (Pvt.) 309
John (Pvt.) 309
MCCLACHEN, Joshua (Pvt.) 362
MCCLACHEY, James (Pvt.) 84, 540
MCCLACHLIN, James (Pvt.) 328
MCCLACKEY, Robert (Pvt.), 127 540
MCCLAIN, Daniel (2nd Lt.) 524, 539
John (Pvt.) 120, 151, 573
Joseph (Pvt.) 450
Neal (Pvt.) 625
Paul (Pvt.) 149, 150
Robert (Pvt.) 134
William (Pvt.) 409

MCCLALON, William (Pvt.) 138
MCCLANAHAN, James (Pvt.) 90
MCCLANAHIN, David (Pvt.) 189
MCCLANLAND, William (Pvt.) 366
MCCLANNAHIN, Robert (Pvt.) 189
MCCLANNAN, James (Pvt.) 547
MCCLAREN, Hugh (Pvt.) 272
  James (Pvt.) 157
MCCLARN, Mathew (Pvt.) 611
MCCLARON, James (Pvt.) 167
MCCLARREN, Hugh (Pvt.) 315
MCCLARTY, John (Pvt.) 566
MCCLATCHEY, James (Pvt.) 75
  Robert (Pvt.) 120, 428
MCCLAUG, William (Pvt.) 229
MCCLAUGHLIN, William (Pvt.) 267
MCCLAY, Charles (Capt.) 609, 658
  Charles (Pvt.) 37, 390, 435, 658
  David (Pvt.) 435
  James (Pvt.) 366
  John (Pvt.) 21, 37, 152, 390, 435(2), 450
  Samuel (Pvt.) 398, 406, 430
MCCLEA, Charles (Capt.) 627
MCCLEAN, Andrew (Pvt.) 57, 135, 415
  Daniel (2nd Lt.) 557
  Daniel (Pvt.) 389
  John 606
  John (Pvt.) 10, 56, 85, 127, 139, 383,
    491, 632
  John (Sgt.) 57
  Robert (Pvt.) 39, 134
MCCLEARY, John (Pvt.) 76
  Jonathan (Pvt.) 84, 115, 130
  Robert (Pvt.) 115
  William (Pvt.) 345
MCCLELAN, Daniel (Capt.) 479, 619
  George (Pvt.) 121
  Hugh (Capt.) 625
  James (Pvt.) 85, 120, 383, 425
  John (Pvt.), 383
  Joseph (Pvt.) 296
  William (Pvt.) 120, 383
MCCLELAND, Daniel (Pvt.) 251
  James (Pvt.) 283
  John (Capt.) 6
  Robert (Pvt.) 643
  William (Pvt.) 200, 643
MCCLELEHAN, Cary (Pvt.) 564
  Robert (Pvt.) 558
MCCLELIN, James (Pvt.) 413
  Thomas (Pvt.) 414, 440
MCCLELLAN, --- (Capt.) 490
  Adam (Pvt.) 177

  Daniel (Capt.) 493, 614
  George (Pvt.) 86, 128, 407
  Henry (Pvt.) 83, 100, 111
  Hugh (Capt.) 551, 557
  Hugh (Pvt.) 331
  Hugh (Scout) 626
  James (Pvt.) 32, 82, 110, 124, 127, 275,
    415, 658
  John (Pvt.) 7, 77, 82, 85, 111, 127, 417
  Joseph (Pvt.) 105, 124
  Josiah (Pvt.) 271
  Nathan (Pvt.) 658
  Robert (Ens.) 91, 137
  Robert (Pvt.) 517, 567, 575, 583, 586
  Thomas (Pvt.) 405
  William (Pvt.) 76, 92, 106, 127, 264,
    266, 278, 417, 576, 583, 596, 658
MCCLELLAND, Daniel (Capt.) 471
  Hendry (Pvt.) 267
  Hugh (Capt.) 649
  James (Pvt.) 42, 140, 269, 285, 516, 637
  John (Pvt.) 10, 29, 41, 140, 141, 243,
    259, 299 (2), 301, 306, 516(2), 636
  Joseph (Pvt.) 313
  Robert (Pvt.) 300, 331, 519
  Samuel (Pvt.) 460
  Thomas 42
  Thomas (Pvt.) 36, 40, 134
  William (Ens.) 323
  William (Pvt.) 36, 42, 287, 298, 301,
    306, 312, 516
MCCLELLEN, Thomas (Pvt.) 401
MCCLELLIN, James (Pvt.) 399
MCCLELON, James (Pvt.) 152
  John (Pvt.) 120
  Robert (Pvt.) 518
  Thomas (Pvt.) 66
MCCLELONS, --- (Capt.) 509
MCCLENAHAN, James (Pvt.) 75, 79,
    93, 101(2), 107, 123, 518, 586
  John (Pvt.), 72, 93, 94, 117, 122 (for
    John Lancaster apprentice)
MCCLENAN, William (Pvt.) 527
MCCLENE, John (2nd Lt.) 368
MCCLENNAHAN, James (Pvt.) 517
MCCLENOHON, James (Pvt.) 79
MCCLEORY, Robert (Pvt.) 130
MCCLERON, Hugh (Pvt.) 285
MCCLERY, Alexander (Pvt.) 540
  John (Pvt.) 541
MCCLESTAN, John (Pvt.) 24
MCCLEVAIN, Andrew (Pvt.) 64, 147
  Joseph (Pvt.) 64

MCCLEWAIN, Robert (Pvt.) 425, 636
MCCLILLAN, William (Pvt.) 530
MCCLINTECK, William (Pvt.) 106
MCCLINTICK, John (Pvt.) 629
MCCLINTIE, Robert (Pvt.) 225
MCCLINTOCH, John (Pvt.) 461
MCCLINTOCK, Alexander (Pvt.), 31,
    33, 68, 443, 444, 446(2)
Alexander (Sgt.) 656
Andrew (Pvt.) 30
Daniel (Pvt.) 78, 97, 296, 313, 353, 362,
    456, 466, 544, 585
Hugh (Pvt.) 343, 353, 355, 364, 365,
    459
James (Pvt.) 365
John (Pvt.) 355, 356, 366
John (Sgt.) 587
Joseph (Pvt.) 169, 355, 364, 528, 599
Joseph (Sgt.) 529, 543, 584
Robert (Pvt.) 219, 356, 366
William (Pvt.) 72, 78, 355, 366, 449,
    457, 544, 585
MCCLINTOCT, Alexander (Pvt.) 448
MCCLINTOG, Daniel (Pvt.) 358
Hugh (Pvt.) 359
Robert (Pvt.) 458
MCCLLAN, George (Pvt.) 412
MCCLOAD, John (Pvt.) 629
MCCLOSKEY, John (Pvt.) 126
MCCLOUD, John (Pvt.) 342, 361
Norman (Pvt.) 341, 361
William (Pvt.) 218, 224
MCCLUCUS, John (Pvt.) 548
MCCLUER, George 592
Hugh (Pvt.) 409, 442
John (Pvt.) 61, 409, 412, 442
MCCLUN, Hugh (Pvt.) 616
Samuel (Pvt.) 351
MCCLUNE, David (Pvt.) 147
John (Pvt.) 479, 631
MCCLUNG, James (Pvt.) 196, 392, 403
Robert (Pvt.) 457
MCCLUNY, Michael (Pvt.) 180
MCCLURE, Alexander (Pvt.) 176, 183,
    193, 617
Charles (Pvt.) 182, 231, 235
Charles (Qtr. Master) 153
Chrs. (Pvt.) 193
Daniel (Pvt.) 181
David (Pvt.) 457, 467
Denny (Pvt.) 198
George (Pvt.) 158, 167, 365
Hugh (Pvt.) 394

James (1st Lt.) 319, 322, 324, 333
James (Light Dragoon) 640
James (Lt. Dn.) 198
James (Lt.) 489, 552, 623(2), 649
James (Pvt.) 160, 176, 181, 182, 193,
    353, 358, 457
John (Ens.) 338, 654
John (Pvt.) 31, 182, 244, 258, 394, 443,
    477, 502, 612(2), 629, 639
Jonathan (Pvt.) 193
Joseph (Pvt.) 207, 214
Robert (Pvt.) 193
Samuel (Pvt.) 92, 99, 102, 104, 355,
    357, 470, 602, 629
Thomas (Pvt.) 350
William (Capt.) 155, 160, 165, 608
William (Pvt.) 158, 159, 167, 176,
    182(2), 186, 193(3), 198, 354, 625,
    647, 655
MCCLURG, William (Pvt.) 232, 633
MCCLWAIN, Andrew (Pvt.) 145
MCCLYMON, David (Pvt.) 287
MCCOEY, James (Pvt.) 326
MCCOLLAM, John (Pvt.) 590
MCCOLLOCH, James (Pvt.) 372
Nathan (Pvt.) 47
Samuel (Pvt.) 523, 536
MCCOLLOM, John (Pvt.) 58, 392, 403,
    419, 437, 635, 656
Michael (Pvt.) 481
Michal (Pvt.) 497
Thomas 608
MCCOLLON, Michael (Pvt.) 502
MCCOLLOUGH, George (Pvt.) 250
Hance (Lt.) 299
James (Pvt.) 196
John (Pvt.) 196
Patrick (Pvt.) 284
MCCOLLUGH, Samuel (Pvt.) 84
MCCOLLUM, Alexander (Pvt.) 209
James (Pvt.) 247, 483, 501
John (Pvt.), 136 (dis.)
Michael (Pvt.) 244
MCCOLLY, Nat. (Pvt.) 127
MCCOLM, Hugh (Pvt.) 143
MCCOLMONT, Robert (Pvt.) 56
MCCOLOCH, Hance (Lt.) 642
MCCOLOM, Hugh (Pvt.) 633
MCCOLOUGH, Robert (Pvt.) 152
Samuel (Pvt.) 540
MCCOMB, James (Pvt.) 39, 52, 68, 418,
    436, 446
James (Troop Lt. Horse) 428

John (Lt.) 386, 397, 429, 656
Robert 596
Robert (2nd Lt.) 12, 22, 25, 43, 54, 62, 444, 447
Robert (Lt.) 27, 67
Robert (Pvt.) 8, 142, 588
Thomas (Pvt.) 20
William (Pvt.) 18, 390, 435, 450
MCCOMBE, Robert (2nd Lt.) 51
MCCOMBES, William (Pvt.), 152
MCCOMBS James (Pvt.) 448
John (Pvt.) 143
Robert (Pvt.) 24
Thomas (Pvt.) 139
MCCOMMON, Robert (Cpl.) 259
Robert (Pvt.) 572, 632
Thomas (Pvt.) 174
MCCOMONING, John (Pvt.) 558
MCCONACY, James (Pvt.) 152
MCCONAGY, Samuel (Pvt.) 303
MCCONAHAY, John (Pvt.) 121
MCCONAHEE, James (Sgt.) 384
MCCONAHEY, James (Pvt.) 120
MCCONAHY, James (Pvt.) 85, 127
John (Pvt.) 128
MCCONAKEE, Samuel (Sgt.) 49
MCCONAL, James (Capt.) 251
MCCONALD, John (Capt.) 639
Robert 639
Robert (3rd Sgt.) 141
MCCONCHAY, Samuel (Pvt.) 643
MCCONEL, Randle (Pvt.) 604
Robert (Pvt.) 309
Robert (Sgt.) 384
MCCONKEY, Jacob (Pvt.) 126
Jacob (Sgt.) 81, 110
MCCONNAGHY, John (Pvt.) 407
MCCONNAL, James (Capt.) 609
James (Pvt.) 281, 286, 497
John (Pvt.) 497
Robert (Capt.) 120
Thomas (Pvt.) 481, 497
William (Pvt.) 288
MCCONNALD, Alexander (Pvt.) 141
MCCONNAUGHY, James (Sgt.) 515
MCCONNEL, Alexander (Pvt.) 287
Charles (2nd Lt.) 241
Gaun. (Pvt.) 193
James (2nd Lt.) 256
James (Capt.) 241, 255, 317
James (Pvt.) 316, 481
John (Capt.) 266, 301, 370, 374, 378
John (Lt.) 34

John (Pvt.) 310, 318, 481
Joseph (Pvt.) 496
Robert (Pvt.) 288
William (Pvt.) 286, 467
MCCONNELL, --- (Capt.) 5
Alexander (Pvt.) 278, 516
Alexander (Sgt.) 309
James (Light Dragoon) 640
James (Lt.) 302
James (Pvt.) 263, 268, 301
John (2nd Lt.) 249
John (Capt.) 260, 308, 614
John (Lt.) 26, 317
Joseph (Pvt.) 247
Matthew (Pvt.) 158
Robert (Ens.) 387
Robert (Pvt.) 267, 301, 516
Robert (Sgt.) 7, 515
Thomas (Pvt.) 502
William (Pvt.) 277, 311, 372, 455
MCCONNO, Redman (Pvt.) 86
MCCONNOL, James (Pvt.) 505
John (Pvt.) 505
MCCONNOUGH, John (Pvt.) 412
MCCONOCHE, Samuel (Sgt.) 25
MCCONOHEY, James (1st Sgt.) 141
MCCONOUGH, Redman (Pvt.) 407
MCCOOMBS, William (Pvt.) 142
MCCORD, Davd (Pvt.) 430
David (Pvt.) 398
James (Pvt.) 328, 561
Mark (Pvt.) 431
Samuel (Pvt.) 268, 303, 310
William (Pvt.), 143, 355, 364, 365, 390, 398, 430(2)
MCCORMACK, James (Pvt.) 84, 114
Jonathan (Pvt.) 84, 114, 130
Robert (Pvt.) 403, 419
MCCORMAK, James (Pvt.) 129
MCCORMIC, Alexander 605
James (Pvt.) 523, 613
Thomas (Pvt.) 613
MCCORMICK, Adam (NCO) 412, 438
Adam (Sgt.) 65, 133, 399, 425, 636
Hugh (Pvt.) 243, 251, 259, 267, 301, 309, 479, 491, 573
Hugh (Waggon Master - commissioned 26 Dec 1776) 5
James (Pvt.) 206, 218, 267, 302, 309, 521, 540, 571
James (Pvt.) 231
James (Sgt.) 224, 425, 434, 449, 636
John (Capt.) 216, 224, 234, 236

John (Ens.) 203, 209, 212
John (Pvt.) 75, 526, 540, 601, 625
Joseph (Pvt.) 402
Patrick (Pvt.) 121, 128, 285, 315
Robert (Pvt.) 41, 64, 128, 147, 246, 285, 315, 392, 437, 650, 657
Samuel (Pvt.) 67, 145, 402, 403, 407, 445, 447
Seth (Pvt.) 175, 179, 186
Thomas (Ens.) 153, 164
Thomas (Pvt.) 178, 653, 654
William (Lt.) 633
William (Pvt.) 209, 219, 225, 246, 479, 490, 494, 506
MCCOSHLIN, John (Pvt.) 67
MCCOSKEY, Robert (Pvt.) 585
MCCOWAN, Francis (Pvt.) 347
Henry (Pvt.) 41
John (Pvt.) 641
MCCOWEN, John (Pvt.) 404
Robert (Pvt.) 433
MCCOWN, Francis (Pvt.) 344, 365
James (Pvt.) 402, 418, 437
John (Pvt.) 30, 403, 419, 437, 457
Robert (Pvt.) 421, 642
MCCOY, --- (Capt.) 359
Alexander (Capt.) 322, 332, 336
Alexander (Pvt.) 342, 371, 459, 574, 579
Daniel (Pvt.) 347, 542
James (Pvt.) 90, 113, 297, 299, 338, 371, 558, 616
James (Scout) 626
John (Pvt.) 251, 297, 300, 305, 455
Joseph (Ens.) 239, 246, 253, 256
Joseph (Pvt.) 244
Mathew (Capt.) 621
Matthew (2nd Lt.) 453, 464
Matthew (Capt.) 339
Nathaniel (Pvt.) 558
Neal 606
Neal (1st Lt.) 239, 470, 602
Neal (2nd Lt.) 245, 253, 257
Neal (Pvt.) 244, 559
Robert (Capt.) 369, 378
Robert (Sub. Lt) 3
Thomas (1st Lt.) 458, 464, 469
William (Pvt.) 455, 467, 622
MCCRACKEN, Hugh (Pvt.) 345, 350, 357
James (Pvt.) 343, 353, 442
John (Pvt.) 271, 628
Joshua (Pvt.) 353, 358

William (Pvt.) 243, 249, 260, 419, 474, 488, 499
MCCRACKIN, William (Pvt.) 64
MCCRAGHAN, Hugh (Pvt.) 458
MCCRAKAN, William (Pvt.) 402, 437
MCCRAY, James (Pvt.) 138, 528, 537
John (Pvt.) 39, 41, 132, 374, 424
Robert (Pvt.) 526, 546, 601
MCCREA, John (Pvt.) 37
Robert (Pvt.) 71, 94, 117, 520, 522, 548
Thomas (Pvt.) 93, 116
MCCREE, Robert (Pvt.) 359
MCCRIGHT, William (Pvt.) 169
MCCROSKEY, Samuel (Pvt.) 200
William (Pvt.) 200
MCCU, Neil (Pvt.) 195
MCCUBBINS, Joseph (Pvt.) 555
MCCUCHON, Alexander (Pvt.) 292
MCCUE, Abraham (Abram) (Pvt.) 220
(none compass mentis), 226 (Aug 1780 - non compus mentus), 616
MCCUILLY, Solomon (Pvt.) 474
MCCULLEY, Hugh (Pvt.) 487
Nathan (Pvt.) 516
Solomon (Pvt.) 499
MCCULLOCH, John (Pvt.) 266
Lewis (Pvt.) 122
Robert (Pvt.) 21, 142
MCCULLOGH, Lewis (Pvt.) 639
MCCULLOH, George (Sgt.) 35
MCCULLOUCH, John (Pvt.) 448
MCCULLOUGH, George (Pvt.) 27, 489, 496
Hance (Lt.) 263, 304
Hans (Lt.) 297
John (Pvt.) 298, 300, 305, 406, 446, 450
Joseph (Fifer) 148
Joseph (Pvt.) 150
Lewis (Pvt.) 638
Patrick (Pvt.) 270, 276, 281
Robert (Pvt.) 18, 139
Robort (Pvt.) 138
Samuel (Pvt.) 114, 129, 521
MCCULLY, Hugh (Pvt.) 480, 494
Solomon (Pvt.) 472, 488, 619
MCCULOUGH, John (Pvt.) 436
Samuel (Pvt.) 581
MCCULTY, James (Pvt.) 249
MCCUM, James (Pvt.) 143
MCCUNE, Andrew (Pvt.) 8, 10, 24, 148, 150
David (Pvt.) 37, 39, 41, 64, 145, 419
Henry (Pvt.) 161

James 405
James (Pvt.) 93, 134, 276, 283, 303, 391, 398, 431, 586, 588, 635
John (Pvt.) 399, 413, 415, 437, 439
John 426
Robert (Pvt.) 32, 136, 388, 396, 404, 444, 589
Samuel (Capt.) 587
Samuel (Pvt.) 31, 34, 134, 135, 270, 388, 400, 440, 443
Thomas (Pvt.) 40, 42, 66, 134, 401, 405, 411, 414, 440, 658
William (Pvt.) 205, 270, 276, 277, 283
MCCUOWN, Robert (Pvt.) 58
MCCUR, Abraham (Pvt.) 223
MCCURDAY, Hugh (Pvt.) 141
John (Pvt.) 199
Joseph (Pvt.) 190
MCCURDEY, Elisha (Pvt.) 199
Hugh (Pvt.) 120
James (Pvt.) 120
John (Pvt.) 185, 199
MCCURDY, Alexander (2nd Lt.) 302
Alexander (Pvt.) 267
David (Pvt.) 145, 147
Elijah (Pvt.) 184
Hugh (Pvt.) 128, 384, 516
James (Capt.) 217, 226, 233, 235, 236
James (Pvt.) 128, 144, 146, 181, 184
John (Pvt.) 168, 185(2), 192
MCCURRY, John (Pvt.) 354, 360, 461, 622
MCCUTCHAN, James (Pvt.) 497
MCCUTCHEN, John (Pvt.) 618
MCCUTCHEON, Alexander (Pvt.) 313
Hugh (Pvt.) 357
John (Pvt.) 621
MCCUTCHIN, James (Pvt.) 247
MCCUTCHON, James (Pvt.) 481
MCDADD, John (Pvt.) 325
MCDADE, John (Pvt.) 336
MCDAID, John (Pvt.) (Scout) 652
MCDALE, Matthew (Pvt.) 233
MCDANIEL, Alexander (Pvt.) 563, 616
Josiah (Pvt.) 233
MCDEAD, Jo. (Pvt.) 565
MCDILL, Jacob (Pvt.) 158, 188
MCDOLE, Mathew (Pvt.) 229
William (Pvt.) 64, 145, 147
MCDONAL, Alexander (Pvt.) 574, 579
Angus (Pvt.) 232, 574, 578
Archibald (Pvt.) 435
Collen (Pvt.) 500

MCDONALD, Alexander (Pvt.) 331, 649
Anges (Pvt.) 648
Angus (Pvt.) 564, 630, 650
Daniel (Pvt.) 446
Edward (Pvt.) 291, 398
James (Pvt.) 205
John (Maj.) 215
John (Pvt.) 236, 294, 637
Murdoch (Pvt.) 342
Robert (Cpl.) 618
Robert (Pvt.) 27, 621
Samuel (Pvt.) 237
Thoph (Pvt.) 248
William 605
William (Pvt.) 99, 582
MCDONALL, Alexander (Pvt.) 568
Dennis (Pvt.) 576, 583
John (Pvt.) 237
Josiah (Pvt.) 229
Michael (Pvt.) 91, 576, 583
Robert (Pvt.) 489
Samuel (Pvt.) 238
Theophilus (Pvt.) 493
William (Pvt.) 91, 92, 575
MCDONALS, Theophlis (Pvt.) 496
MCDONALT, Angis (Pvt.) 228
MCDONEL, Robert (Pvt.) 35
MCDONNAL, Collin (Pvt.) 475
John (Pvt.) 274
MCDONNALD, Robert (Pvt.) 250
Thomas (Pvt.) 199
William (Pvt.) 329
MCDONNEL, Archibald (Pvt.) 450
MCDONNOLD, Daniel (Pvt.) 68
MCDONOL, Michal (Pvt.) 114
MCDONOUGH, Redmond (Pvt.), 59, 603d
MCDORMICK, James (Pvt.) 234
MCDOWAL, Robert (Pvt.) 478
MCDOWALL, Alexander (Pvt.) 200
Collin (Pvt.) 486
Thomas (1st Lt.) 377
MCDOWEL, Alexander (Pvt.) 197
Alexander (Sgt.) 642
Andrew (Pvt.) 119
George (Pvt.) 133, 403
John (Pvt.) 182, 489
Jonathan (Pvt.) 193
Mark 606
Math. (Pvt.) 129
Mathew (Pvt.) 84, 114
William (Pvt.) 403, 419, 437, 657
MCDOWELL, Alexander (Pvt.) 200,

265, 271, 272, 285(2), 314, 315, 615
Andrew (Pvt.) 284
George (Pvt.) 152, 392
James (Pvt.) 272, 281, 286, 316, 330,
  560, 567, 615, 630
James (Sub. Lt.), 3(2)
John (Pvt.) 158, 186, 271, 272, 285(2),
  314, 315, 372, 554, 558, 624, 650
John (unfit for service) 316
Mathew (Pvt.) 586
Matthew (Pvt.) 124
Nathan (Pvt.) 271, 380
Nathan. (Pvt.) 314
Nathaniel (Pvt.) 373
Robert (Pvt.) 272, 285, 504
Thomas (1st Lt.) 368, 372, 382
Thomas (Capt.) 314, 615
William (Pvt.) 392
MCELHANEY, James (Cpl.) 286
MCELHANY, James (Cpl.) 311
MCELHATEN, Alexander (Maj.) 549
MCELHATON, Archibald (Pvt.) 643
MCELHATTEN, James (Pvt.) 289
Samuel (Pvt.) 285
MCELHATTON, Archibald (Pvt.) 285
James (Pvt.) 284
Michael (Pvt.) 271
MCELHENNEY, Hugh (Pvt.) 445
MCELHENNY, Hugh (Pvt.) 67
John (Pvt.) 477
MCELHENY, Hugh (Pvt.) 447
Samuel (Pvt.) 447
MCELHINNEY, John (Pvt.) 485
MCELNOL, Robert (Pvt.) 585
MCELROY, James (Pvt.), 476, 479, 484,
  491, 572(2)
John (Pvt.) 419
Thomas (Pvt.) 478, 504, 509
William (Pvt.) 350
MCELVAIN, Andrew (Pvt.), 151, 437,
  447(2)
Andrew (Sgt.) 67, 445
James (Pvt.) 67, 445, 447
Robert (Pvt.) 67, 445, 447
MCELVAINE, James (Pvt.) 24
Robert (Pvt.) 24
MCELVANE, Andrew (Pvt.) 95
Samuel (Pvt.) 251
MCELVANY, James (Pvt.) 225
MCELVENY, James (Pvt.) 219
MCELVONE, George (Pvt.) 66
MCELWAIN, Andrew (Pvt.) 403, 419,
  656

Joseph (Pvt.) 403, 419, 437
MCELWAINE, George 28
MCELWANE, Andrew (Pvt.) 392
Joseph (Pvt.) 391
Robert (Pvt.), 197 (mov'd.)
MCELWAYN, Samuel (Ens.) 477
MCENLOE, Robert (Pvt.) 544
MCENTAG, Henry (Pvt.) 185, 191
Hugh (Pvt.) 185, 191
MCENTIRE, Alexander (Pvt.) 604
John (Pvt.) 481, 497, 506
Thomas (Pvt.) 362
MCEWING, Charles (Pvt.) 567
MCFALL, Archibald (Pvt.) 347, 349
William (Pvt.) 348, 349
MCFARINE, James (Capt.) 192
MCFARLAIN, James 201
MCFARLAN, James (2nd Lt.) 369
James (Ens.) 587
James (Pvt.) 292, 403, 419
William (Pvt.) 419, 437, 402
MCFARLAND, Andrew (Capt.) 6
James (Pvt.) 270, 276, 284, 296, 313
John (Pvt.) 68, 446
Robert (Pvt.) 269, 270, 275, 282
William (Pvt.) 23, 68
MCFARLANE, James (2nd Lt.) 378
James (Capt.) 171, 182, 183, 647
William (Maj.) 169, 171
William (Pvt.) 446
MCFARLEN, James (Pvt.) 88
MCFARLIN, James (Light Dragoon) 640
James (Pvt.) 64, 74, 163, 281, 538
James (Troop Lt. Horse) 392
John (Pvt.) 448, 642, 404
Patrick (Pvt.) 7, 144, 146
William (Pvt.) 25, 54, 62, 64, 130, 145,
  147, 448
MCFARLINE, James (2nd Lt.) 374
William (Pvt.) 112
MCFARLING, William (Pvt.) 195
MCFARLNE, James (Capt.) 192
MCFARREN, Andrew (Pvt.) 435
Mathew (Pvt.) 542
Matthew (Pvt.) 89
MCFARRON, Andrew (Pvt.) 450
MCFARSON, Robert (Pvt.) 181
William (Pvt.) 27, 35, 250
MCFEAR, Robert (Pvt.) 618
MCFEE, John (Pvt.) 265, 293
Robert (Pvt.) 266, 285
MCFEELY, John (Pvt.) 191
MCFEETERS, James (Pvt.) 482, 497

MCFERLIN, James (Pvt.) 119
MCFERRAN, Samuel (Pvt.) 282
MCFERREN, Henry (Pvt.) 113
MCFERRON, Mathew (Pvt.) 112
MCFERSON, Robert (Pvt.) 198
MCFOOSE, Jacob (Pvt.) 292
MCFUSE, Jacob (Pvt.) 313
MCGACHEN, Samuel (Pvt.) 221
MCGACHIN, Samuel (Pvt.) 227
MCGAFFAGE, James (Pvt.) 95
MCGAFFICK, James (Pvt.) 96
MCGAFFOG, James (Pvt.) 30
MCGAFFOGE, James (Pvt.) 403, 419,
437
John (Pvt.) 402 (smith), 403, 418, 419,
437
Joseph (Pvt.) 15, 402, 418
Robert (Pvt.) 402, 403, 418, 419, 436
William (Pvt.) 418, 437
MCGAFFOGUE, James (Pvt.) 32
William (Pvt.) 37
MCGAFOG, Joseph (Pvt.) 627
MCGAFOGE, James (Pvt.) 147
John (Pvt.) 146
Robert (Pvt.) 146
MCGAFOGF, Robert (Pvt.) 628
MCGAFOGUE, James (Pvt.) 145
Joseph (Pvt.) 144
Joshua (Pvt.) 146
Robert (Pvt.) 144
William (Pvt.) 145
MCGAHY, Samuel (Pvt.) 616
MCGANAUGAY, Samuel (Pvt.) 268
MCGARVEY, Francis (Pvt.) 454
MCGAUGHAN, John (Pvt.) 206
MCGAUGHER, Archibald (Pvt.) 281
MCGAUGHEY, Samuel (Pvt.) 310
William (Pvt.) 651
MCGEE, Alexander (Pvt.) 247
Henery (Pvt.) 141
Henry (Pvt.) 516
James (Pvt.) 561
John (Ens.) 551, 560, 630, 649
John (Pvt.) 58, 136, 406, 590
Michael (Pvt.) 306
Patrick (Pvt.) 92, 99, 429, 441
Pattrick (Pvt.) 408
Ramsey (Pvt.) 158
Samuel 605
MCGEEHAN, Benjamin (Pvt.) 161
James (Pvt.) 144, 145
MCGEHAN, John (Pvt.) 644
MCGHEE, Alick (Pvt.) 35

Patrick (Pvt.) 423
MCGIGAN, Mark (Pvt.) 546
MCGIGHEN, Alexander (Pvt.) 157
MCGIHAN, Samuel (Pvt.) 446
MCGILL, Arthur (Pvt.) 200
Aurthur (Pvt.) 200
Hugh (Pvt.) 566, 567, 581, 635
James (Pvt.) 565, 570, 574, 579, 581,
635, 649
John (Pvt.) 207, 215, 356, 365
MCGINES, James (Pvt.) 196
Patrick (Pvt.), 195 ("run away")
MCGINNES, John (2nd Lt.) 163 (March
1778 - "ordered not to march"), 166
MCGINNEYS, John (Pvt.) 570
MCGINNIS, John (Pvt.) 558
Michael (Pvt.) 430
MCGLAUGHLIN, Edward (Pvt.) 271
William (Pvt.) 309
MCGOFFOG, James (Pvt.) 391
John (Pvt.) 392
Robert (Pvt.) 391, 428
William (Pvt.) 39
MCGOMERY, Humphrey (Pvt.) 31
Humphry (Pvt.) 34
James (Pvt.) 139
John (Pvt.) 328
Robert (Pvt.) 39
Samuel (Pvt.) 39
Samuel (Sgt.) 641
William (Pvt.) 30, 32, 40, 382, 641
MCGONAGLE, Roger (Pvt.) 655
MCGONIGAL, Roger (Pvt.) 625
MCGONIGALE, George (Pvt.), 200(2)
MCGONNEGLE, George (Pvt.) 168
MCGOWAN, Charles 606
Charles (Pvt.) 581, 635
Francis (Pvt.) 349
MCGOWEN, John (Pvt.) 391
MCGRADEY, Alexander (Pvt.) 633
MCGRAGH, Morris (Pvt.) 84
MCGRAH, James (Pvt.) 518
MCGRANAHAN, James (Pvt.), 160, 197
(mov'd.)
MCGRANAHIN, John (Pvt.) 189
MCGRATH, Morras (Pvt.) 115, 130
Morris (Pvt.) 540
MCGRAW, James 607
James (Pvt.) 597
Maurice (Pvt.) 597
Morris 608
Morris (Pvt.) 75, 572, 601, 647
MCGREADY, James (Pvt.) 280, 290

MCGREW, Moses 606
Patrick (Pvt.) 226
MCGRIER, William (Pvt.) 446
MCGRUE, Patrick (Pvt.) 220
MCGUFFEN, William (Pvt.) 41
MCGUFFY, John (Pvt.) 160
MCGUIER, James (Ens.) 647
Robert (Pvt.) 121
William (Pvt.) 448
MCGUIR, Robert (Pvt.) 128
MCGUIRE, --- (Pvt.) 225
Andrew (Pvt.) 243
Archibald (Pvt.) 219
Daniel (Pvt.) 42
James (Ens.) 216
John (Pvt.) 149, 150, 356, 366
Robert (Pvt.) 141, 384, 407, 516
Samuel (Pvt.) 353, 358, 442
William (Pvt.) 343, 353, 359
MCGWIRE, Andrew (Pvt.) 260
MCHAFFEY, Andrew (Pvt.) 214
MACHAN, Able 410
MCHAN, James (Pvt.) 449
MACHAN, John (Clerk) 301
John (Pvt.) 318
Robert (Pvt.) 310
William (Pvt.) 136, 152, 657
MCHARG, Robert (Pvt.) 336
MCHARGE, Robert (Pvt.) 560
MCHARRY, Robert (Pvt.) 344, 360, 622
MCHATTEN, --- (Maj.) 38
MCHATTON, Archibald (Pvt.) 315
Samuel (Ens.) 314
MCHELLEN, Ned (Pvt.) 425
MACHEN, David (Pvt.) 54
John (Clerk) 308
John (Pvt.) 53, 288, 492
Joseph (Pvt.) 486
MCHENERY, Hugh (Pvt.) 628
MCHENEY, George 606
Hugh (Pvt.) 16, 47
Samuel (Pvt.) 30
MCHENY, Thomas (Pvt.) 380
MACHIN, William (Pvt.) 31
MACHLAN, James (Pvt.) 27, 250
MCHOLM, Alexander (Pvt.), 229, 232
(sent his son)
MCHOLYING, John (Pvt.) 562
MACHON, John (Pvt.) 152
William (Pvt.) 443, 444
MCILHATTON, Alexander (Maj.) 332
MCILHENNEY, Hugh (Pvt.) 16
MCILHENNY, Hugh (Pvt.) 48, 55

James (Cpl.) 277
James (Pvt.) 318
James (Sgt.) 545
MCILLHATTEN, Alexander (Maj.) 319, 323
MCILLVAIN, Andrew (Pvt.) 587
MCILROY, James (Pvt.) 35, 56, 508, 632
Thomas (Pvt.) 508
MCILVAIN, Andrew (Pvt.) 588
Samuel (Pvt.) 243, 259
MCILVAINE, Andrew (Pvt.) 34
Andrew (Sgt.) 16, 48, 55
George (Pvt.) 26
James (Pvt.) 7
Robert (Pvt.) 7
MCINTGER, Alexander (Pvt.) 189
MCINTIER, James (Pvt.) 130
MCINTIRE, Alexander (Pvt.) 209
Hugh (Pvt.) 73, 80, 102, 527, 623
James (Pvt.) 73, 80, 102, 523, 526, 527, 623
John (Pvt.) 81, 98, 102
Thomas 608
Thomas (Pvt.) 455, 461, 654
MACK, Alexander (Pvt.) 71, 94, 117
William (Pvt.) 117, 308
MCKAHAN, Alexander (Pvt.) 199
MCKAIN, James (Pvt.) 329
James (Scout) 626
MCKAY, Alexander (Capt.) 609
Alexander (Pvt.) 291, 313
MCKEAN, Alexander (Pvt.) 72, 106
James (Pvt.) 554, 558
Robert (Pvt.) 430
Thomas (Pvt.) 82, 110, 125
William (Pvt.) 394, 424
MCKEB, Robert (Pvt.) 467
MCKEBE, James (Pvt.) 461
John (Pvt.) 461
Robert (Pvt.) 456
William (Pvt.) 461
MCKEE, Alex (Pvt.) 282
Alexander (Pvt.) 269, 275, 304
Andrew (Capt.) 154, 158, 165, 247, 595
Andrew (Pvt.) 461
David (Pvt.) 345, 352, 365, 460, 612
Hugh (2nd Lt.) 367, 372, 376, 383
Hugh (Pvt.) 93, 116, 220, 223, 371
James 405
James (Capt.) 5
James (Pvt.) 64, 76, 92, 104, 145, 147, 149, 151, 390, 392, 403, 435, 437, 450, 522, 526, 583, 419

James (Sgt.) 623
John 405
John (Ens.) 65
John (Pvt.) 134, 157, 159, 184, 190,
    247, 352, 355, 388, 400, 414, 440,
    496, 612, 633
Patrick (Pvt.) 104, 138
Robert (Pvt.) 269, 275, 283, 343, 353
Thomas (Pvt.) 247, 306, 353, 358, 362,
    455, 467, 493, 496, 573, 576
William 91
William (Pvt.) 103, 109, 137, 184, 248,
    289, 297, 299, 305, 459, 460, 575,
    582, 622
William (Sgt.) 364
MCKEEHAN, Alexander (Pvt.) 200
MCKEENAN, James O. (Pvt.) 243, 260
MCKEENE, Robert (Pvt.) 130
MCKEEVER, John (Pvt.) 243, 246, 257,
    259, 470, 473, 491, 498, 506
MCKEILLAN, Edward (Pvt.) 636
MCKELIPS, James (Pvt.) 137
MCKELVEY, John (Pvt.) 314
MCKELVIE, Patrick (Pvt.) 400
MCKELVY, John (Pvt.) 284
MCKENEY, Samuel (Pvt.) 134
MCKENNEY, Robert (Pvt.) 264
MCKENNY, John (Pvt.) 290
 Joseph (Pvt.) 371
 Robert (Pvt.) 280, 290
 Samuel (Light Dragoon) 640
 Samuel (Pvt.) 33
 William (Pvt.) 350
MCKENRIE, Thomas (Pvt.) 134
MCKENSTREY, Samuel (Pvt.) 653
MCKENY, Joseph (Pvt.) 286
MCKENZIE, Thomas (Pvt.) 36
MCKERNY, John (Pvt.) 373
MCKEVER, John (Pvt.) 602
MACKEY, James (Pvt.) 36, 40, 42, 141,
    516, 658
 John (Pvt.) 121, 141, 384, 407, 516
MCKEY, John (Pvt.) 629
MACKEY, Robert (Pvt.) 273, 293, 307
 Samuel (Pvt.) 437
 Stephen (Pvt.) 274, 294, 307
MCKGROGER, Daniel (Pvt.) 290
MCKIBBEN, James 24
 Joseph (Lt.) 386
 Joseph (Pvt.) 148, 560
 Joshua (Pvt.) 8
 William (Pvt.) 120
MCKIBBENS, Joseph (Pvt.) 150

MCKIBBER, Joseph (Pvt.) 331
MCKIBBIN, Jeremiah (Wagon Master) 4
 Joseph (Pvt.) 10, 489, 624
 William 426
MCKIBBON, Jeremiah (Pvt.) 66, 401
MCKIBBONS, William (Pvt.) 417, 516
MCKIBIN, William (Pvt.) 140
MCKIBINS, Joseph (Lt.) 434
MCKICHAN, James (Pvt.) 68
 Samuel (Pvt.) 68
MCKICKEN, George (Pvt.) 180
MCKIGHAN, Alexander (Pvt.) 188
MCKIGHEN, George (Pvt.), 197
MCKILLIPS, James (Pvt.) 104
MCKIM James (Pvt.) 267, 302
 John (Pvt.) 302
 Robert (Pvt.) 650
MCKINDLEY, James (Pvt.) 237
MCKINEY, Samuel (Pvt.) 66
MCKINLEY, Henry (Pvt.) 177, 179
 James (Pvt.) 235
 Samuel (Pvt.) 217, 222, 223
 Walter (Capt.) 263
MCKINLY, James (Pvt.) 214
 John (Pvt.) 207
MCKINNEY, John (Pvt.) 305, 380
 Samuel (Pvt.) 400
 Samuel (Troop Lt. Horse) 387
 Thomas (Pvt.) 66, 401
 Walter (Capt.) 299
 Walter (Ens.) 378
MCKINNIE, John (Pvt.) 297
 Walter (Capt.) 297, 304
MCKINNY, Walter (Ens.) 370
 William (Pvt.) 357
MCKINSEY, Alexander (Pvt.) 175, 353,
    358
 Robert (Cpl.) 129
 Samuel (Pvt.) 95, 96
 Thomas (Pvt.) 405
MCKINSTOY, Alexander (Pvt.) 644
MCKINSTREY, Alexander (Pvt.) 325,
    569
MCKINSTRY, James (Pvt.) 207
 Samuel (Pvt.) 490, 654
MCKINZAY, Robert (Pvt.) 84
MCKINZEY, Robert (Pvt.) 114
MCKINZIE, Alexander (Pvt.) 184
 David (Pvt.) 413, 439
 Thomas (Pvt.) 414, 440
 William (Pvt.) 635
MCKISSEK, Daniel (Pvt.), 91, 575 582
MCKISSEN, John (Pvt.) 93, 116

MCKITCHEN, Samuel (Pvt.) 323
MACKLE, Martin (Pvt.) 123
MCKLEWAIN, Robert (Pvt.) 180
MCKNIGHT, Alexander (Pvt.) 96
John (Pvt.) 149, 150, 435, 450
MCKNITT, Robert (Pvt.) 329
William (Pvt.), 328, 374
MCKOY, Hugh (Pvt.) 226
MCKUNE, William (Pvt.) 278
MCLAIN, Richard (Sgt.) 580
MCLANE, Andrew (Pvt.) 395, 420, 432
Daniel (2nd Lt.) 525
Daniel (Lt.) 420, 432
Daniel (Pvt.) 130, 396, 656
John (Pvt.) 7, 18, 33, 296, 313
John (Sgt.) 395, 420, 432
Richard (Lt.) 83, 129
Richard (Sgt.) 514
Robert (Pvt.) 37
Thomas (Pvt.) 129
MCLAUGHLIN, Patrick (Pvt.) 351
William (Pvt.) 288, 300, 301
MACLAY, Charles (Capt.) 6, 14, 35, 39,
41, 45, 148
Charles (Pvt.), 39, 149(2), 150, 151
John (Pvt.), 151
MCLAY, Charls (Pvt.) 450
David (Pvt.) 449
MACLAY, James H. 588
John (Pvt.) 19, 39, 148, 149, 150, 151
Nat. (Pvt.) 383
MCLEAN, Alexander (Pvt.) 78
Andrew (Pvt.) 10, 24, 589
Daniel (2nd Lt.) 511, 519
John (Pvt.) 21, 24, 292, 457, 589
Richard (Lt.) 70, 113
Richard (Sgt.) 539
MCLEANE, Daniel (Pvt.) 114
John (Cpl.) 19
Thomas (Pvt.) 114
MCLEARN, Matthias (Pvt.) 650
MCLEARY, Joseph (Pvt.) 205
MCLELAND, Henry (Pvt.) 126
Hugh (Pvt.) 597
James (Pvt.) 125
John (Pvt.) 126
Joseph (Pvt.) 125
MCLELLAND, Robert (Pvt.) 311
William (Pvt.) 104
MCLELLON, Robart (Ens.) 103
MCLENE, Daniel (2nd Lt.) 532
James (2nd Lt.) 376
Thomas (Pvt.) 84

MCLERENS, William (Pvt.) 345
MCLERON, Mathew (Pvt.) 350
MCLEVE, George (Pvt.) 455
MCLINTOCK, Daniel (Pvt.) 126
William (Pvt.) 435
MCLONEY, James (Pvt.) 643
MACLUCHEY, Robert (Pvt.) 85
MCLUER, John (Pvt.) 132
MCLURE, Abdiel (Pvt.) 58, 395
Francis (Pvt.) 420
Hugh (Pvt.) 424
James (Lt.) 559
John (Pvt.) 424
MACMAAN, Benjamin (Pvt.) 632
MCMAGHAN, John (Pvt.) 497
Joseph (Pvt.) 482
MCMAHAN, Benjamin (Pvt.) 56
John (1st Lt.) 241, 250, 255
MCMAHON, Benjamin (Pvt.) 572
MCMANAGAL, Neil (Pvt.) 624
MCMANEGIL, John (Sgt.) 581
MCMANEGLE, John (Sgt.) 634
MCMANIGEL, John (Sgt.) 635
MCMANIGLE, James (Pvt.) 650
John (Pvt.) 650
Neal (Pvt.) 490, 650
MCMANNAMY, Daniel (Pvt.) 588
MCMATH, Alla (Pvt.) 402, 419
Samuel (Pvt.) 61, 131
MCMEAN, John (Pvt.) 205
Robert (Pvt.) 209
William (Pvt.) 206, 616
MCMEATH, James (Pvt.) 247
MCMEEN, John (Pvt.) 214, 238
Robert (Lt.) 216, 615
William (Pvt.) 214
MCMEGHAN, Joseph (Pvt.) 497
MCMEIN, John (Pvt.) 236
MCMICALL, Daniel (Pvt.) 188
MCMICHAEL, James (Pvt.) 299, 301,
306
John (Pvt.) 624
Robert (Pvt.) 42, 298, 300, 306
MCMICHEL, James (Pvt.) 281
MCMILLAN, George (Pvt.) 355
James (Pvt.) 16
MCMILLEN, George (Pvt.) 364
Hugh (Pvt.) 414, 440
John (Pvt.) 54
Samuel (Pvt.) 91
Thomas (Pvt.) 91
MCMILLIGAN, William (Ens.) 320, 324
MCMILLIN, George (Pvt.) 629

MCMILLION, William (Ens.) 644
MCMOLLEN, James (Pvt.) 412
John (Pvt.) 297, 299, 412
MCMULEN, James (Pvt.) 227, 131
MCMULLAN, William (Ens.) 334
MCMULLEN, Daniel (Pvt.) 61, 132, 393, 409, 423
George (Pvt.) 74, 119
Hugh (Pvt.) 248, 388, 401
James (Pvt.) 61, 107, 116, 209, 220, 407, 410, 442, 447, 588
John (Pvt.) 51, 61, 82, 110, 289, 379, 409, 423, 442, 631, 131
Larence (Pvt.) 62, 132
Laurence (Pvt.) 394
Michael (Pvt.) 365
Thomas (Pvt.) 103, 137, 424
William (Ens.) 550
MCMULLER, Daniel (Pvt.) 442
MCMULLIN, James (Pvt.) 15, 67, 445, 628
John (Pvt.) 125, 371
MCMUNNIGAL, Neal (Pvt.) 646
MCMURRAY, John (Pvt.) 353
Samuel (Ens.) 170
MCMURREY, Samuel (Ens.) 617
MCMURRIS, Daniel (Pvt.) 196
MCMURRY, John (Pvt.) 278, 358
Joseph (Pvt.) 287, 311
Samuel (Pvt.) 161
MCNAB, William 608
MCNABB, William (Pvt.) 572
MCNAIR, John 608
John (Pvt.) 472, 619
Robert (1st Lt.) 495
Robert (Lt.) 507
Robert (Pvt.) 653, 654
MCNARY, Charles (Pvt.) (Scout) 652
MCNAUGHTON, John (Pvt.) 347, 349, 456
MCNAUL, John (Pvt.) 179
MCNEAL, Andrew (Pvt.) 283
Daniel (2nd Lt.) 203, 205
Daniel (Pvt.) 231, 234
John (Pvt.) 72, 244, 527
Patrick (Pvt.) 269, 276
Patrick (Sgt.) 284
MCNEALLEY, James (Pvt.) 423
MCNEARY, James (Pvt.) 561
MCNECKLE, Alexander (Lt.) 67
MCNEEL, Daniel (2nd Lt.) 212
John (Pvt.) 94
MCNEELEY, George (Pvt.) 17, 65

James (Pvt.) 441
MCNEELLEY, George (Pvt.) 133
MCNEELY, George (Pvt.) 16, 400, 588, 627
James (Pvt.) 429
MCNEIL, Hector (Pvt.) 58, 590
John (Pvt.) 530, 596
MCNELLY, John (Pvt.) 157, 174, 178, 187
Robert (Pvt.) 195
MCNICHOL, Alexander (1st Lt.) 49
Alexander (Lt.) 385
Alexander (Pvt.) 32
MCNICKEL, Alexander (Pvt.) 418
MCNICKLE, Alexander (Pvt.) 39, 68, 446
MCNICOL, Alexander (Pvt.), 448(2)
MCNIGHT, James (Pvt.) 200
MCNIT, Alexander (Pvt.) 326
MCNITT, Alexander (Pvt.) 338, 650
Anthony (Pvt.) 296
John (Pvt.) 624
Robert (Pvt.) 489, 624, 650
William (Pvt.) 489, 624, 650
MCNOE, Robert (Pvt.) 527
MCNULTY, John (Pvt.) 524, 557
MCNUT, Alexander (Pvt.) 559
William (Pvt.) 560
MCNUTT, Anthony (Pvt.) 292, 313
James (Pvt.) 560
John (Pvt.) 555, 559
Robert (Pvt.) 555, 559
William (Pvt.) 266, 281, 298, 299, 300, 301, 306(2), 555
MACONOHY, John (Pvt.) 384
MCOWEN, James (Pvt.) 63, 146
John (Pvt.) 64, 95, 145, 147
Patr. (Pvt.) 147
MCPHAREN, Samuel (Pvt.) 269
MCPHERSON, Samuel (Pvt.) 615
MCQUEAD, Hugh (Pvt.) 351
MCQUEE, Patrick (Pvt.) 617
MCQUILKEN, John (Pvt.) 617
MCQUITKIN, John (Pvt.) 176
MCQUITTERY, Samuel (Pvt.) 269
MCQUOAN, Francis (Pvt.) 459
MCQUOWN, Francis (Pvt.) 181
Henry (Pvt.) 179, 181
William (Sgt.) 180
MCREA, James (Pvt.) 138
MCREADY, Lorans (Pvt.) 601, 610
MCREIHAN, Benjamin (Pvt.) 195
James (Pvt.) 195

MCROBERT, David (Pvt.) 292
MCROBERTS, David (Pvt.) 296
MCROY, James (Pvt.) 26, 249
Thomas (Pvt.) 245, 258
MCSWINE, Edward (Pvt.) 336
George (Pvt.) 316
MCTEAR, Robert (Ens.) 508
Samuel (Pvt.) 619
MCTEE, Thomas (Pvt.) 456
MCTEEAR, Robert (Capt.) 242
MCTEER, James (Pvt.) 208, 220, 223, 226
John (Capt.) 204, 213
John (Pvt.) 236, 238
Matthew (Pvt.) 249, 252
Robert (Capt.) 250, 256, 609
Samuel (Pvt.) 229, 233, 633
William (Pvt.) 205, 219, 225, 231, 234
MCTIER, Robert (Ens.) 651
MCTIRE, Thomas (Pvt.) 624
MCVANE, Andrew (Pvt.) 47
George (Pvt.) 23
MCVEAN, Andrew (Pvt.) 31
MCVENAN, James (Pvt.) 249
MCVICAR, Duncan (Pvt.) 188
MCWANE, Grier (Pvt.) 400
MCWEAN, Andrew (Pvt.) 15
James (Pvt.) 10
Robert (Pvt.) 10
MCWHARTER, William (Pvt.) 399, 413, 415, 439
MCWHINNY, Thomas (Pvt.) 305
MCWILLIAMS, Henry (Pvt.) 323, 558, 574, 578, 648
Hugh (Pvt.) 119
James (2nd Lt.), 512, 533, 535, 545, 599(2)
James (Pvt.) 118, 123, 87
Joseph (2nd Lt.) 518
MCWINNEY, Thomas (Pvt.) 278
MCWINNIE, Thomas (Pvt.) 297
MCWRIGHT, William (Pvt.) 536, 543, 584, 587, 599, 600
MAFFAT, William (Pvt.) 448
MAFFET, William (Pvt.) 22
William (Sgt.) 67
MAFFETT, John (Pvt.) 287
MAFFIT, William (Sgt.) 27
MAFFOT, William (Sgt.) 445
MAGAFOGE, James (Pvt.) 64
John (Pvt.) 63
Joseph (Pvt.) 63
Robert (Pvt.) 63

MAGAIN, Joseph (Pvt.) 141
MAGAW, Robert (Committee of Observation) 4
MAGE, George (Pvt.) 120
MAGEE, John (Ens.) 6
John (Pvt.) 396, 422, 433
MAGHAN, James (Clerk) 267
John (Pvt.) 59, 482, 603
MAGILL, Joseph (Pvt.) (Scout) 652
MAGINNIS, John (Scout) 625
MAHAN, Abel (Pvt.) 406
Alexander (Pvt.) 563
Arcd. (Pvt.) 450
Archibald (Pvt.) 36, 149, 151, 435
David (Pvt.) 36, 58, 62, 396, 398, 406, 422, 433
James (Pvt.) 435
John (Pvt.) 18, 397, 562
Robert (Pvt.) 50, 397, 416
William (Pvt.) 18, 34, 58, 389, 396, 397
MAHAUN, Alexander (Pvt.) 331
Archibald (Pvt.) 40
David (Pvt.) 40
John (Pvt.) 21, 52
William (Pvt.) 21
MAHEN, D. 42
MAHON, Alexander (Pvt.) 597
David (Pvt.) 430, 590
Henry (Pvt.) 143
John (Pvt.) 52, 142, 342, 352, 361, 430
Robert (Pvt.) 142, 425, 430, 636
William (Pvt.) 139, 142, 430, 590
MAIERS, Methais (Pvt.) 59, 603
MAIR, John (Pvt.) 47
MAIRES, John (Pvt.) 55
MAIRS, John (Pvt.) 16, 17, 48, 383
Samuel (Pvt.) 620
William (Pvt.) 642
MAIRTAIN, Christy (Pvt.) 565
MAISE, Christian (Pvt.) 391
James (Pvt.) 273
MALENY, James (Pvt.) 279
MALONEY, James (Pvt.) 290
MALOY, Arthur (Pvt.) 635
Edward (Pvt.) 647
John (Pvt.) 493
MAN, John (Pvt.) 221, 227
MANAHAN, John (Pvt.) 102
MANESSMITH, Henry (Pvt.) 637
MANHIRTER, William (Pvt.) 280
MANN, Samuel (Pvt.) 207
MANNAH, Archibald (Pvt.) 449
MANNER, Henry (Pvt.) 117

John (Pvt.) 71, 94, 117
MANNON, Edward (Pvt.) 276, 283
MANSFIELD, John (Pvt.) 482, 487, 497
MANSIL, William (Pvt.) 125
MANTEER, David (Pvt.) 85
  William (Pvt.) 85
MANTOOTH, David (Pvt.) 219
  William (Pvt.) 114, 129
MANYSMITH, Christian (Pvt.) 206
MARARTY, Hugh (Pvt.) 409
MARCH, George (Pvt.) 646
MARCHAL, Jonathan (Pvt.) 84
MARES, John (Pvt.) 429
  Samuel (Pvt.) 393
  Soffel (Pvt.) 218
  William (Pvt.) 390
MARK, William (Pvt.) 251, 492, 495,
  573
MARKE, William (Pvt.) 480
MARKLE, Martain (Pvt.) 112
MARLIN, John (Pvt.) 344, 360, 365, 622
  Joshua (Pvt.) 163, 189
MARRIN, Archibald (Pvt.) 460
MARRIT, Daniel (Pvt.) 460
MARRON, Archibald 608
MARS, William (Pvt.) 404
MARSDALL, John (Pvt.) 579
MARSDEN, John (Pvt.) 326, 338
MARSDON, John (Pvt.) 564
MARSHAL, David (1st Lt.) 451, 465
  Henry (Pvt.) 380, 610
  John (Pvt.) 347, 401, 405, 411, 414, 457
  Jonathan (Pvt.) 115
  Joseph (Pvt.) 445, 447
  Michael (Pvt.) 457, 459
MARSHALL, Andrew (Pvt.) 278, 287,
  311
  David (1st Lt.) 454, 462
  David (Capt.) 339, 346, 348
  Henry (Pvt.) 269, 275, 282, 601
  John (Pvt.) 41, 75, 269, 275, 282,
    349(2), 459, 540, 574, 631
  John (Sgt.) 346
  Joseph (Pvt.) 68
  Michael (Ens.) 339, 348
  Michael (Pvt.) 347
  Samuel (Pvt.) 347, 348, 363
  William (Pvt.) 209, 276, 522, 526, 540,
    544, 633, 526
MARSHEL, John (Pvt.) 130
MARTAIN, James (Pvt.) 129
  William (Pvt.) 81, 130
MARTAN, Rodger (Pvt.) 366

MARTEN, Niclas (Pvt.) 251
  William (Pvt.) 251
MARTIN, Adam (Sgt.) 81, 100, 110, 125
  Alexander (Pvt.) 176, 617
  Archibald 605(2), 607
  Archibald (Pvt.) 20, 24, 448
  Archibald (Sub.) 140
  Charles (Pvt.) 445
  Christian (Pvt.) 336, 568
  Christopher (Pvt.) 323
  Daniel (Pvt.) 221, 228, 342
  David (Pvt.) 87, 246, 457, 478, 490,
    504, 538, 653, 654
  Henry (Cpl.) 35
  Henry (Pvt.) 122, 244, 258, 477, 502,
    638, 639
  Hugh (Pvt.) 207
  Isaac (Pvt.) 302
  Isaac (invalid) 310
  James (Ens.) 649
  James (Pvt.) 266, 296, 300, 331, 332,
    489, 561, 624, 643
  John (Ens.) 6
  John (Pvt.) 110, 126, 210, 229, 232,
    252, 265, 270, 276, 283, 331, 382,
    604
  Jonathan (J'n't.) (Pvt.) 23, 26, 149
  Joseph (Capt.) 5
  Moses (Pvt.) 629
  Paul (Pvt.) 447
  Robert (Pvt.) 330, 567, 574, 579, 597,
    649
  Roger (Pvt.) 356
  Samuel (Pvt.) 209, 222, 228
  Thomas (Ens.) 15, 48, 515
  Thomas (Pvt.) 67, 445, 447
  Thomas 425
  William (Pvt.) 56, 58, 102, 136, 265,
    270, 276, 283, 325, 336, 371, 381,
    389, 396, 458, 479, 491, 569, 573,
    574, 578, 590, 633, 646, 648, 649
MARTING, Alexander (Pvt.) 195
  Robart (Pvt.) 561
  William (Pvt.) 196
MARTON, Charles (Pvt.) 151
  Charls (Pvt.) 447
MARYHAL, William (Pvt.) 597
MASDON, John (Pvt.) 568
MASE, Christian (Pvt.) 398
MASHALL, William (Pvt.) 585
MASON, John (Pvt.) 643
  William (Sgt.) 19
MASONER, Jacob (Pvt.) 185, 191

MASTING, James (Ens.) 646
MATEER, John (Capt.) 202
Matthew (Pvt.) 56
MATES, SUrban (Pvt.) 312
MATHER, Samuel (1st Lt.) 162
MATHERS, Samuel (1st Lt.) 156
Samuel (Pvt.) 196 ,
Thomas (Pvt.) 67, 315, 447
William (Pvt.) 177, 410, 631, 657
MATHEW, James (Pvt.) 310
MATHEWS, George (Pvt.) 278, 287, 311
James (Pvt.) 184, 190, 268, 303
Philip (Capt.) 482, 500
Samuel (1st Lt.) 166
MATHIAS, --- (Capt.) 510
James (Pvt.) 281
John (Cpl.), 286 (weaver)
Philip (Capt.) 240, 609
MATHIES, George (Pvt.) 303
MATHISWEVER, John (Pvt.) 602
MATIN, William (Pvt.) 98
MATLACK, Timothy 595, 596
MATTHERS, Alexander (Pvt.) 375
MATTHEWS, --- (Capt.) 318
George (Capt.) 5, 318
James (Pvt.) 157
John (Pvt.) 615
Philip (Capt.) 254
MATTHIAS, John (Pvt.), 309, 380
(weaver)
Philip (Capt.) 246
MAUGHAN, David (Pvt.) 51, 411
MAWK, Michael (Pvt.) 198
MAXEL, William (Pvt.) 180
MAXWEL, Robert (Pvt.) 184, 191
MAXWELL, Alexander (Pvt.) 354, 360,
461, 622, 629
James (Pvt.) 266, 267, 298, 300, 305,
344, 355, 360, 364, 365, 382, 457,
458, 622
James (Sgt.) 364
John (Pvt.) 195
Patric(k) (Pvt.) 266, 298, 300, 305
William (Pvt.) 68, 422, 434, 446
MAY, Andrew (Pvt.) 301, 307
George (Pvt.) 620
MAYBRIER, Jacob (Pvt.) 77, 82
MAYS, Silvanas (Pvt.) 472
William (Pvt.) 400
MEAINS, James (Ens.) 329
MEALMAN, Adam (Pvt.) 270, 283
MEALY, Levans (Pvt.) 349
Lorans (Pvt.) 347

MEANAH, James (Pvt.) 466
MEANER, William (Pvt.) 315
MEANES, Robart (Capt.) 555
MEANOR, William (Pvt.) 91, 575, 583
MEANOUGH, Samuel (Pvt.) 269
William (Pvt.) 269
MEANS, George (Pvt.) 650
James (Ens.) 322, 335
James (Pvt.) 566, 630
John (1st Lt.) 322, 324, 331, 335
John (Ens.) 324
John (Pvt.) 269, 282, 283, 516, 566, 630
Joseph (Pvt.) (Scout) 652
Robert (2nd Lt.) 322, 324, 328, 335
Robert (Capt.) 551, 555, 556, 564, 576,
577
Robert (Capt.) (Scout) 652
Robert (Pvt.) 401, 405, 440
MEARES, Alexander (Pvt.) 288, 312
MEARS, Alexander (Pvt.) 279
James (Pvt.) 85, 128
Joh. (Pvt.) 120
John (Pvt.) 85, 140, 626
Samuel (Pvt.) 86, 121, 384, 516
MEAS, James (Pvt.) 121, 293
MEATHERS, Thomas (Pvt.) 445
MEEK, Abner (Pvt.) 292
Abner (Sgt.) 295, 312
George (Pvt.) 332, 490, 597, 624, 650
Hugh (Pvt.) 291
Hugh (Sgt.) 295, 312
James (Drummer) 295
John (Pvt.) 265, 292, 296, 313, 643
Thomas (Pvt.) 293
William (Pvt.) 635, 640
MEEKEY, James (Pvt.) 416
Robert (Pvt.) 271, 285
MEEKLAN, John (Ens.) 358
MEEKLAND, John (Ens.) 339
MEELROY, Thomas (Pvt.) 476
MEENES, James (Pvt.) 567
John (Pvt.) 567
MEERE, John (Pvt.) 284
MEFEATERS, James (Pvt.) 487
MEGILL, Hugh (Pvt.) 331
MEGRAW, James (Pvt.) 603
MEGREGAR, Daniel (Pvt.) 280
MEHAFFEY, Andrew (Pvt.) 604
Josep (Pvt.) 206
Samuel (Pvt.) 208
MEHAFFY, Andrew (Pvt.) 207
John (Pvt.) 207
MEHARG, Robert (Pvt.) 325

MEILROY, James (Sgt.) 632
MELAN, John (Pvt.) 365
MELK, William (Pvt.) 195
MELLAN, John (Pvt.) 252
MELLAR, Matthew (Pvt.), 228 ("in the troop")
MELLON, John (Pvt.) 505
MELORY, Arthur (Pvt.) 187
MELOY, Arthur (Pvt.) 180, 197
John 606
John (Pvt.) 496, 510, 651
MELROY, John (Pvt.) 188
MELTON, John (Pvt.) 501
MENAS, Robert (Pvt.) 414
MENER, Edward 607
MENES, John (Pvt.) 479, 491
MENNER, Henry (Pvt.) 94, 97
MENNON, Edward (Pvt.) 265
MENOCH, James (Pvt.) 455
William (Pvt.) 586
MENOUGH, Isaac (Pvt.) 270, 284
John (Pvt.) 269, 275, 282
Samuel (Pvt.) 283
William (Pvt.) 275, 282
MENSER, Abel (Pvt.) 71, 94, 117
Jepha (Pvt.) 117
Joseph (Pvt.) 71, 94, 117
Zephtha (Pvt.) 97
MENSURE, Jonas (Pvt.) 586
MENTOOTH, Henry (Pvt.) 630
William 606
MENTREATH, David (Pvt.) 225
MERCER, Amos (Pvt.) 245
Joseph (Pvt.) 160
MEREDITH, Jesse (Pvt.) 491, 506
MEREDY, Jesse (Pvt.), 498
MERES, George (Pvt.) 230
MERICLE Martin (Pvt.), 89
MERIDITH Jess (Pvt.) 473
MERIN, Archibald (Pvt.) 612
MEROITY, Hugh (Pvt.) 24
MERORTY, Hugh (Pvt.) 441
MERRIOTT, Daniel (Sgt.) 357
MERRIT, Daniel (Sgt.) 350
MERROT, Matthew (Pvt.) 458
MERROW, Richard (Pvt.) 658
MERTAIN, Jonathan (Pvt.) 150
MERTIN, David (Pvt.), 119
MERVAN, John (Pvt.) 408
MESSER, Joseph 594, 607
Joseph (Pvt.) 198, 594
MESSOR, Joseph (Pvt.) 181
MESURE, Joseph (Pvt.) 617

METEER, Mathew (Pvt.) 489, 573
Matthew (Cpl.) 632
Robert (Pvt.) 478, 504
METEOR, Mathew (Pvt.) 496
METSER, George (Pvt.) 542
MEUSER, Jepha (Pvt.) 94
MEYERS, Mathias (Pvt.) 298
MIARS, John (Pvt.) 127
Jonathan (Pvt.) 84, 130
Stofel (Pvt.) 222
MICKEL, Robert (Pvt.) 440
MICKEY, Daniel (Pvt.) 353, 359
David (Pvt.) 418, 428, 436
James (Pvt.) 10, 68, 144, 146, 402, 418, 436, 587
Robert (Pvt.) 23, 25, 64, 147, 314, 402, 419, 437
MICKLESANE, George (Pvt.) 400
MICKLEWANE, George (Pvt.) 413, 439
Grier (Pvt.) 413, 439
MICKY, Robert (Pvt.) 145
MIERS, Geoarge (Pvt.) 9
George (Pvt.) 234
Stofel (Pvt.) 224
Stophel (Pvt.) 9
MIGRAW, James (Sgt. Maj.) 59
MIHOLMAN, John (Pvt.) 20
MILER, John (Pvt.) 79
Philip (Pvt.) 248
MILES, Michal (Pvt.) 144
Robert (Pvt.) 360
MILFORD, Joseph (Pvt.) 474
MILHOUSE, John (Pvt.) 273, 293, 307
MILIGAN, Andrew (Pvt.) 231
James (Pvt.) 356, 366
MILIGIN, Andrew (Pvt.) 235
MILIRON, John (Pvt.) 603
MILKOY, Henry (Pvt.) 559
MILLAR, Benjamin (Pvt.) 630
Christopher (Pvt.) 642
Isaac (Pvt.) 642
James (Drummer) 641
John (Pvt.) 586
Philip (Pvt.) 184
Phillip (Pvt.) 473
MILLARS, John (Pvt.) 228
MILLEGAN, John (Pvt.) 330, 650
Joseph (Pvt.) 330
Samuel (Pvt.) 328, 490, 650
MILLER, --- (Capt.) 62
Abraham (Pvt.) 236, 238
Alexander (Pvt.) 270, 276, 283, 382, 450

Andrew (2nd Lt.) 513, 534
Andrew (Pvt.) 29, 32, 61, 95, 96(2),
    132, 393, 409, 412, 423, 442, 520,
    524, 631
Benjamin (Pvt.) 563, 566
Chambers (Col.) 549
Chans. 98
Christley (Pvt.) 221
Christn. (Pvt.) 396
Christofor (Pvt.) 404
Christopher (Pvt.) 200(2), 388, 421, 433
Christy (Pvt.) 58, 136, 278, 589
Cristy (Pvt.) 227
Daniel (Pvt.) 79, 101, 123
David (Pvt.) 457
Elias (Cpl.) 19
Elias (Pvt.) 32, 139, 647
George (Pvt.) 116, 122, 246, 461
Henry (Ens.) 204, 209, 213
Henry (Pvt.) 144, 199, 389, 396, 421,
    433, 589
Henry (Sgt.) 79, 101
Hon. 102
Hugh (Pvt.) 344, 360, 458, 622
Isaac (1st Lt.) 14, 38, 45
Isaac (Capt.) 40, 386
Isaac (Lt.) 37, 148, 609
Isaac (Pvt.) 143, 388, 390, 400, 404,
    414, 440
Isaack (Pvt.) 398
J. (Capt.) 449, 450
Jacob (Ens.) 13, 45, 142
Jacob (Fifer) 19
Jacob (Pvt.) 9, 79, 101, 123, 136, 144,
    218, 222, 224
Jacob 102
James (Capt.) 434, 436
James (Pvt.) 149, 151, 273, 293, 297,
    299, 305, 307, 318, 343, 353, 359,
    390, 404, 435, 450, 458, 546, 625
Jerah (Pvt.) 200
Jeremiah (Sgt.) 617
John (Pvt.) 41, 81, 82, 93, 98, 101,
    102(2), 107, 111, 116, 126, 200(2),
    209, 222, 405 (for John Speer), 421,
    433, 460, 642
Joseph (Cpl.) 79, 101
Joseph (Pvt.) 297, 300, 304, 305, 372
Mathew (Pvt.) (Lt. Dragoon), 221
Michael (Pvt.), 48, 50, 162, 177, 200(2)
Peater (Pvt.) 9
Peter (Pvt.) 80, 102, 218, 224
Petter (Pvt.) 222

Philip (Pvt.) 159, 191, 498, 617, 632
Phillip (Pvt.) 200(2), 573
Robert (Committee of Observation) 4
Robert (Pvt.) 184, 198, 558
Samuel 605, 607
Samuel (Pvt.) 20, 143
Samuel (Sub.) 140
Stephen (Pvt.) 80
Steven (Pvt.) 101
Stophel (Pvt.) 158
Thomas (Pvt.) 134, 144, 303, 310
Thomas 81
William (Pvt.) 66, 134, 206, 325, 336,
    353, 358, 362, 388, 400, 414, 440,
    456, 558, 570, 650, 657
William (Scout) 625
MILLERON, Jacob (Pvt.) 15
MILLERONS, John (Pvt.) 52
MILLERS, Alexandrew (Pvt.) 435
MILLHOLLAND, Daniel (Pvt.) 366
MILLIARD, Thomas (Cpl.) 81, 110
MILLICAN, Joseph (Scout) 626
MILLIGAN, John (Pvt.) 53, 221, 227,
    646
Joseph (Pvt.) 558, 567, 650
Samuel (Pvt.) 553, 624
William (Pvt.) 195
MILLIRON, Jacob (Pvt.) 57, 136
John (Pvt.) 57, 59, 136
MILLIRONS, Jacob (Pvt.) 421, 427, 432
John (Pvt.) 421
MILLISON, Jacob (Pvt.) 17, 589
John (Pvt.) 395, 589
MILLISONE, Jacob (Pvt.) 395
MILLROY, Henry (Pvt.) 649
MILLS, George (Pvt.) 143, 352, 355,
    612, 629
Jacob (Pvt.) 351
James (Pvt.) 643
John (Pvt.) 184, 404
MINCHER, Even (Pvt.) 441
MINER, Isaac (Pvt.) 47, 148, 150, 427
J. (Pvt.) 449
John Conrod (Pvt.) 373
MINES, John (Pvt.) 573
MINIS, John (Pvt.) 56, 632
MINK, Mical (Pvt.) 398
Michael (Pvt.) 430
Peter (Pvt.) 431
MINKE, Michel (Pvt.) 144
MINOR, Isaac (Pvt.) 49
Isac (Pvt.), 59, 603d
Joseph (Pvt.) 434

80

Samuel (Pvt.) 643
MINOUGH, Isaac (Pvt.) 276
MINSCAL, Evan 605
MINSTONE, William (Pvt.) 21
MIRCLE, Martain (Pvt.) 585
MIRROW, Richard (Pvt.) 450
MISH, Jacob (Pvt.) 236, 238
MISHEY, James (Pvt.) 7
MISKELLY, Robert (Pvt.) 634, 650
MISSER, Joseph (Pvt.) 176
MISSKELLEY, Robert (Pvt.) 568, 636
MISSKELLY, Robert (Pvt.) 559, 582
MITCHAL, James (Pvt.) 66, 120
 John (Pvt.) 66
 Samuel (Pvt.) 66
 William (Pvt.), 556, 577(2)
 William 645
MITCHEL, Alexander (Pvt.) 63, 146,
 402, 418, 437
 Andrew (Pvt.) 380
 David (Lt. Col.) 338, 404
 David (Maj.) 451
 David (Pvt.) 413, 426, 439
 Ebinezer (Pvt.) 585
 Ezekeiel (Ens.) 436
 Ezekiel (Ens.) 386, 401, 418, 656
 Ezekiel (Pvt.) 64
 Ezkl. (Pvt.) 147
 George (Pvt.) 563
 James (Pvt.) 86, 133, 141, 149, 151,
 219, 225, 235, 237, 380 (3rd), 384,
 390, 392, 435
 Jesse (Pvt.) 263
 John (Pvt.) 133, 186, 400, 413, 439,
 563, 568, 655
 Joseph (Pvt.) 167, 187
 Nathaniel (Pvt.) 380
 Robert 605
 Robert (Pvt.) 66, 134(2), 401(2), 405(2),
 414(2), 440
 Samuel (Pvt.) 42, 56, 134, 168, 195,
 259, 401, 405, 414, 440, 446, 448,
 491, 553, 555, 562
 Samuel (Sgt.) 489
 Thomas (Pvt.) 561, 570, 574, 579
 William (Pvt.) 380, 555, 574, 579
MITCHELL, --- (Col.) 352
 --- (Lt. Col.) 346
 Andrew (Pvt.) 163, 267, 302, 311
 David (Maj.) 29, 462
 George (Pvt.) 331
 James 28
 James (Pvt.) 23, 26, 267 (3d.), 302, 309,

 372, 516
 James (Sgt.) 309
 Jesse (Ens.) 6
 Jesse (Pvt.) 267, 302, 309
 John (Pvt.) 23, 26, 68, 163, 302, 315,
 323, 331, 461, 565, 631
 John (Sgt.) 194, 581, 635
 Joseph (Pvt.) 174, 178, 267, 268, 281,
 302, 303, 310, 374, 544, 613
 Mathew (Pvt.) 655
 Michael (Ens.) 346
 Nathaniel (Pvt.) 267, 302, 309, 318, 372
 Robert (Pvt.) 40, 268, 303, 310, 631,
 658
 Ross (Pvt.) 174, 178, 187, 455
 Samuel (Pvt.) 36, 40, 68, 243, 251, 329,
 479, 559, 573, 624, 631(2), 633, 650
 Samuel (Sgt.) 267
 Thomas (Pvt.) 326, 338, 649
 William (Pvt.) 331, 341, 361, 372, 560,
 564, 630, 648, 650
MITCHHAL, William (Pvt.) 556
MITHEL, John (Pvt.) 411
 Robert (Pvt.) 411
 Samuel (Pvt.), 411(2)
MITSAR, George (Pvt.) 90
MITSER, George (Pvt.) 113
MITTEN, John (Pvt.) 342
 Thomas (Pvt.) 342, 361
MITZER, George (Pvt.) 74
MIVALE, Andrew (Pvt.) 276
MOAR, George (Pvt.) 478, 490
 Henry (Pvt.) 341, 473
 Robert (Pvt.) 479
MOCK, Michael (Pvt.) 176, 181
MOCKEN, David (Pvt.) 658
MODY, John (Pvt.) 414
MOER, Amos (Pvt.) 409
MOHANY, John (Pvt.) 616
MOIRARTY, Hugh (Pvt.) 423
MONAHAN, John (Pvt.) 80
MONEY, Patrick (Pvt.) 117
MONEYPENNY, Robert (Pvt.) 247
MONSEN, William (Pvt.) 110
MONTEER, William (Pvt.) 384
MONTEETH, William (Pvt.) 221, 227,
 519, 542
MONTGOMERY (Mongomery),
 Alexander (Pvt.) 356
 Angass (Pvt.) 346, 366
 Angus (Pvt.) 356
 George (Pvt.) 276
 Hugh (Pvt.) 236, 238

Humphrey (Hum. Humphry, Umph'y) (Pvt.), 15, 41, 142, 428, 627
James (Pvt.) 18, 20, 21, 52, 53, 184, 191, 423, 516
John (Col.) 5
John (Committee of Observation) 4
John (Pvt.) 220, 222, 226, 228, 341, 361, 454, 516
John (Sgt.) 616
Robert (Pvt.) 37, 41, 143
Samuel (Pvt.) 37, 41, 143, 391
William (Clerk) 439
William (Pvt.) 41, 95, 96, 272, 285, 315, 389, 396, 400, 406, 413
MONTGUMRY, James (Pvt.) 383
MONTOOTH, Henry (Pvt.) 331, 566
William (Pvt.) 89
MONTOUR, Andrew (Pvt.) 624, 655
MOODY, David (Pvt.) 248, 483, 485, 501, 510
John (Pvt.) 26, 35, 249
Patrick (Pvt.) 314
William (Pvt.) 87
MOON, John (Cpl.) 242, 259
Joseph (Pvt.) 539
Nathaniel 607
Nathaniel (Drummer/Fifer) 243, 259
William (Pvt.) 540
MOOR, Aaron (Ens.) 321
Alexander (Pvt.) 140, 152, 516
Ames (Pvt.) 442
Aron (Ens.) 324
Fergis (Pvt.) 117
Henry (Pvt.) 506
Howard (Pvt.) 220, 226
James (Pvt.) 62, 132, 139, 152, 251, 265, 375, 394, 479, 491, 541, 589
John 605
John (Pvt.) 180, 188, 197, 271, 351
Jonathan (Pvt.) 258
Lodwick (Pvt.) 169
Patrick (Pvt.), 186, 198 (out w't his wagon)
Robert (Pvt.) 365, 494, 506, 553
Robert (Sgt.) 364
Samuel (Pvt.) 84, 114, 129, 604
Thomas (2nd Lt.) 320, 324
Thomas (Ens.) 559
Thomas (Pvt.) 183, 193
William (Capt.) 170, 175
William (Pvt.) 128, 130
MOORE, Aaron (Ens.) 334, 549
Alexander (Pvt.) 196, 544, 572, 585

Amos (Pvt.) 423
David (Pvt.) 292, 297, 313, 646, 650
George (Pvt.) 484
Henry (Pvt.) 498
James (Pvt.), 18, 20, 37, 56, 57, 99, 136, 264, 290, 292, 296, 313, 395, 421, 432, 632, 643(2)
John (Pvt.) 158, 187, 269, 279, 282, 287, 292, 296, 312, 313, 326, 372, 558, 646
Joseph (Pvt.) 514, 517
Moses (Pvt.) 296, 313
Patrick (Pvt.) 174
Robert (Pvt.) 56, 122, 489, 633, 638, 639, 646
Samuel (Cpl.) 539
Samuel (Pvt.) 291, 295, 313
Thomas (2nd Lt.) 322, 333
Thomas (Pvt.) 646
William (Capt.) 171, 183, 185, 190, 192, 634
William (Pvt.) 650
MOOREHEAD, Alexander (Pvt.) 74, 542
James (Pvt.) 94, 597
William (2nd Lt.) 95
William (Pvt.) 292
MOORHEAD, Alexander (Pvt.) 90, 113
Fergis (Pvt.) 264, 350
Fergus (Pvt.) 274
James (Pvt.) 72, 117, 527
William (2nd Lt.) 14, 29, 32, 45, 133
William (Capt.) 385, 399, 401, 412, 414, 438, 440
William (Pvt.) 296
MOOS, Silvanus (Pvt.) 244
MOOSE, Samuel (Pvt.) 535
MORASON, James (Pvt.) 178
MORDOCK, Patrick (Sgt.) 194
MORE, Aaron (Ens.) 331
David (Pvt.) 328
George (Pvt.) 249
James (Pvt.) 21, 637
Rob (Pvt.) 200
Robert (Pvt.) 161, 624
Samuel (Pvt.) 208
MOREHEAD, Fergus (Pvt.) 294
Forgis (Pvt.) 308
James (Pvt.) 530
MORELAN, John (Pvt.) 323
MORELAND, John (Pvt.) 559
Moses (Pvt.) 323
William (Pvt.) 325, 336
MORESON, John (Pvt.), 405 (for James

Henderson)
MORGAN, Abel (Pvt.) 246
Jacob 598
John (Pvt.) 251
MORHEAD, William (Capt.) 65
William (Pvt.) 436
MORIARTY, Hugh (Pvt.) 588
MORISON, John (Pvt.) 449
MORN, Henry (Pvt.) 361
MORNEY, Rodger (Pvt.) 134
MORNING, Rodger (Pvt.) 133, 152
Roger (Pvt.) 18, 21
MOROSON, James 639
MORPHY, Androw (Pvt.) 152
MORRAH, Alexander (Pvt.) 40
Charles (Pvt.) 248
George (Pvt.) 461
Richard (Pvt.) 40
Thomas (Pvt.) 40
MORRASON, William (Pvt.) 447
MORREHEAD, Fergus (Pvt.) 313
MORRESON, James (Pvt.) 574, 579
MORRIS, John (Pvt.) 544
Ritchard (Pvt.) 151
MORRISON, David 605
George (Pvt.) 366
James (Pvt.) 184, 354(2), 359, 371, 566,
    649
John (Pvt.) 19, 53, 148, 150, 152, 196,
    268, 343, 353, 375, 435, 627, 640,
    642
Mathew (Pvt.) 354(2), 359
Matthew (Pvt.) 461, 629
Noble (Pvt.) 174, 366
William (Pvt.) 273, 293, 307
William (Sgt.) 18, 67, 139
MORRISTOWN, William (Sgt.) 445
MORROSON, James 639
James (Pvt.) 645
MORROW, Alexander (Pvt.) 145
Andrew (Pvt.) 244
Charles (Pvt.) 435, 450, 472, 496, 619
Gaun (Pvt.) 148, 150
Henry (Pvt.) 305
James (Pvt.) 306
John (Pvt.) 24, 61, 131, 417, 423, 441
Richard (Pvt.) 36, 149, 406, 442, 458,
    658
Ritchard (Pvt.) 435
Thomas (Clark) 408
Thomas (Pvt.) 36, 41, 62, 132, 424, 658
Thoms. (Pvt.) 412
William (Pvt.) 64, 145, 147, 169, 220,
    223, 226, 356, 366, 403, 407, 420,
    438, 535, 544, 547, 580, 588, 599,
    616, 624
William (Pvt.) (Light Dragoon) 109, 110
MORTAN, Thomas (Ens.) 140
MORTHLAND, Alexander (Pvt.) 219,
    225
MORTIN, Charles (Pvt.) 68
MORTING, John (Pvt.) 561
MORTLAND, Alexander (Pvt.) 209
MORTON, James (Pvt.) 292, 313
John 201
Thomas (Ens.) 12, 16, 43, 46, 55, 383,
    626
Thomas (Pvt.) 113
William (Pvt.) 404, 641
MOSES, Joseph (Pvt.) 103
MOSGROVE, Samuel (Pvt.) 371
Thomas (Pvt.) 167
MOSHOLDER, John (Pvt.) 586
Jonathan (Pvt.) 119
MOSS, James (Pvt.) 91, 103, 124, 137
Joseph (Pvt.) 91, 109, 137
Silvanis (Pvt.) 503
Silvanus (Pvt.) 619
Silveus (Pvt.) 473
Sylvanus (Pvt.) 258, 498
Sylvinus (Pvt.) 243, 260
MOSSHOLDER, John (Pvt.), 87, 547
MOUNTAIN David Elder (Pvt.) 394
MOUR, James (Pvt.) 573
MOURN, John (Pvt.) 31, 64, 145, 147
MOWAN, Balser (Pvt.) 101
Balson (Pvt.) 80
MOWEN, Lodwick (Pvt.) 600
Ludwick (Pvt.) 599
MOWER, Stephen (Pvt.) 80
MOWON, Steven (Pvt.) 101
MQUOWN, Francis (Pvt.) 179
MT. GOMARY, James (Pvt.) 152, 441
MT. GOMERY, Humphrey (Pvt.) 397
Umphrey (Pvt.) 143
William (Pvt.), 36, 66, 143(2)
MT. GOMORY, John (Pvt.) 141
MT. GOMREY, William (Pvt.) 398
MT. GORMORY, James (Pvt.) 140
MT. GUMERY, Samuel (Sgt.) 404
William (Pvt.), 404
MT. GUMREY, James (Pvt.) 408
MTGOMERY, Humphey (Pvt.) 430
Samuel (Sgt.) 429
William (Pvt.) 431
MT'GOMREY, Samuel (Pvt.) 398

MUGMORE, Samuel (Pvt.) 443
MUKEY, James (Pvt.) 24
MULE, Henry (Pvt.) 93
MULHALEN, Arthur (Pvt.) 61
MULHOLAN, Daniel (Pvt.) 356
MULHOLAND, Rodger (Pvt.) 181
MULHOLLAM, Hugh (Pvt.) 174
MULHOLLAN, James (Pvt.) 174
MULHOLLEN, Daniel (Pvt.) 466
MULHOLLIN, Daniel (Pvt.) 456
MULHOLLON, Arthur (Pvt.) 151
MULHOLM, Arthur (Pvt.) 174
MULHOLN, Arthur (Pvt.) 178
  Hugh (Pvt.) 179
  James (Pvt.) 179
  Roger (Pvt.) 179
MULL, Henry (Pvt.) 116
MULLAN, Joseph (Pvt.) 480, 494
MULLIN, Charles (Ens.) 217
  George (Pvt.) 647
  Joseph (Pvt.) 249, 487
MULLISON, Jacob (Drummer/Fifer) 139
MULLON, George (Pvt.) 88
MULLOY, Edward (Pvt.) 116, 122
MULNOLAND, Henry (Pvt.) 180
MULOY, Edward (Pvt.) 93
MUNTEETH, Henry (Pvt.) 645
MUNTOOTH, William (Pvt.) 108
MURDOCK, Patrick (Sgt.) 176, 617
MURFEY, Andrew (Pvt.) 21
  Cornelous (Pvt.) 656
  John (Pvt.) 434
MURN, John (Pvt.) 392
MURPHEY, Andrew (Pvt.) 150
  Cornelius (Pvt.) 151, 390
  Edward (Pvt.) 237
  John (Pvt.) 117, 427, 629
  Patrick (Pvt.) 393
  Patt. (Pvt.) 132
  Pattrick (Pvt.) 409
MURPHY, --- (Lt.) 6
  Andrew (Pvt.) 19, 20, 139, 148, 435,
    449
  Cornelius (Pvt.) 149
  Daniel 605
  Edward (Pvt.) 236
  John (Cpl.) 596
  John (Pvt.) 150, 273, 449
  Patrick (Patt.) (Pvt.) 30, 61, 302, 423,
    442, 620
  Patrick (invalid) 310
  William (Pvt.) 352, 355, 461
MURRAY, Alexander (Pvt.) 460

  Charles 608
  Charles (Pvt.) 252, 480, 487, 494, 619
  Edward (Pvt.) 518
  George (Pvt.) 351
  Henry (Pvt.) 298
  James (Pvt.) 299, 301, 477, 485, 542
  John (Pvt.) 10, 353
  Michael (Pvt.) 625
  Richard (Pvt.) 343, 353, 359
  Robert (Pvt.) 354, 359, 461
  Thomas (Ens.) 173
  Thomas (Pvt.) 625
  William (2nd Lt.) 452, 455, 463, 466
  William (Pvt.), 353, 456, 625, 655(2)
  William (Pvt.) 358
MURREY, Thomas (Pvt.) 629
MURRON, John (Pvt.) 403, 419, 437,
    656
MURRY, Charles (Pvt.) 472
  Henry (Pvt.) 300
  Thomas (Pvt.) 119
MUSELMAN, Benjamin (Pvt.) 93
MUSGROVE, Elijah (Pvt.) 294, 300, 308
  Samuel (Pvt.) 299
  Thomas (Pvt.) 157, 175, 187, 190, 635
MUSKETOYS, John (Pvt.) 84
MUSSIN, John (Pvt.) 34
MUTERSPAUGH, Philip (Pvt.) 58
MUTRSPACK, Philip (Pvt.) 590
MVICKER, Duncan (Pvt.) 366
MYAR, Jonathan (Pvt.) 115
MYERS, George (Pvt.) 206
  John (Pvt.) 76
  Mathias (Pvt.) 300
MYLER, Elias (Pvt.) 448
  Michal (Pvt.) 63
  Titus (Pvt.) 64, 419
  Tytus (Pvt.) 402, 437
MYLIER, Eli. (Pvt.) 146
  Titus (Pvt.) 147
MYLLER, Michael (Pvt.) 146
MYRAS, John (Pvt.) 206

-N-

NACY, Samuel (Pvt.) 648
NAE, thomas (Pvt.) 19
NAILER, John (Pvt.) 233
  Ralph (Pvt.) 177
NALER, John (Pvt.) 229
NALES, John (Pvt.) 142
NANCE, John (Pvt.) 538
NAPIER, Joseph (1st Lt.) 465
NAPLE, Christian (Pvt.) 260

NAUGIN, Arthur (Pvt.) 563
NAUSS, Philip (Pvt.) 517
NAVE, John (Pvt.) 94, 97, 117
NEAIGIN, Thomas (Pvt.) 564
NEAL, Arthur (Pvt.) 160
  Charles (Pvt.) 139
  David (Pvt.) 86, 121, 128, 384, 516
  James (Pvt.) 182, 193
  John 607
  John (Pvt.) 518
  Thomas (Pvt.) 418, 428, 436
  William (Pvt.) 73, 80, 102, 527
NEALER, Robert (Pvt.) 220
NEALSON, William (Pvt.) 361
NEALY, James (Pvt.) 85, 313, 383, 516
NEARN, John (Pvt.) 189
NECHODEMIS, Andrew (Pvt.) 116
NEEL, Abraham (Pvt.) 87
  David (Pvt.) 393
  Mathew (Pvt.) 189
NEELEY, David (Pvt.) 555
  James (Pvt.) 17, 296
  William 497
  William (Pvt.) 481
NEELSON, Andrew (2nd Lt.) 248
  David (1st Lt.) 251
  John (2nd Lt.) 459
  John (Pvt.) 29
  Nathaniel (Pvt.) 237
  Robert (Pvt.) 460
  William (1st Lt.) 461
NEELY, David (Pvt.) 328, 577, 650
  Doved (Pvt.) 556
  James (Pvt.) 15
  John (Pvt.) 328
  Matthew 606
NEEMAN, George (Pvt.) 158
NEEPER, John (Pvt.) 355, 365, 456
  Joseph (1st Lt.) 454, 460
  Joseph (Pvt.) 346, 356, 366
  William (Pvt.) 366, 458
NEESBIT, Allen (Ens.) 454, 466
  Francis (Pvt.) 23
  Samuel (Pvt.) 460
  William (Pvt.) 527
NEETLES, Robert (Pvt.) 362
NEETLY, James (Pvt.) 626
NEEVANS, Daniel (Pvt.) 39
NEFF, John (Pvt.) 220, 227
NEGLE, Richard (Pvt.) 441
NEIGH, Jacob (Cpl.) 520
NEIL, David (Pvt.) 141
  William (Pvt.) 530

NEILS, David (Pvt.) 620
NEILSON, Daniel (Pvt.) 446
  David (1st Lt.) 256
  John (Pvt.) 267, 302, 446
NELLSON, Andrew (Sgt.) 259
  James (Pvt.) 145
  Robert 594
NELLY, David (Pvt.) 560
  John (Pvt.) 560
NELSON, Abram (Ens.) 240
  Andrew (2nd Lt.) 242
  Andrew (Pvt.) 484
  Andrew (Sgt.) 242
  David (1st Lt.) 242
  David (Pvt.) 478, 484, 619
  James (Pvt.) 356, 365, 366, 459, 484, 619
  John 355
  John (2nd Lt.) 465, 469
  John (Capt.) 341, 366
  John (Lt.) 609
  John (Pvt.) 32(2), 121, 303, 372, 459, 502, 587, 619, 638, 639, 647
  Joseph (Pvt.) 366, 458
  Nathaniel (Pvt.) 238
  Robart (Pvt.) 366
  Robert 607
  Robert (Ens.) 322
  Robert (Pvt.), 116, 346, 356, 366, 594
  Thomas (Pvt.) 318
  William (1st Lt.) 464, 469
  William (Pvt.) 342, 365
NEPPER, Abraham (Pvt.) 90
NESBIT, Allan (Ens.) 463
  Allan (Pvt.) 358
  Allen (Pvt.) 588
  Francis 28
  Francis (Pvt.) 26, 400
  William (Pvt.) 104, 138, 623
NESBITT, Allen (Pvt.) 352
  John (Pvt.) 589
NETLEY, James (Pvt.) 140
NETTLES, Robert (Pvt.) 624, 655
NEULS, John (Pvt.) 416
NEVILLE, Thomas (Sgt.) 7
NEVIN, Daniel (Pvt.) 37
NEVINS, Daniel (Pvt.) 41, 143, 391, 398
NEWAL, Robert (Pvt.) 269
  Thomas (Sgt.) 448
NEWCOMER, Peter (Pvt.) 93, 116
NEWEL, Thomas (Pvt.) 24, 197
  Thomas (Sgt.) 67, 445
  William (Pvt.) 524

NEWELL, John (Pvt.) 271, 284, 289, 314, 371, 379
Robert (Pvt.) 271, 275, 283, 285, 314
William (Cpl.) 519, 575, 582
William (Pvt.) 138, 270, 276, 277, 283, 382, 557
NEWILL, John (Pvt.) 615
NEWTON, Edward (Pvt.) 110, 601
NIBSON, John (Pvt.) 127
NICHELSON, John (Pvt.) 291
NICHOLAS, Alexander (1st Lt.) 47
John (Pvt.) 169, 526, 599
Thomas (Pvt.) 16
NICHOLES, Thomas (Pvt.) 136
NICHOLS, John (Pvt.) 522
Thomas (Pvt.) 17, 589
NICHOLSON, Daniel (Pvt.) 356
Edward (Pvt.) 355, 455, 466
James (Pvt.) 78, 105, 520, 524, 544, 585, 597
John (Pvt.) 78, 295, 313, 316, 543
John (Sgt.) 105
Richard (Pvt.) 356
Samuel (Pvt.) 78(2), 105, 106, 544
Samuel 78
William (Pvt.) 68, 145
William 78
NICKEL, Thomas (Pvt.) 347
NICKELSON, James (Pvt.) 445
NICKLE, Alexander (1st Lt.) 52
Thomas (Pvt.) 344, 360, 622, 628
NICKLES, John (Pvt.) 71, 117
Joseph (Pvt.) 71, 94, 117
Thomas (Pvt.) 344, 365
William (Pvt.) 93, 107, 116
NICKLON, Joseph (Pvt.) 644
NICKLSON, Daniel (Pvt.) 366
Edward (Pvt.) 365
Richard (Pvt.) 366
NICKSON, Samuel (Pvt.), 80
NICOLASON, James (Pvt.) 67
NICOLS Thomas (Pvt.), 57
NICOLSON, James (Pvt.) 447
NIELSON, John (Capt.) 628
Nathaniel (Pvt.) 637
NIGH, George (Pvt.) 101
Jacob (Cpl.) 571
Jacob (Pvt.) 523
John (Pvt.) 101
NIGHTCAP, Solomon (Pvt.) 160
NILES, Robert (Pvt.) 612
NILSON, Andrew (Pvt.) 478
Daniel (Pvt.) 448

David (Pvt.) 472
James (Pvt.) 95, 419, 472, 478
John (Pvt.) 85, 96, 120, 309, 383, 448
Joseph (Pvt.) 307, 413
Robert (Ens.) 324
Robert (Pvt.) 356
NIMAN, George (Pvt.) 184, 190
NIMMON, Alexander (Pvt.) 631
NIMMONS, George (Pvt.) 248
NIPER, Abraham (Pvt.) 113, 542
David (Pvt.) 112
Peter (Pvt.) 113, 542
NIPPER, Abraham (Pvt.) 75
Peter (Pvt.) 74, 90
NISBET, Francis (Pvt.) 413, 439
Francis N. (Pvt.) 66
John (Pvt.) 58, 388, 401, 414, 440
William (Pvt.) 76, 92, 413, 426, 439, 576, 583
NISBETT, Frances (Pvt.) 133
NISBIT, Allen (Ens.) 452
Allen (Pvt.) 362
James (Sgt.) 8
William (Pvt.) 522
NISWANGER, Joseph (Pvt.) 143
NIVANS, Daniel (Pvt.) 657
NIVVANS, Daniel (Pvt.) 431
NIXCON, Robert (Pvt.) 131
NIXON, Mervin (Pvt.) 41
Robert (Pvt.) 61
Robr. (Pvt.) 393
NIXSON, Samuel (Pvt.) 114, 130
NOBEL, Joseph (Pvt.) 62
NOBELE, John (Pvt.) 120
NOBLE, Andrew (Pvt.) 345, 350, 357, 629
Barkly (Pvt.) 57
Bartly (Pvt.) 587
James (Pvt.) 221, 227
John (Pvt.) 86, 128, 180, 197, 392
Joseph (Pvt.) 51, 120, 128
Joseph (2nd Sgt.) 54, 141, 384, 515
Thomas (Pvt.) 402, 418, 428, 436, 457
William (Pvt.) 65, 400, 413, 439
NOGLE, George (Pvt.) 94
Jacob (Pvt.) 73, 80, 102
Richard (Pvt.) 429
NOOP, Michael (Pvt.) 236, 238
NOP, Jacob (Pvt.) 221
NOPLE, Christian (Pvt.) 243
NORMAN, Charles (Pvt.) 93
NORRINGER, Walter (Pvt.) 509
NORTH, Joshua (Pvt.) 476, 490, 505

NORTON, Thomas (Pvt.) 189
NOSE, Adam (Pvt.) 228, 232
NOUCE, Micahel (Pvt.) 72
NOUSE, Michael (Pvt.) 117
Michall (Pvt.) 94
Philip (Pvt.) 515
NOVINGAL, Taroll (Pvt.) 491
NOVINGER, Tevalt (Pvt.) 477
Walter (Pvt.) 651
NOWLS, John (Pvt.) 397
NOX, John (Pvt.) 195
Patrick (Pvt.) 371
Thomas (Pvt.) 21, 52, 139, 151, 447
NUGEN, Arthur (Pvt.) 597
NUGENT, Arthur (Pvt.) 323, 336
Patrick (Pvt.) 330
NYE, John (Pvt.) 80

-O-
OAR, John (Pvt.) 188, 556
OATLEY, Joshua (Pvt.) 654
OBORN, Joseph (Pvt.) 650
OBRIAN, Martin (Pvt.) 110
Murthey (Pvt.), Inlisted in the Army.
123
OBRYAN, Murthy (Pvt.) 118
OBSON, James (Sgt.) 642
O'DONALD, Edward (Pvt.) 458
O'DONNAL, Edward (Pvt.) 347
O'DONNEL, Edward (Pvt.) 349
OFFICER, Alexander (Pvt.) 183
James (Pvt.) 160, 182, 193, 354, 461,
625, 629, 655
John (Pvt.) 433
Jonathan (Pvt.) 193
William (Pvt.) 343, 625, 655
OGDEN, Alexander 608
Isaac (Pvt.) 56, 573
OGDON, Isaac (Pvt.) 473, 498, 503, 632
OGELBEY, John (Pvt.) 65
OGELBY, John (Pvt.) 134
OGELVY, John (Pvt.) 50
OGILBAY, John (Pvt.) 636
OGILBEE, John (Pvt.) 425
OGLE, William (Pvt.) 352
OGLEBEY, John (Pvt.) 133, 399, 413,
415, 439
OGLEBY, John (Pvt.) 52
OHARRANE, Patrick (Pvt.) 283
OLD, Cowin (Pvt.) 85
OLDMAN, Christian (Pvt.) 355
Christy (Pvt.) 352
OLIVER, James (Lt.) 6

James (Pvt.) 206, 214
John (Pvt.) 325, 326, 336, 553, 560,
561, 570, 574, 578
John (Sgt.) 648
John 644
Thomas (Pvt.) 574, 579, 649
OLLERY, John (Pvt.), 307, 308
OLONE, Patrick (Pvt.) 635
OLTS, Henry (Pvt.) 477, 491
OMBARGER, Henry (Pvt.) 9
OMELLS, Charles (Pvt.) 617
O'NAIL, Charles (Pvt.) 248
ONAIL, Henry (Pvt.) 233
ONALE, Charles (Pvt.) 180, 197
ONALL, James (Pvt.) 486
O'NEAL, Henry (Pvt.) 230
James (Pvt.) 481, 497
Richard (Pvt.) 629
O'NEIL, Charles (Pvt.) 19
ONSTETT, George (Pvt.) 430
ORBISON, James (Pvt.) 389, 396
John (1st Lt.) 367, 371, 376, 379
John (Capt.) 261, 273, 293, 307
John (Pvt.) 570
ORE, John (Pvt.) 198
John 645
ORGAN, John (Pvt.) 252, 472, 480, 487,
494, 508, 619
ORIN, John (Pvt.) 588
ORNER, David (Pvt.) 474, 499
OROO, George (Pvt.) 633
ORR, John (Pvt.) 210, 493, 496, 573
Samuel (Pvt.) 207, 215, 496
William (Pvt.) 251, 493, 496
ORRIS, George (Pvt.) 604, 616
ORRNER, David (Pvt.) 488
ORTMAN, John (Pvt.) 143
OSTEN, Owen (Pvt.) 110
OTTENBERGER, George (Pvt.) 160
OTTER, Abraham (Pvt.) 651
Samuel (Pvt.) 243, 244, 259, 260
OTTERWORTH, Andrew (Sgt.) 410
OWENS, Levi (Pvt.) 352
Levy (Pvt.) 345
Levy (Sgt.) 364
William (Pvt.) Hatter. 125

-P-
PACEHORE, John (Pvt.) 575, 582
PACKMAN, Jonathan (Pvt.) 130
PAGE, David (Pvt.) 222
PAINTS, Nathaniel (Pvt.) 597
PAKE, John 405

John (Pvt.) 32, 143, 398, 430
PALEY, Thomas (Pvt.) 474
PALL, Nathaniel (Pvt.) 151
PALMAR, Henry (Pvt.) 384
PALMER, Hendy (Pvt.) 309
Henery (Pvt.) 141
Solomon (Pvt.) 326
PALMORE, Henry (Pvt.) 302
PALSEBEY, Christn. (Pvt.) 185
PALSEY, Christin (Pvt.) 192
PALSLEY, Christin (Pvt.) 185
John (Pvt.) 190, 635
PALSLY, John (Pvt.) 186
PARDEY, James (Pvt.) 35
PARK, James (Pvt.) 516
Robert (Pvt.) 268
PARKE, John (Pvt.) 407
Robert (Pvt.) 303
PARKER, Abraham (Pvt.) 258
Abram (Pvt.) 245
Alexander (2nd Lt.), 613
Alexander (Pvt.) 161, 198
James (Pvt.) 181, 198
John (Lt. Dn.) 197
John (Pvt.) 26, 159, 180, 248, 249, 601,
    610, 613
Joshua (Pvt.) 651
Richard (2nd Lt.) 202, 211
Robert (Pvt.) 312
William (Pvt.) 161, 181, 185, 191, 198
PARKES, Robert (Pvt.) 281
Samuel (Pvt.) 264, 287, 311
PARKESON, David (Ens.) 213
PARKHILL, James (Pvt.) 266, 272, 285,
    315
PARKINGTON, George (Pvt.) 616
PARKINSON, David (Ens.) 204
Richard (Pvt.) 224
PARKISON, Daniel (Pvt.) 587
John (Pvt.) 206
Richard (Pvt.) 208, 218
PARKS, Arthur (Pvt.) 57, 589
David (Pvt.) 72, 94, 117, 527, 530, 599
James (Pvt.) 71, 94, 117, 181, 198, 398
John (Pvt.) 94, 116
Joseph (Pvt.) 32, 64, 145, 147
Samuel (Pvt.) 381, 643, 278
Thomas (Pvt.) 438
PARSCHAL, Caleb (Pvt.) 330
PARSHAL, Caleb (Pvt.) 567
PARSHELL, Caleb (Pvt.) 566
PASCO, John (Pvt.) 62, 132, 410, 424,
    442

PATERSON, George (Pvt.) 624
James (Pvt.) 19, 435, 449
Peter (Pvt.) 360
Thomas (Pvt.) 27
William (Pvt.) 36
PATICHAL, Caleb (Pvt.) 630
PATIN, Joseph (Pvt.) 358
PATON, James (Pvt.) 285
Robert (Pvt.) 138
PATRSON, John (Pvt.) 185, 191
William (Pvt.) 185, 191
PATTAN, John (Pvt.) 445
William (Clark) 174
PATTARSON, James (Pvt.) 152
PATTEN, Hugh (Pvt.) 160
James (Capt.) 381
James (Pvt.) 244, 258
John (Pvt.) 68
Joseph (Pvt.) 104, 461
Robort (Pvt.) 104
Samuel (Capt.) 380
Thomas (Pvt.) 508
William (Pvt.) 654
PATTERSON, Alexander (Ens.) 172
Alexander (Pvt.) 243, 249, 260, 572,
    632
Andrew (Pvt.) 158
George (Pvt.) 362, 474, 493, 499, 654
James (Pvt.) 148, 150, 222, 243, 251,
    259, 264, 290, 310, 375, 479, 494,
    506, 643
John (Pvt.) 8, 10, 133, 175, 188, 195,
    245, 258, 617, 635
Joseph (1st Lt.) 532
Josiah (Pvt.) 195
Nicoles (Pvt.) 309
Obadiah (Pvt.) 195
Peter (Pvt.) 460
Petter (Pvt.), 200(2)
Robert (Pvt.) 206, 243, 246, 247, 260,
    473, 476, 489, 498, 506, 618, 651
Samuel (Pvt.) 245
Solomon (Pvt.) 309
Thomas (Pvt.) 130, 250, 290, 309
William (Ens.) 534
William (Pvt.) 42, 208, 380, 602, 610,
    629
William (Sgt.) 277, 286, 311
PATTESON, Jonathan (Pvt.) 130
Thomas (Pvt.) 130
PATTIN, John (Pvt.) 64
PATTISON, Peter (Pvt.) 344
William (Ens.) 513

PATTON, --- (Capt.) 601
Alexander (Ens.) 194
Hugh (Pvt.) 640
James (Capt.) 262, 271, 368, 377
James (Ens.) 499, 638
James (Pvt.) 121, 315, 615, 638
James (Waggon master) 4, 598
John (Lt.) 172, 194, 640
John (Pvt.) 56, 160, 161, 195(2: one
    identified as Irish, the other as Jr.),
    447, 475, 572
Joseph (1st Lt.) 519, 524, 525, 556, 575,
    582
Joseph (Pvt.) 91, 138, 350, 357
Joshua (Pvt.) 353
Robert (Pvt.) 91, 179, 279, 287, 312,
    375, 419, 437, 576, 583, 613
Samuel (Capt.) 6, 261, 277, 286, 310,
    368, 372, 376, 382, 601, 602, 609,
    610
Thomas (Pvt.) 653, 654
William (Clerk) 178
William (Pvt.) 121, 187, 195(2), 638,
    639, 640, 653
PATTSON, Hugh (Pvt.) 195
PATTY, William (Pvt.) 75, 84, 115, 130,
    540
PAUGE, John (Pvt.) 421
PAUL, Nahomel (Pvt.) 131
Nathaniel (Pvt.) 61, 423
William (Pvt.) 394, 424
PAULEY, John (Pvt.) 245
Thomas (Pvt.) 249, 499
PAULL, Nathaniel (Pvt.) 409, 441
Obediah (Pvt.) (Scout) 652
William (Pvt.) 409, 442
PAWLING, Henry (Pvt.) 81, 98
PAXTON, James (Pvt.) 292, 296, 313,
    419, 438
John (Pvt.) 58, 398, 430
Nathaniel (Pvt.) 548
Richard (Pvt.) 437
Samuel (Pvt.) 207
Thomas (Pvt.) 143, 390, 398, 430
PEACAKER, Abraham (Pvt.) 107
PEACE, Patrick (Pvt.) 276
PEACEACRE, Abraham (Pvt.), 93,
    116(2)
PEACHEL, Daniel (Pvt.) 79
PEACOCK, William (Pvt.), 181, 198
    (removed)
PEADON, Isaac (Pvt.) 342
Thomas (Pvt.) 151, 447

PEAHEL, Daniel (Pvt.) 101
PEAHILL, Daniel (Pvt.) 107
PEAL, Thomas (Pvt.) 484
PEARCE, Obedia 565
Obida (Pvt.) 565
Thomas (Pvt.) 565
PEARS, Dudley (Pvt.) 624
PEASRY, William (Pvt.) 426
PEBLES, Robert (Pvt.) 431
PECHLEY, Phelty (Pvt.) 72, 94, 117
PECKMAN, Jonathan (Pvt.) (Clarck) 114
PEDAN, Thomas (Pvt.) 182
PEDEN, John (Pvt.) 185, 191
Thomas (Pvt.) 193, 445
PEDON, Isaac (Pvt.) 361
PEEBLE, Alexander (Capt.) 394, 396
PEEBLES, Alexander 596
Alexander (Capt.) 25, 44, 54, 56, 96,
    385, 420, 432, 588, 628
James (Pvt.) 428
Robert (Col.) 5
Robert (Pvt.) 26, 34, 51, 54, 134, 286,
    388, 657
William (Pvt.) 268
PEEL, James (Pvt.) 143, 391, 431
Thomas (Pvt.) 243, 252, 260, 472, 478,
    619
PEELER, Jacob (Sgt.) 8
PEELMAN, Peter (Pvt.) 219
PEEPBLES, Alexander (Capt.) 12
PEEPLES, Alexander (Capt.) 135
Robert (Pvt.) 143
William (Pvt.) 310
PEIRCE, Thomas (Pvt.) (Scout) 652
PENER, Peter (Pvt.) 94, 117
PENERANCE, John (Pvt.) 78
PENTER, Jonathan (Pvt.) 194
PENTON, Samuel (Capt.) 55
PENWEL, Aaron (Pvt.) 160
PENWELL, Aaron (Pvt.) 617
PEOBLES, Robert (Pvt.) 398
PEOPELS, Mathew (Pvt.) 66
PEOPLES, Alexander (Capt.) 22, 50, 608
Robert (Pvt.) 31, 66, 278, 400, 414, 440
William (Pvt.) 296, 312
PEORRIE, William (Pvt.) 303
PEPBLES, James (Pvt.) 430
PEPLES, Alexander (Capt.) 27, 28, 62(2),
    422, 434
PEPPER, George (Pvt.) 189
Philip (Pvt.) 189
PERCE, Obediya (Pvt.) 579
PERRY, James (Pvt.) 24

William (Pvt.) 16, 17, 148, 150, 439, 627
PETER, Peter (Pvt.) 308
PETERSON, James (Pvt.) 228
William (Pvt.) 273
PETTERSON, Ezekial (Pvt.) 196
William (Pvt.) 372
PETTY, John (Pvt.) 191
PFOUTS, David (Pvt.) 509
George (Pvt.) 509
PHILIPS, Henry (Pvt.) 289, 295, 643
Jacob (Pvt.) 431
John (Pvt.) 292
PHILIPSS, John (Pvt.) 505
PHILLIPS, Henry (Pvt.) 291, 313
John (Pvt.) 200(2), 246, 296, 313, 456, 476, 477, 485, 618, 621
PHOUTS, David (Pvt.) 476, 502
George (Pvt.) 476
John (Pvt.) 476
Lonard (Pvt.) 476
Michael (Pvt.) 476
PICKENS, John 606
PIERCE, Joseph (Pvt.) 181, 198
Obediah (Pvt.) 649
PIKE, John (Pvt.) 390
PILE, Larance (Pvt.) 9
PILLARS, William (Pvt.) 589
PILLERS, William (Pvt.) 152
PILSAN, Robert (Pvt.) 110
PILSON, Robert (Pvt.) 287, 311
PIMM, William (Pvt.) 315
PIN, William (Pvt.) 272
PINE, James (Pvt.) 79
PINES, John Tate (Pvt.) 396
PINKERTEN, Joseph (Pvt.) 612
PINKERTON, Henry (Pvt.) 548
Joseph (Pvt.) 345, 352, 365
PINNAGE, Simon (Pvt.) 214
PIPER, James (Pvt.) 195, 401, 405, 414, 440
James (Sgt.) 312
John (Pvt.) 80, 102, 352, 358, 362, 455
Samuel (Pvt.) 64, 145, 147, 392, 403, 419, 437, 656
William (Pvt.) 157, 277, 286
William (Sgt.) 184, 187, 190, 634
PIPIR, James (Pvt.) 191
PIRCE, Obedya (Pvt.) 574
PIRKINS, William (Pvt.) 353
PITTS, Joseph (Pvt.) 66, 401, 411, 414, 440, 587, 631
PITZER, Jacob (Pvt.) 371, 643

PLANTS, Christian (Pvt.) 501
Jacob (Pvt.) 247, 257, 483
Jacob (Pvt.) 501
Tobias (Pvt.) 501
PLUMER, John (Pvt.) 82
PLUMITH, John (Pvt.) 549
PLUMMER, John (Pvt.) 110, 126
PLUNKET, Thomas (Pvt.) 442
POAKE, Robert (Pvt.) 195
POALLY, John (Pvt.) 559
POE, --- (Capt.) 586
James (Capt.) 512, 520, 523, 525, 532, 571, 575, 582
James (Pvt.) 91, 103
POILARD, John (Pvt.) 281
POINTS, John (Pvt.) 523, 526, 623
Nathaniel 606
POLAN, Henry (1st Lt.) 513, 533
POLAND, Robert (Pvt.) 549
POLICK, William (Pvt.) 128
POLINGER, Abraham (Pvt.) 233
POLK, John (Pvt.) 111
POLLACK, John (Pvt.) 126, 188
POLLARD, John (Pvt.) 299, 301, 306
POLLINE, Master (Pvt.) 195
POLLINGER, Abraham (Pvt.) 229
POLLOCK, Charles (Pvt.) 249, 472, 480, 487, 494
James (Pvt.) 168
John (Pvt.) 163, 199, 548
Thomas (Pvt.) 188, 199, 635
William (Pvt.) 361
POLLY, Thomas (Pvt.) 488
POLOCK, John (Pvt.) 77, 198
POLTNEY, Joseph (Pvt.) 474, 499
POLTON, John (Pvt.) 444
POMERY, George (Pvt.) 374
POMROY, George (Pvt.) 318
PONSLAR, Henry (Pvt.) 219
PONSLER, Charles (Pvt.) 9
Henry (Pvt.) 225
POO, James (Pvt.) 137
POOREMAN, Daniel (Pvt.) 88
POORMAN, Daniel (Pvt.) 98, 119, 539, 546
John 605
John (Pvt.) 208
POPE, John (Pvt.) 191
PORDY, John (Pvt.) 35
PORTER, --- (Pvt.) 127, 128
David (Pvt.) 143, 398, 406, 431
Hugh (Pvt.) 290, 400
Jacob (Pvt.) 431

James (Pvt.) 400, 431
John (Pvt.) 115, 279, 281, 288
Jonathan (Pvt.) 130
Joseph (Pvt.) 290
Robert (Pvt.) 65, 400
Thomas (Pvt.) 144, 397
William (Pvt.) 278, 287
PORTERFIELD, John (Pvt.) 23, 68, 445, 447
John (Sgt.) 27
Samuel (Pvt.) 15, 16, 67, 402, 436, 445, 447, 628
Samuel (Troop Lt. Horse) 428
William (Pvt.) 657
PORTNEY, Joseph (Pvt.) 488
POSHWAIT, Samuel (Pvt.) 200
POSTEL, Henry 605
POSTEN, Henery (Pvt.) 197
POSTLE, William (Pvt.) 642
POSTLETHWAITE, Samuel (Capt.), 5
POTERFIELD, John (Pvt.) 25
POTS, Alexander (Pvt.) 393
Allexander (Pvt.) 86, 128, 384
John (Pvt.) 85, 127
POTTER, John (Pvt.) 94, 97, 117
Simon (Pvt.) 94, 97, 117
POTTS, Alexander (Pvt.) 121
Hance (Pvt.) 437
John (Pvt.) 120
POULTNEY, Joseph (Pvt.) 252
POWER, James (Capt.) 451, 455, 462, 466, 609
James (Lt.) 612
James (Pvt.) 347, 348, 363
Peter (Pvt.) 107, 116
Samuel (Pvt.) 347, 348, 363
William (Pvt.) 347, 349
POWLING, Henry (Pvt.) 102
PRATES, Simon (Pvt.) 230, 233
PRAYLE, William (Pvt.) 279
PREATHER, Thomas (Pvt.) 80, 101
PREATS, George (Pvt.) 298, 305
PREMER, Felty (Pvt.) 80, 101
PRENTICE, J. Senr., (Pvt.), 129
PRETTS, Adam (Pvt.) 89
PRIAR, Nathan (Pvt.) 503
PRICAN, --- (Pvt.) 93
PRICE, Daniel (Pvt.) 94, 117
Dorintine (Sgt.) 489
Jacob (Pvt.) 94, 97, 117
John (Pvt.) 93, 107, 116
Joseph (Pvt.) 654
Joseph (Sgt.) 653

PRIER, John (Pvt.) 505
Nathan (Pvt.) 473
Nathani (Pvt.) 510
Timothy (Pvt.) 474, 488
PRIGMAN, Henry (Pvt.) 305
PRINGHAM, Frederick (Pvt.) 299
PRINGMAN, Frederick (Pvt.) 306
PRIOR, John (Pvt.) 501
Nathan (Pvt.) 243, 260, 498
Timothy (Pvt.) 472, 499
PRISSELL, Henry (Pvt.) 543
PRITH, Adam (Pvt.) 112
PRITS, Joseph (Pvt.) 405
PRITTS, Adam (Pvt.) 542
George (Pvt.) 542, 585
PRYOR, Peter (Pvt.) 643
Timothy (Pvt.) 619
PUMERY, Thomas (Pvt.) 449
PUMMERY, Thomas (Pvt.) 427
PUMREY, Thomas (Pvt.) 434
PUMROY, Thomas (Pvt.) 148, 150
PURDAY, William (Pvt.) 365
PURDY, --- (Col.) 476, 477
James (Capt.) 6
James (Col.) 471, 473, 474, 479, 482, 489, 493, 495, 498, 499, 500, 508, 509(2), 510
James (Lt. Col.) 483
James (Pvt.), 27, 35, 250
John (Pvt.) 27, 35, 68, 250, 446, 448
John (Pvt.) 484
Robert (Pvt.) 352, 358, 455, 466
Thomas (Pvt.) 343, 353, 359, 458
William (Pvt.) 355
PURIANCE, John (Pvt.) 585
PURSLEY, James (Pvt.) 349
PURSLY, James (Pvt.) 347
PURVEONS, John (Pvt.) 527
PURVIANCE, John (Pvt.) 73, 106, 530, 544, 597
Samuel (Pvt.) 82, 110, 126
PUTMAN, Peter (Pvt.) 225

-Q-
QEEN, William (Pvt.) 61, 131, 442
QUERY, Charles (Pvt.) 127
QUIGEL, Philip (Drummer/Fifer) 243
Phillip (Drummer/Fifer) 259
QUIGGLE, Philip (Ens.) On 23 April 1778 it was reported that he had "gone to the enemy" and was replaced by William Rea. 252
QUIGLE, Michael (Pvt.) 488, 499

Michel (Pvt.) 474
Philip (Pvt.) 56
Phillip (Pvt.) 573
QUIGLEY, Christopher (1st Lt.) 202,
205, 211
Henry (Pvt.) 229, 233
John (Pvt.), 7, 57, 135, 221, 227, 589(2)
Michael (Pvt.) 249
Philip (Pvt.) 632
Phillip (Ens.) 241
Robert (1st Lt.) 14, 36, 40, 45, 65
Robert (2nd Lt.) 587
Robert (Capt.) 614, 636
Robert (Lt.) 385, 424, 426, 658
Rt. (Capt.) 636
Samuel 28
Samuel (Pvt.) 7, 24, 49, 57, 135, 395,
415, 420, 425, 432, 589, 636
QUIGLY, John (Pvt.) 10
Robert (1st Lt.) 132
Robert (Lt.) 399, 412, 438
Robert (Pvt.) 134
Samuel (Pvt.) 10
QUILON, Ambris (Pvt.) 347
QUOWN, William M. (Pvt.) 179

-R-
RAB, John (Pvt.) 506
RABB, David (Pvt.) 363
RACHFORD, Alexander (Pvt.) 194
RAGAN, Daniel (Pvt.) 409
RAIGH, John (Pvt.) 176
RAILER, Robert (Pvt.) 227
RAIRDON, Thomas (Pvt.) 208
RALFSNIDER, Henry (Ens.) 528
RALPH, Henry (Ens.) 519
Matthias (Pvt.) 325
RALPH-SNYDER, John (Pvt.) 77
RALPHSCHNEIDER, Henry (Ens.) 529
RALPHSNYDER, Henry (Ens.) 547, 533
John (Pvt.) 548, 526
RALSON, David (Pvt.) 496
James (Pvt.) 248
RALSTON, Andrew (Pvt.) 196, 431
David (Pvt.) 251, 493
James (Pvt.) 159, 195
John 27
John (Pvt.) 25, 144, 447
RAMAGE, Josiah (Pvt.) 515
Josias (Pvt.) 517
RAMBURGH, Phillip (Pvt.) 657
RAMER, Abraham (Pvt.) 225
RAMMAGE, Josiah (Pvt.) 78, 543, 584

RAMMER, Abraham (Pvt.) 219
RAMSAY, James (Pvt.) 124
Thomas (Pvt.) 311, 647
William (Ens.) 377
William (Pvt.) 311
RAMSEY, Benjamin (Pvt.) 279, 288, 312
David (Pvt.) 68
Hugh (Pvt.) 68
James (Pvt.) 84, 114, 275, 540
John (Pvt.) 264, 278, 287, 311, 643
Nathan (Pvt.) 189
Samuel (Pvt.) 175, 185, 191
Thomas (Pvt.) 278, 287, 303, 318, 372
William (Ens.) 368, 372, 380
William (Pvt.) 278, 287, 303, 318
RAMSON, William (Pvt.) 27
RANAX, Alexander (Pvt.) 316
RANDAL, James (Pvt.) 588
RANDELL, Thomas (Pvt.) 625
RANDELS, James (Pvt.) 114
RANDFRO, John (Pvt.) 87
RANDLES, Thomas (Pvt.) 655
RANDLS, James (Pvt.) 84
RANECK, Samuel (Pvt.) 538
RANFREW, John (Pvt.) 584
RANGLEBURY, Philip (Pvt.) 403
RANISON, William (Pvt.) 250
RANKAN, David (Pvt.) 275
James (Pvt.) 275
Jeremiah (Ens.) 282
RANKEN, William (Pvt.) 257
RANKIN, James (Pvt.) 269, 283, 373
Jeremiah (Ens.) 262, 269
Jeremiah (Lt.) 274
Jeremiah 374
John (Pvt.) 143, 243, 249, 259, 269,
306, 488, 499, 552
John (Sgt.) 555
Richard (Pvt.) 27, 243, 250, 260, 472,
619
William (Pvt.) 269, 275, 282, 372, 528,
529, 576, 583
RANKINS, John (Pvt.) 564
RANNELLS, James (Pvt.) 125
William (Lt.) 291, 295, 312
RANNELS, John (Pvt.) 427
RANNILL, John (Pvt.) 89
RANOLDS, John (Pvt.) 142
RANSBERRY, Philip (Pvt.) 392
RAPIN, David (Pvt.) 187
RAPINE, Daniel (Pvt.) 184, 190
RAPWING, Daniel (Pvt.) 635
RASENBERY, John (Pvt.) 620

92

RAUHAUS, John (Sgt.) 577
RAWLSTON, Robert (Pvt.) 508
RAY, James (Pvt.) (deserted 29 April
1779) 59 127, 400, 413, 435, 450,
603
John (Capt.) 514
John (Pvt.) 139, 399, 413, 636
Mathew (Pvt.) 104, 138
William (Pvt.) 137, 576, 583
RAYACK, Thomas (Pvt.) 449
RAYEN, Michael (Pvt.) 111
Timothy (Pvt.) 388
RAYLE, William (Pvt.) 289
RAYN, Michael (Pvt.) 82
RAYNE, Michael (Pvt.) 77
RAYNEY, Samuel (Pvt.) 459
REA, --- (Capt.) 587
Alexander (Pvt.) 304
James (Pvt.) 18, 65, 135, 479, 490, 494,
506
John (Capt.) 69, 77, 78, 105, 528, 534,
584
John (Lt.) 6
John (Pvt.) 19, 415, 425, 459
Jonathan (Pvt.) 129
Samuel (Pvt.) 72, 78, 106, 119, 310
William (Ens.) 252, 255
William (Lt.) 473, 632
William (Pvt.) 72, 78, 106
William (Sgt.) 543, 584, 600
READ, James (Pvt.) 630
John (2nd Lt.) 254
John (Ens.) 649
Steaphen (Pvt.) 9
William (Pvt.) 56
READERS, Casper (Pvt.) 224
REAFSNYDER, John (Pvt.) 601
REAGER, Conrod (Pvt.) 102
Michall (Pvt.) 80
REAGLE, Jacob (Pvt.) 501
REAL, William (Cpl.) 529
REAMER, Abraham (Pvt.) 217
Abram (Pvt.) 222, 223
REANY, William (Pvt.) 196
REAR, John (Pvt.) 640
REARDAN, Thomas (Pvt.) 402, 436
REARDON, Thomas (Pvt.) 418
REAUGH, John (Pvt.) 195, 617
REAY, William (Ens.) 250
RECORD, Michel (Pvt.) 473
REDDART, John (Pvt.) 395
REDDY, James (Pvt.) 624
Josiah (Pvt.) 624

Thomas (Pvt.) 624
REDLEBERGER, John (2nd Lt.) 511
REED, Adam (Pvt.) 247
Alexander 606
Alexander (Pvt.) 249, 252, 472, 489,
496, 619
Andrew (Pvt.) 76, 92, 104, 138, 291,
306, 576, 583
David (Pvt.) 138, 176, 183, 184, 186,
190, 193, 617
David (Sgt.) 634
Henry (Pvt.) 292, 296, 313, 373
Jacob (Pvt.) 89
James (Pvt.) 91, 244, 290, 292, 306,
316, 332, 490, 505, 567(2), 576, 583,
630, 646, 650, 653, 654
James (Sgt.) 653
John (2nd Lt.) 239, 246, 256
John (Capt.) 536, 543
John (Ens.) 555, 557, 577
John (Lt.) 638
John (Pvt.) 48, 49, 52, 57, 67, 122, 137,
181, 182, 187, 195, 263, 267, 280,
290, 302, 315, 343, 353, 359, 419,
438, 445, 447, 523, 527, 549, 623
John (Sgt.) 642
Jonathan (Pvt.) 192
Joseph (Pvt.) 19, 148, 150, 152, 327
Joseph (Sgt.) 19, 449
Joseph 612
Joshua (Sgt.) 139
Paul (Pvt.) 280, 290, 316
Richard (Pvt.) 629
Samuel (Pvt.) 68, 159, 184, 191, 246,
248, 263, 268, 302, 310, 445, 447,
476, 490, 504, 643, 653, 654
Stefe (Pvt.) 219
Stephen (Pvt.) 225
Thomas (Pvt.) 77, 82, 558, 576, 583
Thomas (Sgt.) 113, 129
William (Clerk) 277
William (Pvt.) 58, 92, 99, 104, 158, 167,
176, 181, 182, 243, 252, 260, 264,
280, 478, 484, 490, 501, 505, 572,
589, 643, 651, 653, 654
William (Sgt.) 632
REEGLE, Jacob (Pvt.) 505
REEP, Jonas (Pvt.) 221
REEVER, Frederick (Pvt.) 274
REEVES, Frederick (Pvt.) 294
REGAN, Daniel (Pvt.) 423, 481, 497
REGAR, Michael (Pvt.) 117
REID, John (Pvt.) 638

REIDBAGGH Michael (Pvt.) 233
REIDIBAUGH, Michael (Pvt.) 230
REIFSNYDER, Henry (Ens.), 537
REIGN, Michael (Cpl.) 545
REILY, Thomas (Pvt.) 544
REIMER, Abraham (Pvt.) 616
REINARD, John (Pvt.) 143
REINHART, Frederick (2nd Lt.) 170
REMSEN, William (Pvt.) 35
REMSON, William (Pvt.) 27
RENCHART, Frederick (Ens.) 172
RENE, Martin (Pvt.) 476
RENESON, harry (Pvt.) 492
  William (Pvt.) 573, 632
RENFREN, John (Pvt.), 118
RENFREW, John (Pvt.) 108
RENICK, Samuel (Pvt.) 546
RENISON, Henry (Pvt.) 480, 495
  William (Pvt.) 480
  William (Pvt.) 494
RENKEN, John (Pvt.) 474
RENKIN, Archebal (Pvt.) 137
RENNICKS, Samuel (Pvt.) 521
RENNISON, William (Pvt.) 487
RENNOLDS, Jonathan (Pvt.) 119
RENSBURGHER, Philip (Pvt.) 419, 438
RENSON, William (Pvt.) 56
REPPEY, William (Pvt.) 152
REREDON, Thomas (Pvt.) 417
RETTED, John (Pvt.) 427
RETTER, Casper (Pvt.) 222
REVOUR, Frederick (Pvt.) 308
REX, George (Pvt.) 476
REYNARD, John (Pvt.) 290
REYNOLDS, Adam (Pvt.) 188
  James (Pvt.) 143, 398, 406, 431, 576, 583
  John (Pvt.) 395, 421, 432
  Robert (Pvt.) 422
  William (1st Lt.) 367, 376
  William (Lt.) 262
RHAY, James (Pvt.) 133, 152
RHEA, --- (Capt.) 609
  Alexander (Pvt.) 269
  Daniel (Pvt.) 274, 294
  James (Pvt.) 21, 269, 455
  John (Capt.) 528
  Robert (Pvt.) 270
  William (Ens.) 521
  William (Lt.) 55
  William (Pvt.) 243, 260, 526, 573
RHEINHART, Frederick (Pvt.) 248
RHINE, Michael (Pvt.) 126

RHYNE, Stephen (Pvt.) 184
  Steven (Pvt.) 191
RIAN, James (Pvt.), 405 (for John Pake)
  Michael (Cpl.) 519
RIANS, John (Pvt.) 347
RICE, Frederick (Pvt.) 490, 654
  Fredrick (Pvt.) 653
  Jeremiah (Pvt.) 207
RICHARD, Allexander (Pvt.) 57
  Barnard (Pvt.) 87
RICHARDS, Alexander (Pvt.) 8, 395, 420, 432
  Henry (Pvt.) 395, 415, 420, 432, 589
RICHARDSON, Edmond (Pvt.) 323, 582
  Edmund (Pvt.) 634, 636
  William (Pvt.) 394, 424
RICHARTS, Hendry (Pvt.) 135
RICHESON, Edward (Pvt.) 345, 568
RICHEY, Alaxander (Pvt.) 135
  Alexander (Pvt.) 10, 415
  Allexander (Pvt.) 133
  Andrew (Pvt.) 549
  Joseph (Pvt.) 294, 374
  Thomas (Pvt.) 125
  William (Pvt.) 215
RICHIE, John (Pvt.) 191
  William (Pvt.) 191
RICHISON, Edmond (Pvt.) 646
  Edward (Pvt.) 352
RICKETS, Robert (Pvt.) 574, 579, 648
  Zacaria (Pvt.) 574, 578
  Zachariah (Pvt.) 648
RICORDS, Robert (Pvt.) 651
RIDDATT, John (Pvt.) 421
RIDDEL, James (Pvt.) 654
  John (Sgt.) 35
RIDDETT, John (Pvt.) 432
RIDDLE, James (Ens.) 473
  James (Lt.) 471, 619
  James (Pvt.) 251(2), 474, 493, 653
  James (Pvt.) 499
  John (Pvt.) 244, 247, 258, 347, 348, 460, 488, 569, 646, 648
  John (Sgt.) 474, 499
  Mathew (Pvt.) 82, 110, 549
  Matthew (Pvt.) 126
  William (Pvt.) 27, 35, 243, 250, 260, 474, 488, 498
RIDDLEBERGER, John (2nd Lt.) 524, 541
RIDDLESBARGER, John (Pvt.) 89
RIDDLESBERGER, John (2nd Lt.) 532
RIDEL, John (Pvt.) 574

RIDER, Thomas (Pvt.) 246
RIDGER, Richard (Pvt.) 414
RIDLE, John (Pvt.) 579
Joseph (Pvt.) 185
RIDLESBARGER, John (Pvt.) 112
RIDSTONE, William (Pvt.), 178
RIELEY George (Pvt.) 200
RIELY, George (Pvt.) 200
RIGAN, Daniel (Pvt.) 502
RIGER, Barnard (Pvt.) 537
RIGGLE, Stephen (Pvt.) 82, 110, 126
RIGHER, Barnert (Pvt.) 545
RIGHT, Charles (Pvt.) 548
Richard (Pvt.) 523
William (Pvt.) 141
RIGN, Michael (Pvt.) 524
RILEY, George (Pvt.) 174
RIMER, Phillip (Pvt.) 647
RINE, Michael (Pvt.) 538, 557
RINEHART, Frederick (Pvt.) 160, 199
RINGLAND, James (Pvt.) 481, 497, 502
RINHART, Frederick (Pvt.) 199
RINIKS, Samuel (Pvt.) 523
RION, Timothy (Pvt.) 139
RIPPEL, Mathias (Pvt.) 141
RIPPELS, Jacob (Pvt.) 141
RIPPEY, Samuel (Pvt.) 23, 57, 395, 421,
433, 589
William (Pvt.) 142, 397, 430
RIPPLE, Jacob (Pvt.) 19
RIPPY, Samuel (Pvt.) 25, 136
RISSNIDER, Henry (Ens.) 81
RITCHARDS, Hendry (Pvt.) 57
RITCHESON, Edmund (Pvt.) 336
RITCHEY, John (Pvt.) 221, 228
Thomas 124
RITCHIE, James (Pvt.) 283
RITCHISON, William (Pvt.) 61, 132,
409, 442
RITE, Gorg (Pvt.) 435
John (Pvt.) 435
RITHERFORD, Isack (Pvt.) 439
RITNOR, John (Pvt.) 138
RITTER, Gasper (Pvt.) 218
ROACH, Morris (Pvt.) 98, 599
ROAN, Charles (Pvt.) 167
David (Pvt.) 206
John (Pvt.) 147
Petor (Pvt.) 138
ROATCH, John (Sgt.), 59, 603d
ROBB, Benjamin (Pvt.) 430
David (Pvt.) 341, 629
John (Pvt.) 431, 473, 498

ROBBINS, Alexander (Pvt.) 630
ROBERTS, James (Pvt.) 75, 84, 114,
130, 540
Richard (Pvt.) 269, 275, 283
Samuel (Pvt.) 473, 498
William (Pvt.) 633
ROBERTSON, Alexander (1st Lt.) 246,
254, 256
Alexander (Pvt.) 174, 268, 303, 310,
331, 374, 617
Francis (Pvt.) 314
George (Pvt.) 314
Hugh (Pvt.) 252
James 606
James (Pvt.) 139, 169, 247, 257
Jeremiah (Pvt.) 208, 296
John (Pvt.) 20, 21, 133, 135, 152, 258,
268, 331, 400, 413, 439
Jonathan (Capt.) 609
Samuel (Pvt.) 275
William (Pvt.) 267, 302, 309, 325, 373,
380, 400, 413, 439, 454, 466
ROBESON, Alexander (Pvt.) 509
Andrew (Pvt.) 586
Hugh (Pvt.) 573, 632
James (Pvt.) 104, 138, 270, 509, 599
John (Pvt.) 52
ROBINSON, Alexander (1st Lt.), 240
Alexander (Pvt.) 503 566, 597, 651
Francis (Pvt.) 271, 284
George (Capt.) 5
George (Pvt.) 284
Hugh (Pvt.) 501, 588
James (Pvt.) 176, 179, 248, 494, 520,
546, 549, 601
Jeremiah (Pvt.) 292
John (Lt.) 654
John (Pvt.) 18, 32, 53, 64, 93, 105, 116,
318, 478, 490, 493, 546, 584, 653,
654, 504
Jonathan (Capt.) Of Sherman's Valley.
255
Jonathan (Pvt.) 475, 500
Joseph (Pvt.) 501
Michael (Pvt.) 347, 348, 362
Robert (Pvt.) 245, 482, 505
Samuel (Pvt.) 200
ROBISON, Alexander (Pvt.) 183
("moved"), 479, 494, 563
Hugh (Pvt.) 56
James (Cpl.) 616
James (Pvt.) 175, 183, 480, 524
John (Lt.) 338

John (Pvt.) 59, 65, 78, 145, 147, 150, 373, 496, 543, 603
Jonathan (Capt.) 241
Joseph (Pvt.) 547
Robert (Pvt.) 80, 101, 501
ROCH, Morrise (Pvt.) 81
ROCK, George (Pvt.) 75, 90, 113
Henry (Pvt.) 90, 99, 113
John (Pvt.) 93, 106, 116
Morris (Pvt.) 102
ROCKEL, Henry (Pvt.) 543
ROD, William (Pvt.) 79, 101, 107
RODDEY, James (Pvt.) 455
RODDY, Alexander (Pvt.) 362
James (Pvt.) 91, 103, 362, 575, 582
John (Pvt.) 109
RODES, Frederick (Pvt.) 504
RODGERS, George (Pvt.) 292
John (Pvt.) 582, 634
Mathew (Pvt.) 221
Richard (1st Lt.) 203, 208
Richard (Pvt.) 388, 401, 440, 657
Ritchard (Pvt.) 66
Robert (Pvt.) 221
Samuel (Pvt.) 73
Thomas (Pvt.) 222
William (Ens.) 341, 629
William (Pvt.) 492, 501
RODMAN, James (Pvt.) 246, 479, 490, 494, 506, 653
Samuel (Pvt.) 654
RODS, Frederick (Pvt.) 476
RODSBERRY, William (Pvt.) 196
RODY, Alexander (Pvt.) 655
James (Pvt.) 655
Josiah (Pvt.) 655
Thomas (Pvt.) 655
ROE, James (Pvt.) 299
Joseph (Pvt.) 182
Thomas (Pvt.) 438
ROGER, John (Pvt.) 102, 179
Samuel (Capt.) 541
ROGERS, John (Pvt.) 175, 318, 636
Matthew 605
Matthew (Pvt.) 228
Richard (1st Lt.) 212
Robert (Pvt.) 228
Samuel (Capt.) 88, 514
Samuel (Pvt.) 80, 102
Thomas (Pvt.) 228
William (Ens.) 360
William (Pvt.) 157, 483
ROLAND, Thomas (Pvt.) 510

ROLE, John (Pvt.) 332
John (Pvt.) 566
Michael (Cpl.) 577
Michal (Cpl.) 555
Michel (Pvt.) 565
Mickle (Pvt.) 574, 578
ROLL, John (Pvt.) 554
Michael (Pvt.) 554, 648
ROLLAN, Thomas (Pvt.) 492
ROLSTON, David (Pvt.) 572, 632
RONBOROUGH, Charles (Pvt.) 26
RONEY, James (Pvt.) 177, 647
RONNELLS, John (Pvt.) 112
ROOCK, Morris (Sgt.) 169
ROOPLEY, Jacob (Lt.) 217
ROOSE, Jeconias (Pvt.) 132
RORK, Michal 565
ROSBERRY, Alexander (Pvt.) 425
ROSBERY, Robert (Pvt.) 435, 450
ROSBOROUGH, Charls (Pvt.) 280
ROSBROGH, Alaxander (Pvt.) 135
ROSBROUGH, Charles (Sgt.) 148
John (Pvt.) 149
ROSE, Jeremias (Pvt.) 620
ROSEBERRY, Alexander (Pvt.) 636
ROSEBOROUGH, Alexander (Pvt.) 395, 415, 420
James (Pvt.) 395, 416, 420
ROSEBROUGH, Charles (Pvt.) 150
John (Pvt.) 151
ROSENBERG, Abraham (Pvt.) 267, 302, 601, 610
Daniel (Pvt.) 301
John (Pvt.) 268
ROSENBERGER, Daniel (Pvt.) 267
George (Pvt.) 238
John (Pvt.) 303, 310
ROSENBOROUGH, Charles (Sgt.) 36
ROSENBURGH, John (Pvt.) 263
ROSENBURY, Abraham (Pvt.) 380
ROSENLAGER, Daniel (Pvt.) 309
ROSIER, John (Pvt.) 472
ROSINBERGER, George (Pvt.), 236
ROSINGERBERGER George (Pvt.) 220
ROSS, Adam (Pvt.) 64, 147
Arch (Pvt.) 354
Charles (Pvt.) 52
George (Pvt.) 655
James 608
James (Pvt.) 76, 92, 104, 143, 147, 184, 191, 246, 274, 294, 307, 390, 398, 430, 472, 482, 489, 496, 501, 505, 507, 547, 576, 583, 586, 619

John (Pvt.) 249, 342, 354, 460, 489, 496
Joseph (Pvt.), 342
Samuel (Lt. Col.) 39, 451, 462
Samuel (Pvt.) 265, 292, 296, 342, 354, 361
Simon (Pvt.) 391, 403, 419, 437
Thomas (Pvt.) 269, 275, 282
William (Pvt.) 84, 245, 284, 291, 295, 314, 323, 482, 501, 505, 540, 567, 581, 635, 643, 644
ROSSENBERGER, Abram (Pvt.) 309
ROTRICK, George (Pvt.) 565
ROUSINGBERGER, George (Pvt.), 226 (Aug 1780 - unfit for duty)
ROWAN, Charles (Pvt.) 158, 174
Charly (Pvt.) 178
David (Pvt.) 199, 200
John (Pvt.) 419, 438
Stewart (Pvt.) 179
Stuart (Pvt.) 175, 186
ROWEN, Flavel (Clerk) 617
ROWLAND, Thomas (Pvt.) 251, 483, 501
ROWNEY, James (Pvt.) 617
ROYAL, Samuel (Capt.) 5
ROYAN, Andrew (Pvt.) 178
ROYAR, Daniel (Ens.) 88
Henry (Pvt.) 389
Samuel (Capt.) 88, 511
ROYER, --- (Capt.) 585
Daniel (Ens.) 70
Hendry (Pvt.) 114
Henry (Pvt.) 396
Samuel (Capt.) 90, 516, 531, 609
RUBLE, Mathias (Pvt.) 559
RUKETS, Robert 644
RULE, William (Pvt.) 98, 102
RULED, William (Pvt.) 81
RUMBLE, George (Pvt.) 116
RUMELL, George (Pvt.) 102
RUMSHEY, John (Pvt.) 435, 450
RUNSHAW, John (Pvt.) 149
RUP, Jones (Pvt.) 227
RUPLEY, George (Pvt.) 208
Jacob (Pvt.) 207
RUPP, Jonas (Pvt.) 9
RUSAL, James (Pvt.) 152
RUSEL, Andrew (Pvt.) 587
James (Pvt.), 59, 603d
RUSSEL, Andrew (Pvt.) 105, 122, 584
Henry (Pvt.) 290
James (Pvt.) 52, 57, 136
Joseph (Pvt.) 267

RUSSELL, Andrew (Pvt.) 78, 517, 518, 519, 543
David (Pvt.) 278, 287, 311, 373
James (Pvt.) 18, 20, 21, 53, 139, 278, 287, 312, 395, 421, 432, 589
John (Pvt.) 352, 358, 362
Joseph (Pvt.) 288, 302
RUTH, Richard (Pvt.) 399, 413, 415
Ritchard (Pvt.) 65
RUTHERFORD, Isaac (Pvt.) 402, 419
RUTLIDG, Jason (Pvt.) 127
RUTLIDGE, Jason (Pvt.) 428
RYAN, Andrew (Pvt.) 635
James (Pvt.) 642
Thomas (Pvt.) 80
Timothy (Pvt.) 20
Timothy (Pvt.) 657
William (Sgt.) 637
RYDON, John (Pvt.) 560
RYHARD, Barnard (Pvt.) 108
Bernard (Pvt.) 118
RYLEY, George (Pvt.) 161
RYMER, Nichles (Pvt.) 102
Peter (Pvt.) 79
RYN, Timothy (Pvt.) 401, 414, 440
RYNOLDS, James (Pvt.) 128
RYON, Timothey (Pvt.) 66

-S-
SACCAT, Joseph (Pvt.) 128
SACHNET, Joseph (Pvt.) 41
SACKET, Asoriah (Pvt.) 127
Azariah (Pvt.) 120
Azariah (Sgt.) 55
Joseph (Pvt.) 39, 394
SACKETS, Joseph (Pvt.) 24
Thomas (Pvt.) 24
SACKETT, Amos (Pvt.) 62, 409, 423
Asiria (Pvt.) 428
Aza. (Sgt.) 48
Azarh. (Sgt.) 16
Azariah (Pvt.) 408
Aziriah (Sgt.) 131
Azoriah (Sgt.) 60
Elijah (Pvt.) 442
Eliza (Pvt.) 61
Joseph 605
Joseph (Pvt.) 37, 62, 409, 620
SADLER, Jacob (Ens.) 154
SAGAROON, Patrick (Pvt.) 115
SAGARSON, Patrick (Pvt.) 130
SAGERSON, Patrick (Pvt.) 542
SAHLER, John (Pvt.) 421, 433

SAIL, Samuel (Pvt.) 586
SAILOR, Jacob (Ens.) 157
ST. CLAIR, Neal (Pvt.) 649
SALSBURY, Nathan (Pvt.) 278
SALSGARE, Casper (Pvt.) 398
SALTSGEBER, Casper (Pvt.) 143
SALTSGIVER, Gasper (Pvt.) 406(2: one
  is substitute for Frederick Bidinger,
  apprentice), 431
SAMIALS, Robert (1st Lt.) 321, 324
SAMLS, Isaac (Pvt.) 359
SAMMIS, Isaac (Pvt.) 621
SAMOS, Isaac (Pvt.) 466
SAMPEL, Ezikel (Lt.) 601, 609
  Joseph (Pvt.) 224
SAMPLE, David (Pvt.) 19, 65, 133, 139,
  400, 413, 439
  Ezekiel (2nd Lt.) 380
  Ezekiel (Ens.) 273, 293, 307
  James (Capt.), 208 (sick - Jan 1778)
  James (Pvt.) 350, 357
  Joseph (Pvt.) 218
SAMUEL, Robert (Capt.) 644
SAMUELS, Robert (1st Lt.) 329, 334
  Robert (Capt.) 550, 573, 574, 578, 579,
  645, 648
SANDERLIN, Samaul (Cpl.) 555
SANDERS, Frederick (Pvt.) 613
SANDERSON, --- (Capt.) 602
  Alexander (Pvt.) 209, 218, 229, 232,
  633
  James (Pvt.) 345, 350, 357
  John (Pvt.) 218, 224 ("run off"), 457,
  624, 655
  Robert (Capt.) 204, 210, 213, 467, 609
  William (Capt.) 452, 456, 463, 468, 470,
  471, 602, 609
  William (Maj.) 338
SANDS, James (Pvt.) 207
SANFORD, Abraham (Pvt.) 568
  Abraham (Pvt.) 565
SANKEY, Richard (Pvt.) 650
SANS, John (Pvt.) 347
SANSEBAUGH, Christian (Pvt.) 162
SANTRY, Dinnass (Pvt.) 439
SANZEBOUGH, Christopher (Pvt.) 179
SARGEANT, Edward (Pvt.) 19
SARVED, Jonathan 645
SATTERLY, Samuel (Pvt.) 395
SAVAGE, Henry (Pvt.) 460, 568, 581,
  636
  John (Pvt.) 79, 393, 409, 424
  Patrick (Pvt.) 265, 272, 285, 315, 643

Richard (Pvt.) 546
SAVIGE, Henry (Pvt.) 560
SAWERS, James (Pvt.) 209
SAWYERS, James (Lt.) 217
SAY, James (Pvt.) 554, 558
  James (Scout) 626
SAYLOR, Jacob (Pvt.) 103, 137
SCALES, William (Pvt.) 492
SCANDRIH, Jacob (Pvt.) 199
SCHNEIDER, Jacob (Pvt.) 530
  John Ralph (Pvt.) 522
SCHOLER, John (Pvt.) 438
SCHOOLER, John (Pvt.) 64, 392, 403,
  419
SCIFFINGTON, Henry (Pvt.) 359
SCINFFINTON, Henry (Pvt.) 354
SCIVENTON, Henry (Pvt.) 629
SCOOP, Oily (Pvt.), 233. See Soop.
SCOOT, John (Pvt.) 574, 578
  William (Pvt.) 645
SCORGS, James (Pvt.) 145, 147
SCOT, Adam (Pvt.) 411, 435
  Adam Co. (Pvt.) 450
  James (Pvt.) 182, 193
  Jo. (Pvt.) 565
SCOTT, Adam (1st Lt.) 33
  Adam (2nd Lt.) 14, 31, 45, 443
  Adam (Lt.) 148
  Adam (Pvt.) 390 ("warned to stay at
  home"), 631
  Archibald (Pvt.) 270, 276, 283
  David (Pvt.) 93, 116, 122, 480, 487,
  494, 580
  James (Pvt.) 117, 273, 293, 303, 307,
  332, 392, 403, 481, 497, 505, 560,
  650
  John (Col.) 293
  John (Ens.) 632
  John (Lt.) 261, 273
  John (Pvt.) 56, 78, 126, 298, 336, 372,
  475, 486, 500, 570, 573, 618, 621,
  648
  John (Pvt.) (Scout) 652
  John (Pvt.) 126
  John (Qtr. Master) 11, 608
  Joseph (Pvt.) 482, 487, 497
  Matthew (Pvt.) 395, 421, 433
  Moses (Pvt.) 290, 430
  Robert (2nd Lt.) 451, 456, 462, 468
  Robert (Pvt.) 292, 296, 313, 496, 624,
  655
  Samuel (Pvt.) 270, 276, 283
  Thomas (Pvt.) 134, 282

William 28
William (Pvt.) 23, 26, 93, 107, 116, 143, 274, 294, 307, 430, 553
SCOUTEN, Adoras (Pvt.) 251
Simon (Pvt.) 490
SCOUTON, Simeon (Ens.) 653
Simon (Ens.) 653
Simon (Pvt.) 476, 504
Theadoris (Pvt.) 491
SCRANTON, James (Pvt.) 442
SCROGGS, Alexander (Pvt.) 176
Ebenr. (Pvt.) 656
James 28
James (Pvt.) 23, 25, 402, 419, 437
Rawlin (Pvt.) 159
SCROGS, Alexander (Pvt.), 195, 388 (not to be found)
Allexander (Pvt.) 401, 414
James (Pvt.) 64
SCULE, Joseph (Pvt.) 200
SCULLY, William (Pvt.) 562
SEACE, Milchar (Pvt.) 74
SEAGART, Abraham (Pvt.) 283
SEAGER, George (Pvt.) 542
SEALER, Mathias (Capt.) 8
SEALES, William (Pvt.) 482, 497
SEAMANS, Edward (Pvt.) 617
SEARIGHT, Gilbert (Pvt.) 158
SEAUTON, Theodoris (Pvt.) 477
SECHLER, Jacob (Pvt.) 290
Philip (Cpl.) 290
SECHRIST, John (Pvt.) 113
SECKET, Elijah (Pvt.) 394
SECKETT, Thomas 605
SECKIT, Azekiah (Pvt.) 626
SECRIST, John (Pvt.) 75
Solomon (Pvt.) 93, 116
SEDGEWICK, Thomas (Pvt.) 347, 349
SEDGWICK, John (Pvt.) 456
SEECHRIST, John (Pvt.) 90, 542
SEEGARD, Abraham (Pvt.) 275
SEERIGHT, Gilbert (Lt.) 183, 190
SEGEL, Jacob (Pvt.) 509
SEGERIST, Solomon (Pvt.) 107
SEIVINGTON, Henry (Pvt.) 354
SELCHER, Michael (Pvt.) 359
SELL, John (Pvt.) 112, 647
Samuel (Pvt.) 93, 116, 122
SELLAR, Jacob (Pvt.) 109
SELLARS, David (Pvt.) 586
SELLER, Jacob (Pvt.) 575, 582
SELLERS, David (Pvt.) 118, 123, 538, 546

Francis (Pvt.) 61
Holmes (Pvt.) 308
Jacob (Pvt.) 118, 123, 538, 580
John (Pvt.) 148, 150
Martin (Pvt.) 540
Matthias (Capt.), 6
Thomas (Pvt.) 264, 274, 294
SELLERSF, Jacob (Pvt.) 247
SEMMERAL, David (Ens.) 33
SEMPLE, David (Pvt.) 18, 21, 152
Ezekiel (Ens.) 261
James (Capt.) 203
Robert (Pvt.) 197
SEMRAL, David (Ens.) 412
SENART, John (Pvt.) 393
SENESSY, Mathias (Pvt.) 347
SENTRY, Denis (Pvt.) 426
Dennis (Pvt.) 128
SERGEANT, Edward (Pvt.) 20, 21, 139, 148
SERGENT, Edward (Pvt.) 152
SERIGHT, Gilbert (Lt.) 171
SERJENT, Edward (Pvt.) 150
SERVER, Jacob (Pvt.) 332, 563
Philip (Pvt.) 563, 630
SESS, Walker 606
SEXON, Alen (Pvt.) 248
SEYHAWK, Timothy (Pvt.) 648
SEYMER, Henry (Pvt.) 542
SHACKLER, Frederick (Pvt.) 274
SHADE, Boston (Pvt.) 488, 499
David (Pvt.) 625, 655
George (Pvt.) 343, 625, 655
SHAFFLETON, George (Pvt.) 243
SHAFTON, George (Pvt.) 252
SHALADY, George (Pvt.) 78
SHALATOE, William (Pvt.) 292
SHALE, William (Pvt.) 618
SHALLEDY, George (Pvt.) 105
SHALS, Samuel (Pvt.) 476
SHANNON, George (Pvt.) 111, 547, 560, 567, 630
Hugh (Pvt.) 244, 615
James (Pvt.) 16(2), 47, 48, 55, 67, 309, 445, 447, 628
John (Pvt.), 206, 269, 270, 275, 276, 282, 283
Joseph (Pvt.) 276, 284, 631
Nathaniel (Pvt.) 276
Robert (Capt.) 11, 15, 16, 27, 609, 628
Robert (Pvt.) 397, 428, 430, 447
Samuel (Pvt.) 446
Thomas (Pvt.) 76, 82, 111, 522, 526,

548
William (Cpl.) 282
William (Pvt.) 82, 110, 269, 275, 278,
  285, 315, 544
SHANON, George (Pvt.) 586
Joseph (Pvt.) 411
Samuel (Pvt.) 290
William (Sgt.) 547
SHARA, Andrew (Pvt.) 336
SHARLATTO, George (Pvt.) 296
SHARON, Hugh (Pvt.) 259, 477
James (Pvt.) 342, 345, 361
Samuel (Pvt.) 477
William (Pvt.) 246
SHARP, Alexander (Pvt.) 195, 398
George 324
George (Pvt.) 362, 624, 654
George (Sub. Lt.) 3
James (Pvt.) 64, 139, 145, 147, 400,
  413, 439
John (Pvt.) 20, 64, 145, 147, 162, 388,
  401, 414
Joseph 608
Joseph (Ens.) 457, 462, 468
Joseph (Pvt.) 461, 478, 504
Mathew (Light Dragoon) 640
Mathew (Pvt.) 78, 523, 544, 623
Mathew (Pvt.) (Light Dragoons) 72
Matthew (Pvt.) 527, 585
Robert (Lt.) 302
Robert (Pvt.) 7, 10, 63, 144, 146, 149,
  150, 267, 309, 390, 398, 402, 416,
  418, 436
Robert 425
William (Pvt.) 78, 105, 536, 543, 584,
  601, 610
SHARPE, Joseph (Ens.) 451
SHARRA, Andrew (Pvt.) 560, 574, 578
SHARRON, Hugh (Pvt.) 502
Samuel (Pvt.) 502
William (Pvt.) 478, 504
SHARROW, Andrew (Pvt.) 648
SHATO, Anthony (Pvt.) 625, 655
John (Pvt.) 625
SHATOE, John (Pvt.) 655
SHAVEL, Frederick 28
SHAVER, Adam (Pvt.) 85, 99, 115, 130
Henry (Pvt.) 116, 122
Jacob (Pvt.) 119
John (Pvt.) 352, 358
Peter (Ens.) 511, 524(2), 532, 557
Peter (Pvt.) 273, 293
Simeon (Pvt.) 79

SHAVOUR, Paul (Pvt.) 308
SHAVR, Henry (Pvt.) 93
SHAW, Alexander (Pvt.) 195
Andrew (Pvt.) 347, 455
Jacob (Pvt.) 538
James (Pvt.) 175
John (Pvt.) 597
Samuel (2nd Lt.) 452, 457, 463, 467,
  468
Samuel (Lt.) 339, 346, 348
Samuel (Pvt.) 245, 504, 612
Thomas (Pvt.) 459
William (Pvt.) 121, 245, 621, 638, 639
SHEAKEL, Peter (Pvt.) 83
SHEARER, Jacob (Pvt.) 237
William (Pvt.) 227
SHEATHY, Edward (Pvt.) 199
SHEAVER, Peter (Ens.) 541
SHEDE, Boston (Pvt.) 474
SHEDSWOCK, Thomas (Pvt.) 458
SHEEHAN, Cornelius (Pvt.) 360, 622
William (Pvt.) 344, 360, 622
SHEEHEN, Jeremiah (Pvt.) 635
SHEEKAN, William (Pvt.) 365
SHEERER, Jacob (Pvt.) 238
William (Pvt.) 221
SHEETS, Henry (Pvt.) 88, 98, 119, 539
Jacob (Pvt.) 119
John (Pvt.) 77, 82, 111, 548
Michael (Cpl.) 545
Michael (Pvt.) 87, 108, 118, 538
SHEFELTEN, George (Pvt.) 474
SHEFFELTON, George (Pvt.) 488
SHEHAN, Jeremiah (Pvt.) 188
William (Pvt.) 460
SHEHOLE, Frederick (Pvt.) 23
SHELDS, David (2nd Lt.) 379
SHELE, Frederick (Pvt.) 51
SHENIFIELD, John (Pvt.) 308
SHERLE, Frederick (Pvt.) 54
SHERMAN, Thomas (Pvt.) 293, 298,
  300, 307
SHERON, George (Pvt.) 126
Thoms. (Pvt.) 126
SHERRA, Andrew (Pvt.) 325
SHERROD, Andrew (Pvt.) 570
SHERRON, Thomas (Pvt.) 184
SHEVELE, Frederick (Pvt.) 421, 433
SHEVIL, Frederich (Pvt.) 57
Frederick (Pvt.) 589
SHEVILE, Frederick (Pvt.) 25, 395
SHIELDS, David (2nd Lt.) 368, 370, 377
David (Lt.) 261, 277, 286, 310, 318

100

James (Pvt.) 455
John (Cpl.) 408, 423
John (Pvt.) 62, 132, 375, 424
Joseph (Lt.) 339, 358
Joseph (Pvt.) 461
Mathew (Pvt.) 267
Matthew (Pvt.) 373
Peter (Pvt.) 87, 119
Robert (Pvt.) 268, 298, 300, 303, 310
William (Pvt.) 343, 353, 359
SHIFT, Adam (Pvt.) 538
SHILLING, Daniel (Pvt.) 87, 119
SHILLITOE, George (Pvt.) 126
SHINBERGER, Francis (Pvt.) 200
SHINING, George (Pvt.) 330
SHIRK, Joseph (Pvt.) 78, 105, 544, 585
SHIRLEY, Thomas (Pvt.) 278, 287, 312
SHIRON, William (Pvt.) 126
SHITLY, Andrew (Pvt.) 167
SHITS, Henry (Pvt.) 546
SHITTS, John (Pvt.) 126
SHIVEL, Frederick (Pvt.) 62
Fredrick (Pvt.) 136
SHOAF, James (Pvt.) 142
Peter (Pvt.) 143
SHOAP, Boston (Pvt.) 307
SHOCKEY, Jacob (Pvt.) 94, 97
SHOFE, James (Pvt.) 397, 430
Peter (Pvt.) 398, 430
SHOFF, James (Pvt.) 428
Peter (Pvt.) 26
SHOFFLETON, George (Pvt.) 259
SHONIFIELD, John (Pvt.) 274
SHONNEFIELD, John (Pvt.) 294
SHORNER, Elias (Pvt.) 93
SHORT, Jacob (Pvt.) 538
SHORTLEY, George 28
SHOT, Jacob (Pvt.) 87, 108, 118
SHROOTF, William (Pvt.) 189
SHUFF, Peter (Pvt.) 23
SHUFFLETON, George (Pvt.) 499
SHUNK, Simon (Pvt.) 87, 110, 124, 125,
  538, 546, 572
SHUPT, Jacob (Pvt.) 220, 226
SHUTLER, Barnet (Pvt.) 429
Barny (Pvt.) 127
SHYHAWK, Stephen (Pvt.) 329
SIGHTS, Henry (Pvt.) 76, 92, 576, 583
Stoffel (Pvt.) 530
Stoffle (Pvt.) 576, 583
Stophel (Pvt.) 76, 92
SIGLAR, John (Pvt.) 325, 574, 578
SIGLER, George (Pvt.) (Scout) 652

Jo. (Pvt.) 565
John (Pvt.) 336
John (Pvt.) (Scout) 652
SIM, Andrew (Pvt.) 268
SIMANS, John (Pvt.) 152
SIMARAL, David (2nd Lt.) 65
SIMER, Henry (Pvt.) 112
SIMERAL, David (Ens.) 385
SIMERALL, David (Ens.) 14
SIMERTON, John (2nd Lt.) 454
SIMMENTON, John (2nd Lt.), 463
SIMMER Jacob (Pvt.), 93
SIMMERAL, John (Pvt.) 587
SIMMERS, Fred. (Pvt.) 129
Frederick (Pvt.) 124
Fridrick (Pvt.) 84, 114
SIMMERSON, Robert (Pvt.) 624
SIMMERVILL, David (Ens.) 31
SIMMISON, Samuel (Pvt.) 588
SIMMON, Frederick (Pvt.) 540
SIMMONS, Edward (Pvt.) 177
SIMOND, Richard (Pvt.) 189
SIMONDS, Edward (Pvt.) 189
William (Pvt.) 189
SIMONS, John (Pvt.) 18, 19, 139, 142,
  230, 233
William (Pvt.) 546
SIMONTON, John (2nd Lt.) 452, 465
William (Pvt.) 650
SIMPSON, George (Pvt.) 91
John (Pvt.) 210, 289, 299, 314, 615, 284
Thomas (Pvt.) 102
SIMRAL, David (Ens.) 399, 438
John (Pvt.) 66, 400, 413, 440
SIMRALL (Simrell), David (Ens.) 133
David (Pvt.) 134
John (Pvt.), 134(2), 405
SIMS, Andrew (Pvt.) 303, 310
Samuel (Pvt.) 276, 283
SIMSON, Robert (Pvt.) 655
Thomas (Pvt.) 85
SINCLAIR, Neal (Pvt.) 649
SINCLEER, Phillip (Cpl.) 280
SINDOLPH, Joseph (Pvt.) 161
SINE, William (Pvt.) 397
SINGAR, Jacob (Pvt.) 617
SINGER, Henery (Pvt.) 200
Henry (Pvt.) 162, 347
Jacob (Pvt.) 158, 199
Simeon (Pvt.) 168
Simon (Pvt.) 159, 200
William (Pvt.) 303
SINKEY, Thomas (Pvt.) 646

William (Pvt.), 569(2), 574(2), 578, 579, 646(2), 648, 649(2)
SINKLER, Neal (Pvt.) 559
Neil (Pvt.) 574, 579
SINQUE, Thomas (Pvt.) 329
SINSABOUGH, Christian (Pvt.) 175
SINTORPH, George (Pvt.) 298
SINTRUMP, George (Pvt.) 306
SIRRET, James (Pvt.) 407
SIRWIN, John (Pvt.) 117
SISNA, Stephen (Pvt.) 54
SISNEY, James (Pvt.) 389
William (Pvt.) 264
SITES, Hendry (Pvt.) 104
Stofel (Pvt.) 104
SITMORE, John (Pvt.) 20
SITS, Henry (Pvt.) 138
SITSE, Stofel (Pvt.) 138
SKAVOUR, Paul (Pvt.) 294
SKIEHAWK, Stephen (Pvt.) 554
SKILES, John (Pvt.) 145, 152
SKINER, George ;(Pvt.) 398
William (Pvt.) 397
SKINNER, George (Pvt.) 439
William (Pvt.) 416, 425, 439, 636
SKIVINTON, Henry (Pvt.) 461
SKYHAUK, Timothy (Pvt.) 578
SKYHAWK, Steephen (Pvt.) 561
Timothy (Pvt.) 574, 630
SKYLES, Isaac (Pvt.) 180, 197
James (Pvt.) 83, 100
SLIDER, Christy (Pvt.) 630
SLIFE, Frederick (Pvt.) 125
SLOAN, David (Pvt.) 616
James (Pvt.) 168, 199, 214
John (Cpl.) 520, 539
John (Pvt.) 101
Robert (Pvt.) 291, 295, 313, 380
Samuel (Pvt.) 207
William (Pvt.) 208, 215, 343, 354, 359
William (Sgt.) 616
SLONE, John (Pvt.) 571
William (Pvt.) 604
SLOWN, Jonathan (Pvt.) 84
SMALEY, Benjamin (Pvt.) 249
Lewis (Pvt.) 35, 621
SMALL, Adam (Pvt.) 89, 112, 123, 542, 585
Andrew (Pvt.) 330, 597, 646, 649
James (Pvt.) 478, 508, 651
SMALLEY, Lewis (Pvt.) 474, 498, 618
Louis (Pvt.) 488
Simon (Pvt.) 245

SMALLMAN, William (Pvt.) 587
SMALY, Simon (Pvt.) 258
SMART, John (Pvt.) 86
SMILEY, Archibald (Pvt.) 475, 500, 509, 651
Archibeld (Pvt.) 505
George (Ens.) 453, 464
George (Pvt.) 351
James (Pvt.) 178
John (Pvt.) 345, 352, 475, 486, 500
Samuel (Pvt.) 351, 363
Thomas (Ens.) 340, 351
Thomas (Pvt.) 457, 475, 500, 505, 509, 651
Thomas (Sgt.) 612
Will (Pvt.) 612
William (Pvt.) 158, 167, 178, 351, 363, 456, 651
SMILY, James (Pvt.) 174
William (Pvt.) 174
SMITH, --- (Col.) 530, 537, 584
Abraham 544
Abraham (Col.) 39, 510, 536, 543, 547, 658
Abraham (Lt.) 3
Abraham (Pvt.) 40, 42, 401, 405, 411, 414, 440, 631, 658
Abraham (Sub. Lt.) 3
Abram (Col.) 518
Abram (Pvt.) 36, 134
Alexander (Pvt.) 354(2), 355, 359, 365
Andrew (Pvt.) 91, 104, 138, 481, 497, 505, 576, 583
Anthony (Pvt.) 105
B. (Pvt.) 409
Ben (Pvt.) 189
Brice (Pvt.) 206
Daniel (1st Lt.) 512, 526, 547
Daniel (Lt.) 522, 623
Daniel (Pvt.) 77, 82, 111, 126
Frederick (Pvt.) 538, 546
George (butcher) 199
George (Pvt.) 82, 110, 126, 199, 520, 524, 548(2), 557, 617, 625
Gideon (Pvt.) 431
Henry (Pvt.) 87, 108, 118, 537, 545
Henry Money (Pvt.) 235, 237
Hugh (Pvt.) 63, 229, 232, 633
Isaac (Pvt.) 413, 426, 439
Jacob (Pvt.) 440
James (Pvt.) 16, 17, 64, 76, 91, 92, 104, 138(2), 142, 157, 181, 186, 188(2), 189, 198, 199, 249, 276, 308, 397,

398, 407, 427, 430(2), 455, 467, 576,
  583, 588, 617, 627, 635
James (Sgt.) 429
John (Adjt.) 388
John (Clerk) 642
John (Lt.) (Light Dragoon) 656
John (Pvt.) 30, 33, 66, 95, 134, 136,
  188, 264, 274, 276, 294, 299 (2), 308,
  345, 352, 360, 365, 371, 379, 381,
  389, 396, 400, 422, 433, 457, 460,
  472, 587, 612, 619, 622
John (Sgt.) 297, 304
John Greer (Pvt.) 225
Joseph (Fifer) 545
Joseph (Pvt.) 83, 100, 111, 275, 347,
  348, 353, 358, 557
Josiah (Pvt.) 269, 283
Michael (Pvt.) 244
Nathanieel (Pvt.) 189
Nathaniel (Pvt.) 177, 588, 617
Nicholas (Pvt.) 219, 225
Patter (Pvt.) 222
Peater (Pvt.) 9
Peter (Pvt.) 101, 185, 191, 217, 223
Robert (Pvt.) 177, 218, 224, 265, 270,
  276, 283, 326, 561
S. 126
Samuel (Pvt.) 75, 84, 115, 130, 269,
  275, 283, 294, 308, 540
Thomas (Pvt.) 278
William 606
William (Capt.) 274
William (Lt.) 262, 268, 282
William (Pvt.) 72, 83, 94, 100, 111, 126,
  133, 134, 306, 327, 397, 436, 478,
  504, 508, 561, 651
William (Sgt.) 615
William Kelley (Pvt.) 394
SMITSMAN, Peter (Pvt.) 329
SMURRAY, William (Pvt.) 362
SMYLIE, John (Pvt.) 459
SMYTH, Abraham (Col.) 531
  Daniel (1st Lt.) 533
  George (Pvt.) 163
  Hugh (Pvt.) 145, 146
  James (Pvt.) 145, 147
  John (Pvt.) 58, 96
SNAKINBERGER, Francis (Pvt.) 158
SNEDER, George (Pvt.) 144
SNIBLEY, Christopher (Pvt.) 540
SNIDER, Adam (Pvt.) 233
  Andrew (Pvt.) 371, 379
  Conrad (Capt.) 70, 86

Conrod (Capt.) 118
Daniel (Pvt.) 80, 102
David (Pvt.) 80, 101
George (Pvt.) 183
Henry (Pvt.) 111, 126
Henry Ralph (Ens.) 110
Jacob (Pvt.) 80, 82, 102, 111, 126, 527
John (Pvt.) 191, 233 (April 1781 -
  dead), 390, 435, 450
John R. (Pvt.) 126
John Ralph (Pvt.) 111
John Rasph (Pvt.) 82
Nicholas (Pvt.) 81, 110, 125
Peter (Cpl.) 87
Peter (Pvt.) 125, 548
Philip (Pvt.) 205, 235
Phillip (Pvt.) 9
Ralph (Ens.) 71
SNIVELY, Andrew (Pvt.) 75, 540
  Hendry (Pvt.) 103
  Henry (Pvt.) 91, 109
  John (Pvt.) 231, 235
  Joseph (Pvt.) 73, 80, 102
SNIVILY, Andrew (Pvt.) 84, 115, 130
  Chrisby. (Pvt.) 130
  Christy (Pvt.) 114
  Crisby (Pvt.) 84
  Jonathan (Pvt.) 130
SNIVLEY, Henry (Pvt.) 575, 582
SNOBARGER, Duley (Pvt.) 586
SNODGRASS, Alexander (Pvt.) 245
  James (Pvt.) 119
  Robert (Ens.) 169, 512, 514, 516, 533,
    535, 537, 580
  Robert (Lt.) 70, 118
  Robert (Pvt.) 545
  Samuel (Pvt.) 119, 521, 523, 538, 546,
    572
  Thomas (Pvt.) 36, 40, 151, 303, 450
  William (Pvt.) 538, 580
  William (Sgt.) 118, 514, 545
SNODGRESS, James (Pvt.) 87
  Robert (Lt.) 86
  Samuel (Pvt.) 87
  Thomas (Pvt.) 149, 406, 435
  William (Sgt.) 87
SNODY, John (Pvt.) 440
SNOWBARGER, Andrew (Pvt.) 89, 112
  Jacob (Pvt.) 74, 90, 542
SNOWBERGER, Andrew (Pvt.) 108, 541
  Auley (Pvt.) 93
  Owley (Pvt.) 116, 122
SNOWBORGER, Jacob (Pvt.) 113

SNUTT, Ludwick (Pvt.) 542
SNYDER, Adam (Pvt.) 229
Conrad (Capt.) 88, 119
Henry (Sgt.) 547
Henry R. (Ens.) 513
Jacob (Pvt.) 73, 77, 169, 546, 599
John (Pvt.) 149, 229
Nicholas (Pvt.) 109, 547
Peter (Cpl.) 118
Philip (Pvt.) 237
SOCKETT, Joseph (Pvt.) 121
SOLENBERGER, Joseph (Pvt.) 357
SOLINBARGER, Peter (Pvt.) 349
SOLINBARIGER, Peter (Pvt.) 347
SOMERS, Isaac (Pvt.) 455
SOMERVILLE, David (Ens.) 45
SOOKE, John (Pvt.) 117
SOOP, Oily (Pvt.) Proved over age as of
   14 March 1781. 229
SOTLOR, John (Pvt.) 138
SOURPIKE, Daniel (Pvt.) 278
SPANGLER, Andrew (Pvt.) 476
Henry (Pvt.) 485
SPEALMAN, George (Pvt.) 22
SPEAR, David (Pvt.) 420, 438
James (Pvt.) 102
Samuel (Pvt.) 656
SPEARE, William (Sgt.) 601, 609
SPEARS, William (Pvt.) 283
SPEEDY, Allen (Pvt.) 269, 275, 283
Andrew (Pvt.) 298, 306
SPEELMAN, George (Pvt.) 25, 589
George (Sgt.) 57, 135, 420, 432
SPEER, David (Pvt.) 400, 414
John 405
John (Pvt.) 58, 389, 396, 422, 431, 433
Samuel (Pvt.) 58, 396, 422, 433
William (Pvt.) 275
SPEERE, Samuel (Pvt.) 136
SPEIR, William (Pvt.) 380
SPELMAN, George (Sgt.) 28
SPENCE, Andrew (Pvt.) 271
SPIELMAN, George (Sgt.) 395
SPIER, John (Pvt.) 136
Samuel (Pvt.) 389
SPOTTWOOD, William (Pvt.) 458
SPOTWOOD, William (Pvt.) 343, 625
SPPITTENGER, George (Pvt.) 87
SPROUT, Alaxander (Pvt.) 196
Alexander (Pvt.) 152, 162, 177, 617
William (Pvt.) 159, 168
SPUNK, Jacob (Pvt.) 233, 229
STACKPOLE, James (Pvt.) 475, 500,

509, 651, 653, 654
STACKPOLN, James (Pvt.) 505
STAFFORD, James 605
STAGAN, John (Pvt.) 243, 260
STAGERS, Jacob (Pvt.) 496
STAGGERS, Conrad (Pvt.) 477
John (Pvt.) 491
STAHL, Henry (Pvt.) 522
John (Pvt.) 8
Leonard (Pvt.) 517
STAKE, Frederick (Pvt.) 302, 310
STAKER, Frederick (Pvt.) 268
STAKLER, George (Pvt.) 143
STAL, Leonard (Pvt.) 536
STALFORD, Alexander (Pvt.) 553
STALL, Henry (Pvt.) 73, 80, 102, 526
Jacob (Pvt.) 102
James (Pvt.) 405 (for John Young), 430,
   642
John (Pvt.) 10, 24, 35, 81, 98, 102, 142,
   397
Leonard (Ens.) 69, 79, 100
Leonard (Pvt.) 169, 519, 586, 599, 600
Matthew (Pvt.) 27, 250
STAMILL, Robert (Pvt.) 20
STANDLEY, Marshal (Lt.) 549
STANDLY, Marshel (2nd Lt.) 321, 324
Nathaniel (Pvt.) 563
STANDS, Leonard (Pvt.) 295
STANFORD, Abraham (Pvt.) 323
STANLEY, Marshal (2nd Lt.) 330
Marshall (Lt.) 563
Nathaniel (Pvt.) 567, 581, 636
STANLY, Marshal (2nd
   Lt.), 334
STANS Leonard (Pvt.) 291, 313
STANTON, Alexander (Pvt.) 88, 98
STAR, Arthur (Pvt.) 443, 569
James (Pvt.) 505
STARET, James (Pvt.) 438
STARK, George (Pvt.) 302
STARN, John (Pvt.) 269
STARR, Arther (Pvt.) 644
Arthur (Pvt.) 31, 33, 443
James (Pvt.) 220, 223, 226, 246, 475,
   500
John (Pvt.) 475, 500
Thomas (Pvt.) 229, 233, 633
STARRET, David (Pvt.) 21
James (Pvt.) 403, 420
Robert (Pvt.) 134
STARRETT, Alexander (Pvt.), 430(2)
STARREY, William (Pvt.) 496

STARRIT, Alexander (Pvt.) 23
STATFORDE, Alexander (Pvt.) 556, 577
STATLER, Emanuel (Pvt.) 138, 522,
    527, 576, 583
  Emmanuel (Pvt.) 76, 92
  Jacob (2nd Lt.) 514, 532, 575, 582
  Jacob (Ens.) 165
  Jacob (Lt.) 70, 90, 137
  John (Pvt.) 92, 99, 576, 583
  Samuel (Pvt.) 536
  Samuel (Sgt.) 91, 137, 517, 575, 580,
    582
STAUNTON, Alexander (Pvt.) 539
STAYMAN, Joseph (Pvt.) 219, 225
STEALY, Jacob (Pvt.) 565
STEAR, John (Pvt.) 9
STEARN, Joseph (Pvt.) 265, 270
STEARRAT, James (Pvt.) 411
STECK, Benjamin (Pvt.) 621
STEEL, Benjamin (Pvt.) 618, 632
  Christifer (Pvt.) 279
  David (Pvt.) 245, 258, 326, 338, 561
  George (Pvt.) 149, 150
  John (Capt.), 6
  Nathaniel (Pvt.) 622
  Nathn. (Pvt.) 360
  Peter (Pvt.) 483, 485
  Robert (Pvt.) 624
  Samuel (Pvt.) 149, 151
  William (Pvt.) 36, 40, 149, 151, 373
STEELE, Benjamin (Pvt.) 56, 572
  Peter (Pvt.) 501
STEELFORD, Alexander (Pvt.) 562
STEELL, Ephm. (Pvt.) 200
  John (Pvt.) 200
STEEN, Alexander (Pvt.) 621
STEER, John (Pvt.) 205, 235, 237
STEESY, George (Pvt.) 249
STEET, John (Sgt.) 599
  William (Pvt.) 529
STEGER, John (Pvt.) 251
STEIGER, Conrod (Pvt.) 485
STEMPAT, Peter (Pvt.) 290
STENGER, William (Pvt.) 268
STEPENSON, Nathaniel (Pvt.) 419
STEPHEN, Alexander (Pvt.) 359, 363
STEPHENS, Jacob (Pvt.) 528
  James (Pvt.) 180, 197
  Nathaniel (Ens.) 18, 43, 444
  Richard (Pvt.) 149, 150
STEPHENSON, George (2nd Lt.) 382
  Nathaniel (Ens.) 21, 53
  Richard (Pvt.) 95, 96

  Robert (Pvt.) 159, 168, 371, 375
  William (Pvt.) 67, 289, 445
STEPHSON, William (Pvt.) 379
STERET, Alexander (Pvt.) 398
STERETT, James (Pvt.) 147
  William (Pvt.) 147
STERICKS, George (Pvt.) 309
STERN, John (Pvt.) 283
  Joseph (Pvt.) 283, 643
STERRET, Alexander (Pvt.) 143
  David (Pvt.) 68, 151, 445, 447
  James (Pvt.) 145, 587
  Robert (Pvt.) 66, 400, 413, 439
  William (Pvt.) 145
STERRETT, Alexander (Pvt.) 26
  Andrew (Pvt.) 371
  David (Pvt.) 18
  James (Pvt.) 64, 277
  William (Lt.) 3
  William (Pvt.) 64, 352
STERRIT, John (Light Dragoon) 640
  John (Pvt.) 283
STERRITT, John (Pvt.) 265, 270
  Robert (Pvt.) 133
STEVENS, Jacob (Pvt.) 81, 98, 102
  Richard (Pvt.) 33
STEVENSON, George (2nd Lt.) 370, 379
  George (Pvt.) 318
  Jacob (Pvt.) 104
  James (Pvt.) 268
  John (Pvt.) 267, 268, 288, 302, 309
  Joseph (1st Lt.) 370, 378
  Joseph (Lt.) 302
  Joseph (Pvt.) 267, 309
  Nathan (Ens.) 12, 52
  Nathaniel (Ens.) 67, 139, 385
  Robert (Light Dragoon) 640
  Robert (Lt.) 303
  Robert (Pvt.) 248, 267, 310
  Thomas (Pvt.) 588
  William (Pvt.) 288, 447
STEVINSON, Nathaniel (Lt.) 603
STEWARD, Archibald (Pvt.) 227
  James (Pvt.) 643
  John (Capt.) 224
STEWART, Alexander (Pvt.) 635
  Archibald (Pvt.) 221
  Charles (Pvt.), 58, 267, 309(2), 625,
    643(2)
  Edward (Pvt.) 285, 315
  George (Sub. Lt.) 3
  James (2nd Lt.) 13, 44
  James (Pvt.) 79, 126, 188, 189, 200,

270, 280, 283, 290, 298, 302, 306, 309, 419, 438, 586
John (Capt.) 216
John (Pvt.) 149, 151, 347, 348, 365, 379, 625
Richard (Pvt.) 458, 629
Robert (Pvt.) 126, 188, 548, 588
William (2nd Lt.) 154, 157, 165
William (Ens.) 621
William (Pvt.) 179, 292, 296, 313, 418, 436, 613, 635
STICKLEMAN, John (Pvt.) 106
Peter (Pvt.) 238
STICKLER, John (Pvt.) 570
STIEVENSON, Nathaniel (Ens.) 447
STIFFEY, Lenordd (Pvt.) 117
STIGLEMAN, Peater (Lt.) 8
STIGLER, John (Pvt.) 572
STILES, Abraham (Pvt.) 493
STINE, William (Pvt.) 285
STINGER, William (Pvt.) 310
STIPHINS, Richard (Pvt.) 30
STITSMAN, Daniel (Pvt.) 80, 101
STITT, James (Pvt.) 74, 89, 112, 526, 542
John 605
John (Lt.) 70, 88, 111
John (Pvt.) 20, 21, 139, 151, 248
John (Pvt.) 24
Thomas (Pvt.) 20
Thomas (Sub.) 140
William (Pvt.) 90, 99, 113, 169, 528, 541, 543, 599, 601
STITTS, James (Pvt.) 522
John (Sgt.) 541
STIVINSON, Nathinel (Lt.) 59
STOCK, William (Pvt.) 144
STOCKDON, Robert (Pvt.) 289, 371
STOCKTON, George (Pvt.) 318
Robert (Pvt.) 318
STOCTON, Robert (Pvt.) 279
STOLL, Henry (Pvt.) 601
STOMBAUGH, Jacob (Pvt.) 431
Philip (Pvt.) 430
STOMBOUGE, Phillp (Pvt.) 398
STOMBOUGH, Jacob (Pvt.) 398
Peter (Sgt.) 397
STONE, James (Pvt.) 342, 344, 361
John (Pvt.) 77, 251
STONEKING, John (Pvt.) 75
Jonathan (Pvt.) 84, 114
STONER, Abraham (Pvt.) 71, 94
Bernard (Pvt.) 541

David (Pvt.), 93, 107, 116(2)
John (Pvt.) 82, 111
Mathew (Sgt.) 19
STONKING, John (Pvt.) 540
Jonathan (Pvt.) 130
STOOP, Hugh (Pvt.) 207
James (Pvt.) 112
STOOPER, John (Pvt.) 542
STOOPES, James (Pvt.) 89
STOOPS, James (Pvt.) 108
John (Pvt.) 526, 601
Robert 608
Robert (Pvt.) 87, 108, 112, 538
Robert (Sgt.) 541
STORY, William (Pvt.) 507
STOTLEN, Samuel (Sgt.) 599
STOTLER, Emanuel (Pvt.) 623
Jacob (2nd Lt.) 512
Jacob (Lt.) 103
John (Pvt.) 104
Samuel (Pvt.) 623
Samuel (Sgt.) 103
STOTLOR, Emanuel (Pvt.) 104
STOTTLER, Jacob (2nd Lt.) 516
STOUP, Jacob (Pvt.) 107
STOUPE, Jacob (Pvt.) 93, 116
John (Pvt.) 93, 116
STOVER (Stovar), Daniel (Pvt.) 84, 114, 124, 129, 542
Emmanuel (Pvt.) 99
Georg(e) (Pvt.) 83, 108, 114, 129, 541
Jacob (Pvt.) 75, 90, 113, 542
Manuel/Manuele (Pvt.) 85, 115, 130
Michael (Pvt.) 89, 112, 123, 542, 585
STRACHEN, Samuel (Pvt.) 411
STRAHAM, Samuel (Pvt.) 152
STRAHAN, Samuel (NCO) 412, 438
Samuel (Pvt.) 19, 133, 139, 427, 434, 435
Samuel (Sgt.) 65, 399
STRAHAUN, Samuel (Pvt.) 21
STRAIN, Hugh (Pvt.) 157
John (Pvt.) 36, 143, 406
Samuel (Pvt.) 18
William 42
William (2nd Lt.) 13, 40, 45, 142
William (Capt.), 386, 397, 399, 404, 405, 429, 431, 641(2)
STRAM, John (Sgt.) 449
STRAN, John (Sgt.) 434
STRANG, Simeon (Pvt.) 89
Simon (Pvt.) 124
STRAPE, George (Pvt.) 570

106

STRATHAN, Samuel (Pvt.) 631
STRATIN, Abraham (Pvt.) 110
STRATTAN, John (Sgt.) 401
STRATTIN, Abraham (Pvt.) 125
STRAUNE, William (Capt.) 614
STRECH, William (Pvt.) 122
STRETCH, William (Pvt.) 638, 639
STREWGANDER, Michael (Pvt.) 143
STRITHOVE, Jacob (Pvt.) 113
STRONG, Simeon (Pvt.) 112
  Simon (Sgt.) 541
STROOPS, John (Pvt.) 522
STROPES, John (Pvt.) 112
STROUCE, Phillap (Pvt.) 479
STROUP, George (Pvt.) 565
STROUPE, John (Pvt.) 107
STROUSE, Philip (Pvt.) 244, 494, 503
STROUT, John (Pvt.) 573
STUARD, Alexander (Pvt.) 563
  Daniel (Pvt.) 460
  James (2nd Lt.) 144, 146
  James (Pvt.) 329, 564
  John (Pvt.) 130
  Jonathan (Pvt.) 84
  Richard (Pvt.) 461
  Robert 606
  Robert (Pvt.) 528
STUART, Alexander (Pvt.) 515, 517,
  543, 567, 581, 584
  Archebald (Pvt.) 616
  Archey (Pvt.) 563
  Archibald (Pvt.) 325, 624, 655
  Charles (Pvt.) 267, 302(2), 354, 655
  Daniel (Pvt.) 625, 655
  Edward (Pvt.) 272
  Francis (Pvt.) 559
  George (Pvt.) 496
  Henry (Pvt.) 584
  James (2nd Lt.) 38
  James (Lt.) 40
  James (Pvt.) 27, 35, 82, 110, 252, 265,
  267, 276, 290, 496, 508, 517, 518,
  519, 522, 526, 544, 585, 596
  John 595, 607
  John (Capt.) 232
  John (Pvt.) 75, 115, 207, 267, 345, 352,
  371, 472, 475, 486, 496, 500, 507,
  540, 619
  John (Pvt.) 594
  Joseph (Pvt.) 27, 250, 475, 492, 500
  Robert (Pvt.) 83, 100, 111, 350, 357,
  537
  William (Ens.) 495, 618

  William (Pvt.) 243, 247, 252, 260, 428,
  473, 475, 478, 484, 486, 498, 500,
  507
  William (Sgt.) 184, 190
STUFF, Michael (Pvt.) 73, 80, 102, 540
  Nichles (Pvt.) 80, 101
  Nicholas (Pvt.) 540
STUKLEMAN, Peter (Pvt.) 236
STUL(L), Felty (Pvt.) 89, 113
  John (Pvt.) 35, 200 (atty.), 653, 654
  Ludwick (Pvt.) 89, 112
  Mathew (Pvt.) 260
  Matthew (Pvt.) 243
STULTS, Herman (Pvt.) 117
STUMBACK, Jacob (Pvt.) 391
STUMBAUCH, Jacob (Pvt.) 143
STUMP, Adam (Pvt.) 87, 521, 523, 538,
  546
  John (Pvt.) 74, 88, 572
  Jonathan (Pvt.) 119
STUMPAUCH, Peter (Pvt.) 143
STUMPS, Phillip (Pvt.) 548
STUPE, Robert (Pvt.) 557
STURGAN, John (Pvt.) 618
STURGEON, John (Pvt.) 249, 483, 485,
  501, 621
  Robert (Pvt.) 501
  William (Pvt.) 500
STURGES, William (Pvt.) 475
STURR, James (Pvt.) 616
STUWART, Hugh (Pvt.) 130
SUCH, Thomas (Pvt.) 247
SULAVAN, Patt. (Pvt.) 61
SULIVAN, Patrick (Pvt.) 620
SULLIVAN, Patrick (Pvt.) 30, 32, 95, 96,
  393, 424, 527, 530, 597
  Pattrick (Pvt.) 409
SULOVAN, Patrick (Pvt.) 132
SUMMER, Jacob (Pvt.) 116
SUMMERS, Jacob (Pvt.) 122, 647
SUMMERVILLE, David (Ens.) 443
SUMP, John (Pvt.) 538
SUNDERLIN, Samuel (Cpl.) 577
SURVER, Jacob (Pvt.) 553, 577
  Jacub (Pvt.) 556
  Philip (Pvt.) 566
SUSENBURG, George (Pvt.) 361
SUSINBURG, George (Pvt.) 342
SUTING, Alexander (Pvt.) 565
SWAGERDY, Frederick (Pvt.) 243, 260
SWAGERTY, Frederick (Pvt.) 258
SWAIN, Benjamin (Pvt.) 126
SWAN, Bazil (Pvt.) 301

James (Pvt.) 381
John (Pvt.) 278, 616
Joseph (Pvt.), 287, 311(2)
William (Pvt.) 278, 287, 311, 318, 372
SWANE, Benjamin (Pvt.) 77, 82, 111
SWANGER, Abin (Pvt.) 163
Jacob (Pvt.) 160
SWANSEY, William (Capt.) 188
SWARTS, Philip (Pvt.) 91, 575, 583
SWARTSEL, Philip (Pvt.) 103, 137
SWEESE, Daniel (Pvt.) 35
George (Cpl.) 35
SWEESY, Daniel (Pvt.) 27, 250, 484,
618
George (Pvt.) 26, 485
John (Pvt.) 502, 618
SWEEZY, Mathias (Pvt.) 362
Matthias (Pvt.) 455
SWEGERTY, Frederick (Pvt.) 245
SWENE, Archibald (Pvt.) 189
SWESEY, Daniel (Pvt.) 476, 621
George (Pvt.) 476
John (Pvt.) 476, 621
SWESY, Daniel (Pvt.) 639
George (Pvt.) 621
SWEZEY, Mathias (Pvt.) 348
SWIM, Jacob (Pvt.) 199
SWINEY, Edmund (Pvt.) 325
SWING, Edward (Pvt.) 562
SWISHER, Jeremiah (Pvt.) 188
Michael (Pvt.) 363
SWITCHALM, John (Pvt.) 205
SWITSER, Jacob (Pvt.) 117
SWITSHELM, George (Pvt.) 207
SWITZER, Frederick (Pvt.) 220, 223,
226
SWITZHELLM, John (Lt.) 637
SWOOPE, Peter (Pvt.) 89
SWOPE, Nicholas (Pvt.) 83, 100, 111,
126, 548
Peter (Pvt.) 112, 542
Stopel (Pvt.) 285
Stophel (Pvt.) 272
SYMER, Frederick (Pvt.) 586
SYMMER, Henry (Pvt.) 89
SYMMONS, Edward (Pvt.) 184
SYMONS, John (Pvt.) 21
SYPO, Henry (Pvt.) 633

-T-
TAGUE, Michael (Pvt.) 117
TAILOR, Henry (Pvt.) 323
TAIREL, John (Pvt.) 34

TAIT, David (Pvt.) 134
John (Pvt.) 297, 300
TALBERT, Joseph (Pvt.) 141
Nathan 27
TALBOUTH, John (Pvt.) 199
TALLOON, Daniel (Pvt.) 135
TALLY, Ferrill (Pvt.) 650
TALOR, George (Pvt.) 193
TALYOR, Matthew (Pvt.) 326
TANNER, John (Pvt.) 338
TANYARD, Jess (Pvt.) 138
TANYEAR, Jesse (Pvt.) 300
TANYER, Jesse (Pvt.) 298
TARBETT, Thomas (Col.) 510
TARDEPOO, Peter (Pvt.) 484
TARDEVOS, Peter (Pvt.) 478
TARDIVEAN, Peter (Pvt.) 619
TARDIVEARE, Peter (Pvt.) 472
TARREL, John (Pvt.) 31
Lawrence (Sgt.) 647
TARROL, John (Pvt.) 41
TATE, John 605
John (Pvt.) 58(2), 76, 92, 136(2), 389,
395, 404, 421, 422, 433(2), 641
Robert (Ens.), 57, 135, 395
Robert (Pvt.) 30, 32, 58, 389 (had
inlisted in the PA Volunteers as of
Aug 1780), 396, 421, 433, 444
Robert (Sgt.) 395
Samuel (Pvt.) 157
Sobt. (Pvt.), 136
TAYLER, Mathers (Pvt.) 579
Mathey (Pvt.) 574
TAYLOR, --- (Capt.) 491
Andrew (Pvt.) 290
Archibald (Pvt.) 246, 482, 501, 505
Charles (Pvt.) 279
Edward (Pvt.) 29, 32, 58, 85, 589
Francis (Pvt.) 612
Frederick (Capt.) 453, 458, 464, 609
Frederick (Pvt.) 344, 360, 365, 622
George (Pvt.) 186
Henry (Capt.) 320, 324, 327, 333, 609,
611
Henry (Pvt.) 646
Hugh (Pvt.) 104, 111
Israel (Pvt.) 474, 499
James (Pvt.) 27, 35, 243(2), 250, 251,
259, 260, 472, 478, 479, 491, 619
James (Pvt.) 484
John (Capt.) 473, 498
John (Pvt.) 26, 249, 279, 281, 288, 312,
327, 337, 457, 476, 485, 549, 565,

108

618, 621
Mat(t)hew (Pvt.) 180, 187, 197
(removed), 338, 353, 358, 359, 569,
635, 646, 649
Richard (Pvt.) 355, 364, 365, 456, 629
Robert (Maj.) 15, 46, 239, 253
Robert (Pvt.) 270
Samuel (Pvt.) 271, 284, 289, 314, 481,
486, 497
William (Pvt.) 278, 344, 360, 423, 441,
458, 563, 622
William (Sgt.) 364
TAYS, Hugh (Pvt.) 144, 435, 449
TEAGARD, Abraham (Pvt.) 269
George (Pvt.) 269
TEALER, Edward (Pvt.) 136
James (Pvt.) 35
TEAT, John (Pvt.) 590
Robert (Pvt.), 443, 589(2)
TEATE, John (Pvt.) 278
TEETER, Abraham (Pvt.), 297
John (Pvt.) 308
TEETUS, Abraham (Pvt.), 300
TEGARD, George (Pvt.) 283
TEMPELTON, John (Pvt.) 442
William (Pvt.) 151
TEMPLE, Robert (Pvt.) 180
TEMPLETAN, William (Pvt.) 409
TEMPLETON, Alexander (Pvt.) 266,
298, 300, 306, 643
George (Pvt.) 625
John (Pvt.) 229, 232, 394, 409, 424
Mathew (Pvt.) 449
William (Pvt.) 292, 296, 313, 423, 441
TENNES, Anthony (Pvt.) 257
TENNIS, Anthony (Pvt.) 473
Samuel (Pvt.) 244, 473
TENNISS, Anthony (Pvt.) 498
Samuel (Pvt.) 498
TERREL, John (Pvt.) 149
TERRELL, John (Pvt.) 151
TERRENCE, Albert (1st Lt.) 596
William (Pvt.) 597
THACHER, Edward (Pvt.) 497
THATCHER, Edward (Pvt.) 482, 487
THOFT, William (Pvt.) 326
THOM, John (Pvt.) 315, 546
THOMAS, George (Pvt.) 437
Henry (Pvt.) 477, 485
Jacob 410
Jacob (Pvt.) 121, 128, 407, 477, 485
John (Pvt.) 181, 198, 372
William 607

William (Pvt.) 437, 604
William (Pvt.) 595
THOMHSON, Alexander (Pvt.) 106
THOMPSON, Alexander (2nd Lt.) 514,
543, 534
Alexander (Lt.) 584
Alexander (Pvt.) 72, 391, 403, 419, 437,
571
Andrew (Pvt.) 68, 388, 404, 446, 642
Andrew (Sgt.) 133
Archibald (Pvt.) 73, 106
Archibald (Sgt.) 529, 543, 584, 596
Caleb (Pvt.) 293, 297
Daniel (Pvt.) 75, 83, 100, 111, 126
David (Pvt.) 68
George (Pvt.) 73, 291, 295, 313
Isaac (1st Lt.) 613
Isaac (Lt.) 242
Isaac (Pvt.) 474, 493, 499, 573
Isaack (Lt.) 259
James (Pvt.) 134, 143, 182, 243, 247,
252(2), 260, 296, 313, 326, 346, 356,
366, 405, 406, 440, 459, 473, 475,
478, 488, 500, 506, 630, 650, 658
James (Sgt.) 192, 259
John 607
John (Pvt.) 75, 77, 82, 84, 91, 103,
111(2), 126(2), 149, 160(2), 161,
181, 198, 220, 277, 278, 286, 303,
311(2: one is identified as stiller),
343, 389, 390, 391, 435, 450, 474,
488, 548, 576, 582, 583, 619, 624,
625, 634, 636, 150, 286
John (Sgt.) 242, 288
Joseph (Pvt.) 68, 392, 403, 419, 446,
448, 588, 656
Mathew (Lt.) 418, 436
Mathew (Pvt.) 25, 64, 145(2), 147(2),
401, 402, 419, 437
Matthew (Lt.) 386, 641
Matthew (Pvt.) 23, 587
Moses (Pvt.) 330, 563, 650, 566
Moses (Sgt.) 630
Robert (Ens.) 262, 295, 641, 642
Robert (Pvt.) 76, 92, 104, 265, 270, 276,
415, 474, 488, 499, 527, 530, 576,
583, 597, 642, 643, 649
Robort (Pvt.) 138
Samuel (Pvt.) 292, 296, 313, 316, 373,
624, 655
Thomas (Capt.) 329
Thomas (Pvt.) 323, 353, 490, 498, 555,
624, 650

William (Capt.) 6
William (Committee of Observation) 4
William (Pvt.) 27, 40, 55, 64, 68, 72, 78,
 106, 147, 180, 197, 250, 251, 258,
 278, 286, 292, 296, 311, 315, 329,
 330, 353, 359, 372, 379, 380, 402,
 403, 419(2), 437(2), 445, 446, 448,
 485, 498, 501, 503, 544, 548, 553(2),
 585, 630, 641, 646, 650, 473, 483,
 562
THOMSON, --- (Col.) 470
 Abraham (Pvt.) 190
 Alexander (Pvt.), 78, 200(2)
 Andrew (Pvt.) 66, 314, 401, 410, 414,
  440
 Archibald (Pvt.) 78
 George (Pvt.) 80, 102
 James (Pvt.) 36, 66, 292, 398, 401, 414,
  644, 651
 John (Col.) 59, 60, 471, 602(2), 603,
  604, 610
 John (Pvt.) 137, 191, 227, 398, 414,
  472, 530, 440
 Mathew 28
 Rice Morgan (Pvt.) 278
 Robert (Ens.) 291, 404
 Robert (Pvt.) 399, 405 (for John
  McKee), 413, 439
 Samuel (Pvt.) 586
 Thomas (Capt.) 321, 324, 334
 Thomas (Pvt.), 559(2)
 William (Cpl.) 35
 William (Pvt.) 318, 404, 586
THOMSPON, Matthew (Lt.) 404
THORN, James (Pvt.) 278, 303
 John (Pvt.) 87, 123, 538
 John 537, 545
 Jonathan (Pvt.) 118
 Joseph (Pvt.), 297
 William (Pvt.) 548
 William (Sgt.) 81, 110
THORNBURY, Joseph (Pvt.) 189
 Thomas (Pvt.) 189
THORNE, James (Pvt.) 287
 Joseph (Pvt.), 293
THRUSE, Richard (Pvt.) 419
TILFORD, Robert (Pvt.) 158, 167
TINNIS, Samuel (Pvt.) 503
TINNY, Edward (Pvt.) 189
TINTARF, Jacob (Pvt.) 102
TINTONE, Nicholas (Pvt.) 379
TIPPER, Charles (Pvt.) 265, 272, 285,
 315, 643

TOD, James (Pvt.) 402
 John (Pvt.) 183
 Jonathan (Pvt.) 194
TODD, Henry (Pvt.) 277, 286, 288, 311
 Henry (Sgt.) 529, 547, 596
 James (Pvt.) 413, 439
 Samuel (Pvt.) 274
TODHUNTER, Abraham (Pvt.) 491, 496,
 507, 653, 654
 Jacob (Pvt.) 507
TOLBOUT, John (Pvt.) 199
TOM, Henry (Pvt.) 9, 219, 225
 John (Pvt.) 94, 116, 265, 272, 285
 Samuel (Pvt.) 117
TOMPSON, Andrew (Pvt.) 84, 114
 Daniel (Pvt.) 84, 130
 James (Pvt.) 42
TOOKES, Peter (Pvt.) 585
TOOL, Richard (Pvt.) 499
 Thomas (Pvt.) 231, 235
TOOPS, Henry (Pvt.) 476, 484
TORBETT, Thomas (Lt. Col.) 51, 253
TORRANCE, Albert (Pvt.) 78
 Hugh (Pvt.) 448
 James (Pvt.) 78, 97
 John (Pvt.) 305, 651
 William (Pvt.) 73, 78
TORRANS, Albert (Pvt.) 106
 Hugh (Adj.) 11
 James (Pvt.) 106
 John (Pvt.) 300
 William (Pvt.) 106
TORRENCE, Albert (1st Lt.) 527, 534
 Albert (Lt.) 584
 David (Pvt.) 305
 Halbert (1st Lt.) 514
 Hugh (Pvt.) 544, 585
 James (Pvt.) 585
 John (Pvt.) 8, 10, 142
 William (Pvt.) 527, 530, 544, 585
TORRENS, David (Pvt.) 298, 300
 Halbert (Pvt.) 119
 John (Pvt.) 297
 Samuel (Pvt.) 299
TOSTER, Joseph (Pvt.) 650
TOWNSLEY, Thomas (Pvt.) 355, 356,
 461, 629
TOWNSLY, Thomas (Pvt.) 366
TOWSDALE, Thomas (Pvt.) 36
TRACE, John (Pvt.) 169
TRACR, William George (Pvt.) 78
TRACY, Matthew (Pvt.) 215
TRATER, James (Pvt.) 477

110

TRAUGH, Peter (Pvt.) 308
TRAWSDAL, William (Pvt.) 588
TRAXLER, Michael (Pvt.) 395
  Michal (Pvt.) 136
  Peter (Pvt.) 421, 427, 432
TRAYER, William George (Pvt.) 105
TREAT, Peter (Pvt.) 195
TREEK, Nicholas (Pvt.) 537
TREES, Andrew (Drummer) 290
  John (Ens.) 125
  John (Pvt.) 110, 599
TREISH, Leonard (Pvt.) 422
  Peter (Pvt.) 421
TREMBLE, James (Pvt.) 434
  William (Pvt.) 400, 413, 439
TRES, John (Pvt.) 279
TREUSDALE, Thomas (Pvt.) 405
TREXLER, Michel (Pvt.) 433
TREXSELL, George (Pvt.) 27
TRIGG, Jesse (Pvt.) 289
TRIMBELL, James (Pvt.), 405 (for
  William Hunter)
TRIMBLE, George (Pvt.) 80, 101
  James (Pvt.) 427, 642
  John (Pvt.) 9, 293, 313, 387, 522, 539,
    544, 585
  Thomas (Pvt.) 85, 384
  William (Pvt.) 23, 26, 66, 133, 134
TRIMER, Anthony (Pvt.) 258
  Paul (Pvt.) 252
TRIMMER, Anthony (Pvt.) 504, 508,
    651
  Paul (Pvt.) 478, 484, 619
TRINDEL, John (Capt.) 205
TRINDLE, Alexander (Capt.) 5
  Alexander (Pvt.), 225 ("in the troop")
  Alexander (Pvt.) (Lt. Dragoon) 219
  John (Capt.) 202, 211, 608
  John (Sub. Lt.) 3
TRINMEN, Paul (Pvt.) 472
TRINSBY, Patt. (Pvt.) 134
TROLINGER, Jacob (Pvt.) 232
TROLLINGER, Jacob (Pvt.) 229
TROTER, James (Pvt.) 485
TROTTER, Richard (Pvt.) 191
TROUGH, Peter (Pvt.), 281, 299, 301
TROUSDALE, Thomas (Pvt.) 66
TROUSDEL, Thomas (Pvt.) 411
TROUT, John (Pvt.) 81, 109, 110, 632
TROVENGER, Henry (Pvt.) 237, 238
TROWSDAL, Thomas (Pvt.) 401
TROWSDALE, Thomas (Pvt.) 134, 135,
    414, 440

TROXEL, George (Pvt.) 474, 488
TROXELL, George (Pvt.) 498
TROXSELL, George (Pvt.) 250
TROXSYL, George (Pvt.) 35
TRUCK, Peter (Pvt.) 136
TRUESDALE, William (Ens.) 350, 357
TRUKENBERGER, Francis (Pvt.) 200
TRUSDALE, Hugh (Pvt.) 163, 351, 355,
    357
  John (Pvt.) 345, 350, 357
TRUSH, Jacob (Pvt.) 58, 396, 399, 590
  Leonard (Pvt.) 396
  Peter (Pvt.) 57, 395, 589
TRYOCK, Jacob (Pvt.) 275
TUCH, Jacob (Pvt.) 136
TULL, Richard (Cpl.) 632
  Richard (Pvt.) 56, 474, 502
TULLY, Farrell (Pvt.) 546
  Richard (Pvt.) 573
TUMMA, Turst (Pvt.) 126
TUNNER, John (Pvt.) 326
TURBET, Thomas (Lt. Col.) 239
TURBETT, Thomas (2nd Lt.) 479, 481,
    495
  Thomas (Capt.) 5
  Thomas (Pvt.) 499
TURBIT, Thomas (Lt. Col.) 20
TURNER, Adam (Pvt.), 149, 151, 406
    (above age as of 17 April 1781)
  Daniel (Pvt.) 189
  James (Pvt.) 590
  John (Pvt.) 168, 189, 390, 404, 435,
    450, 564, 642
  Robert (Pvt.) 19, 52, 53, 150, 148
  Thomas (Adj.) 253
  Thomas P. (Pvt.) 245
  William (Pvt.) 19(2), 21, 139, 148, 150,
    152
TWEED, John (Pvt.) 158, 195
TYLER, --- (Capt.) 510
  William (Pvt.) 409
TYSOR, James (Pvt.) 411

-U-

ULBINS, John (Ens.) 642
UMBERGER, Henry (Pvt.) 222
UMSTEAD, George (Pvt.) 58
UNANGST, Andrew (Pvt.) 280
UNANKE, Andrew (Pvt.) 290
UNONSENKS (Unangst), Andrew (Pvt.)
    280
UNSTEAD, George (Pvt.) 136
UPTON, William (Pvt.) 247

UTLER, Samuel (Pvt.) 472
UTTER, Abraham (Pvt.) 56
Samuel (Pvt.) 56, 619

-V-
VALKER, David (Pvt.) 222
John (Pvt.) 222
VAN CAMP, William (Pvt.) 622
VAN LEAR, Joseph (Pvt.) 294
William (Pvt.) 546
VANCAMP, William (Pvt.) 360
VANCE, David (Pvt.) 185, 191
George (Pvt.) 281, 299, 301
John (Pvt.) 87, 119, 287, 300
Jons. (Pvt.) 546
Patrick (Pvt.) 74, 88, 119, 538, 546
VANHORN, Joseph (Pvt.), 200(2)
VANLEAR, Joseph (Pvt.) 274, 307
Matthew (Pvt.) 374
VANLEER, Christ (Pvt.) 199
VARNER, George (Pvt.) 272
Henery (Pvt.) 121, 141, 384
Henry (Pvt.) 128, 516
VARNNER, Henery (Pvt.) 86
VASEY, John (Pvt.) 472, 619
VAUGH, Gilbert (Pvt.) 336
John (Pvt.) 554
John (Pvt.) (Scout) 652
VAUGHAN, Thomas (Pvt.) 633
VAUGHN, Alexander (Pvt.) 287, 311
VAUGHT, John (Pvt.) 630
William (Pvt.) 630
VEAL, Samuel (Pvt.) 565
VEASEY, John (Pvt.) 478, 508
VEASY, John (Pvt.) 484
VELE, Samuel (Pvt.) 611
VERNOR, Henry (Pvt.) 393
VINCENT, William (Pvt.) 182
VOTRICK, Henry (Pvt.) 565
VOUGH, Gilbert (Pvt.) 565
John (Pvt.) 565
William (Pvt.) 567, 566
VOUGHT, Gabriel (Pvt.) 325
Gilbert (Pvt.) (Scout), 652
VURTUE James (Pvt.), 278

-W-
WADDELL William (Pvt.), 318
WADDELLE, William (Sgt.) 616
WADDLE, John (Pvt.) 218
Joseph (Pvt.) 309
William (Pvt.) 205, 288, 301, 309, 371
WADE, Thomas (Pvt.) 330, 567

WAGERMAN, Jacob (Pvt.) 75, 90, 542
Phillip (Pvt.) 542
WAGGONER, Jacob (Pvt.), 174(2), 178, 179
John (Sgt.) 93, 115
Martin (Pvt.) 93, 116
Peter (Pvt.) 237, 238
Stophel (Pvt.) 94, 116
WAGGRMAN, Jacob (Pvt.) 113
WAGONER, John (Pvt.) 305
WAIDEN, James (Pvt.) 41
WAKEFIELD, James (Pvt.) 442
John (2nd Lt.) 321, 324, 331, 334
John (Lt.) 562, 581, 635
John (Pvt.) 407, 424, 442
Thomas (Pvt.) 393, 409, 424, 620
WAKELY, Edward (Pvt.) 175
WAKER, James (Pvt.) 352
William (Pvt.) 354
WAKFIELD, John (Pvt.) 410
WALACE, James (Pvt.) 61, 131, 409
John (Pvt.) 61, 151
Moses (Pvt.) 220
William (Pvt.) 61
WALAHAN, Pierce (Pvt.) 100
WALAS, Patrick (Pvt.) 194
WALASE, John (Pvt.) 410
WALCH, James (Pvt.) 547
WALES, Jonathan (Pvt.) 646, 650
WALH, Niclas (Pvt.) 188
WALICK, Philip (Pvt.) 236
WALIHIN, Pierce (Pvt.) 119
WALKEL, Robert (Pvt.) 402
WALKER, Alexander (Ens.) 471, 619
Andrew (Pvt.) 7, 10, 24, 63, 144, 146, 271, 302, 311, 314, 380, 402, 416, 418, 436
Archibald (Pvt.) 647
Benjamin (Pvt.) 121, 128
David (Pvt.) 218, 224, 243, 252, 259, 326, 327, 338, 478, 484, 564, 569, 616
David (Pvt.) 644
George (Pvt.) 116, 573
Hugh (Pvt.) 573
James (Pvt.) 63, 146, 272, 276, 283, 285, 315, 358, 382, 402, 418, 437, 615
John (Pvt.) 209, 272, 286, 315, 374, 633
John (Qtr. Master) 218
John (Waggon master) 598
John (Wagon Master) 4
Jonathan (Pvt.) 604

Joseph (Pvt.) 64, 145, 147, 403, 407, 411, 420, 438, 631
Philip (Pvt.) 507
Phillip (Pvt.) 246, 496
Robert (Pvt.) 18, 19, 21, 52, 53, 63, 139, 141, 145, 146, 152, 251, 418, 437, 455, 466, 516
Samuel (2nd Lt.) 7, 10, 12, 23, 43, 47, 49, 52, 140, 383, 515
Samuel (Ens.) 424, 434, 449, 636
Samuel (Pvt.) 37, 39, 120, 149, 151, 271, 284, 289, 314, 371, 390, 404, 417, 641
William (Pvt.) 18, 19, 21, 59 (deserted 29 April 1779), 63, 139, 145, 146, 152, 206, 214, 300, 429, 441, 603
WALKIN, John (Qtr. Master) 224
WALLACE, Benjamin (Pvt.) 506
David (Pvt.) 72, 78
George (Lt.) 6
George (Pvt.) 99, 456
Hugh (Pvt.) 352
James (Pvt.) 151, 161, 423
John (Clerk) 60
John (Pvt.) 36, 40, 42, 68, 97, 117, 269, 275, 282, 446, 528, 537, 588, 631
John (Sgt.) 33, 148, 443
Jonathan (Pvt.) 332
Joseph (Pvt.) 287, 311
Moses (Pvt.) 226
Patrick (Pvt.) 183, 185
Robert (Pvt.) 352, 371
Samuel (Capt.) 203, 212
Samuel (Pvt.) 220, 226, 548
Thomas (1st Lt.) 513, 528(2), 534, 536
Thomas (Lt.) 69, 647
Thomas (Sgt.) 267, 301
William (Pvt.) 16, 17, 123, 142, 268, 271, 284, 289, 290, 291, 303, 314, 350, 357, 397, 427, 430, 597
WALLACK, Philip (Pvt.) 238
WALLAHER, Pierce (Pvt.) 111
WALLAKER, Pierce (Pvt.) 546
WALLANGHER, Pierce (Pvt.) 83
WALLAS, Benjamin (Pvt.) 481, 497
John (Pvt.) 94, 135
Thomas (Lt.) 92, 115
William (Pvt.) 87
WALLES, William (Pvt.), 538
WALLICE, William (Pvt.) 118
WALLIE, John (Pvt.) 66
WALLIS, George (Pvt.) 85, 115, 130, 347

William (Pvt.) 348
WALLOWS, Thomas (Sgt.) 308
William (Pvt.) 310
WALTER, Gasper (Pvt.) 71, 94
John (Pvt.) 393, 409, 423
WALTERS, Jacob (Pvt.) 236, 238
John (Pvt.) 121, 200(2), 360, 472, 618, 619, 622, 638, 639
Michael (Pvt.) 351, 461
Stophel (Pvt.) 122, 638, 639
WALTNER, Samuel (Pvt.) 41
WALVEL, James (Pvt.) 441
WARD, Edward (Pvt.) 407, 410, 424, 442
John (Pvt.) 113, 297
Joseph (Pvt.) 62, 132, 394, 409, 424, 442
Thomas (Pvt.) 561
William (Pvt.) 61, 131, 408, 423
William (Sgt.) 630
WARNACH, Joseph (Pvt.) 306
WARNER, Henry (Pvt.) 620
WART, Conrode (Pvt.) 112
WARTIN, Thomas (Pvt.) 616
WARTON, Samuel (Pvt.) 35
Thomas (Pvt.) 221
WARTS, Conrad (Pvt.) 89
George (Pvt.) 74, 90
John (Pvt.) 75, 90, 113
WASON, Daniel (Pvt.) 285, 306
John (Pvt.) 326
Thomas (Pvt.) 289, 297, 299, 305
William (Pvt.) 176, 315
WASSON, William (Pvt.) 276
WASTERBROOK, Richard (Pvt.) 597
WATERS, Robert (Pvt.) 86, 128, 141, 393
WATHERAW, Samuel (Pvt.) 120
WATSON, Aaron (Pvt.) 196
Andrew (Pvt.) 72, 78, 106, 522, 585
Daniel (Pvt.) 617
David (Pvt.) 136, 389 ("took up a deserter"), 396
James (Pvt.) 91, 103, 124, 137, 161, 183, 193, 575, 583
John (Pvt.) 56, 159, 189, 360, 479, 491, 572, 622, 632
John (Sgt.) 247
Mosas (Pvt.) 189
Moses (Pvt.) 160
Moses (Sgt.) 247
Robert (Pvt.) 150, 157, 435, 450
Robert (Sgt.) 148

Samuel (Pvt.) 516
Thomas (Ens.) 453, 461, 464
Thomas (Pvt.) 371
William (Pvt.) 360, 458
William (Pvt.) 126
WATT, --- 5
James (Pvt.) 82, 431
John (Pvt.) 82, 431
Samuel (Pvt.) 548
Thomas (Pvt.) 145
WATTERS, John (Pvt.) 157
Robert (Pvt.) 121
WATTS, --- 5, 6
Archibald (Pvt.) 343, 353, 359
Francis (Pvt.) 612
Frederick (Col.) 38, 451, 462, 608
Frederick (Lt. Col.) 5
Frederick (Pvt.) 360, 622
Frederick (Sub. Lt.) 3
James (Pvt.) 353, 358, 362, 629
WAUGH, Isaac (Pvt.) 219, 225
James (Pvt.) 199, 200
John (Pvt.) 219, 225
WAUH, Simon (Pvt.) 331
WAYBORN, Samuel (Pvt.) 323
WAYBURN, Samuel (Pvt.) 648
WCOLF, Jacob (Pvt.) 174
W'DROW, Samuel (Pvt.) 434
WEABURN, Samuel (Pvt.) 574, 578, 644
WEAKFEEL, John (Lt.) 550
WEAKLEY, James (Pvt.) 185
Robert (Pvt.) 191
WEAKLY, Edward (Pvt.) 185, 191
James (1st Lt.) 166
James (Pvt.) 185, 191
Nathn. (Pvt.) 184
Natt. (Pvt.) 191
Robert (Pvt.) 159, 184
Samuel (Pvt.) 189
WEAR, Aaron (Pvt.) 16, 148, 150
Andrew (Pvt.) 274, 281, 308
George (Pvt.) 15, 63, 144, 146, 149, 150, 402, 418, 436
Robert (Pvt.) 270
Samuel (Pvt.) 63, 144, 146, 402, 418, 436
Thomas (Pvt.) 309
WEARHAM, John (Pvt.) 159
Phillip (Pvt.) 160
WEAVE, Aaron (Pvt.) 627
WEAVER, Aaron (Pvt.) 148
Adam (Pvt.) 236, 238
Balser (Pvt.) 124

Balsor (Pvt.) 125
Bolser (Pvt.) 110
Conrod (Pvt.) 231, 234
George (Pvt.) 272, 627
Henry (Pvt.) 119
Jacob (Pvt.) 83, 199, 221, 227, 539, 546
John (Cpl.) 277
Philip (Pvt.) 220, 226
Phillip (Pvt.) 223
William Smith (Pvt.) 93
WEBB, Michael (Pvt.) 567
WEBSTER, James (Pvt.) 222, 228
William (Pvt.) 222, 228
WEDDLE, William (Pvt.) 267
WEEBLE, Fredrick (Pvt.) 136
WEED, Michael (Pvt.) 630
WEEKS, George (Pvt.) 567
WEER, Aaron (Pvt.) 427
George (Pvt.) 54, 428
Samuel (Pvt.) 428
WEESBROOKE, Richar (Pvt.) 556, 577
WEIR, George (Pvt.) 49, 62, 587
Robert (Pvt.) 281
Thomas (Pvt.) 278, 302, 318
William (Pvt.) 302
WEIRICK, Vallentine (Pvt.) 78
WEKELY, James (1st Lt.) 155
WELCH, Andrew (Pvt.) 271, 615
Edward (Pvt.) 286, 374
James (Pvt.) 313, 315
John (2nd Lt.) 368, 377
John (Pvt.) 143, 602, 610, 643
Joseph (Pvt.) 227
Samuel (Pvt.) 209, 227
Walter (Pvt.) 42
Walter (Sgt.) 37, 142
WELDING, Patrick 605
WELDON, Joseph (Pvt.) 630
Patrick (Pvt.) 24, 132
WELLS, Abraham (Pvt.) 488, 474, 499

Abram (Pvt.) 252
James (Pvt.) 251, 573
WELSH, Andrew (Pvt.) 285, 314
Casper (Pvt.) 543
Danell (Pvt.) 200
Edward (Pvt.) 315
Gasper (Pvt.) 90, 99
James (Pvt.) 296, 359, 621
Jasper (Pvt.) 113
John (2nd Lt.) 371, 380
John (Pvt.) 271, 540
Joseph (Pvt.) 220

Robert (Pvt.) 342, 361
Samuel (Pvt.) 220
Walter (Pvt.) 658
Walter (Pvt.) 23
WERRICK, Valentine (Drummer) 543
WESSLY, Joseph (Pvt.) 558
WEST, Edward (Pvt.) 342, 344, 361, 459, 612
WESTBROOK, Joseph (Pvt.) 330
Leavy (Pvt.) 645
Levi (Pvt.) 553
Richard (Pvt.) 553, 630, 645
WETHEROW, Samuel (Pvt.) 52, 150
WETTEROW, James (Sgt.) 410
WETZEL, George (Pvt.) 178
WEVER, John Mathis (Pvt.) 610
WHARRY, David (Pvt.) 42, 134
John (Pvt.) 134, 414, 440
Samuel (Pvt.) 133, 400, 413, 439
WHARTON, Henry (Pvt.) 210
Samuel (Pvt.) 27, 250, 328, 645
Thomas 531
Thomas (Pvt.) 208, 227
WHERREY, Samuel (Pvt.) 65
WHERRY, David (Pvt.) 36, 40, 658
Samuel (Pvt.) 18, 19, 21, 139, 152
WHETSTONE, Michael (Pvt.) 308
WHIRRY, John (Pvt.) 588
WHISNER, John (Pvt.) 134
WHISTNER(Whistnor), John (Pvt.) 66, 388, 400, 414, 440
WHITAKER(Whitacre), Samuel (2nd Lt.) 453, 461, 464
Thomas (Pvt.) 243, 260
WHITAYER, Samuel (Pvt.) 352
WHITCOMB, William (Pvt.) 236, 238
WHITE, Alexander (Pvt.) 246, 298, 301, 306, 359, 622
David (Capt.) 233, 235
Edward (Pvt.) 135, 421
George (Pvt.) 122, 251, 480, 492, 495, 638, 639
James (Cpl.) 617
James (Pvt.) 176, 328, 345, 352, 365, 456, 553, 562, 563, 567, 653, 654
John (Pvt.) 36, 40, 149, 151, 159, 174, 182, 252, 352, 355, 406, 435, 450, 461, 480, 487, 494, 562
Joshua (Pvt.) 562
Mathew (Pvt.) 298, 350
Matthew (Pvt.) 365, 459
Peter (Pvt.) 130
Robert (Pvt.) 294

Samuel (Pvt.) 265, 272, 285, 315, 643
Shaving (Pvt.) 556
Steaving (Pvt.) 577
Thomas (Pvt.) 205, 508
Wathew (Pvt.) 345
William (Pvt.) 58, 77, 82, 248, 332, 507, 553, 556, 563, 577, 613, 637
WHITECOMBE, William (Pvt.) 637
WHITEFIELD, Peter (Pvt.) 294
WHITEHEAD, Jacob (Pvt.) 248
WHITEMORE, Peter (Pvt.), 103
WHITESIDES, Peter (Pvt.) 307
WHITING John (Pvt.) 182
Jonathan (Pvt.) 193
WHITMAN, Joseph (Pvt.) 544
WHITMER, John (Pvt.) 477
Peter (Pvt.) 137
WHITMIRE, Jacob (Pvt.) 398
WHITMOR, Jacob (Pvt.) 390
WHITMORE, John (Pvt.) 252, 485
Joseph (Pvt.) 78, 97, 106, 585
Michael (Pvt.) 82, 124, 125, 519, 547
Micheal (Pvt.) 586
Peter (Pvt.) 91, 576, 583
WHITSET, George (Pvt.) 174
WHITSTONE, Michael (Pvt.) 294
WHITTMORE, Michael (Pvt.) 110
WHOOLTREE, Joseph (Drummer) 19
WHOREY, David (Pvt.) 436
WIBBLE, Daniel (Pvt.) 102
Frederick (Pvt.) 91
WIBLE, Fredrick (Pvt.) 103
WIBURN, Samuel (Pvt.) 567
WICK, Jacob (Pvt.) 538
WIDDEROW, William (Pvt.) 86
WIDEROW, John (Pvt.) 127
Samuel (Pvt.) 383
WIDERROW, Samuel (Pvt.) 127
William (Pvt.) 128, 384
WIDNER, Jacob (Pvt.) 80, 102
WIDNOR, Jacob (Pvt.) 73
WIDROW, John (Pvt.) 85
Samuel (Pvt.) 449
WIELY, William (Pvt.) 344
WIER, Aaron (Pvt.) 17, 434, 449
George 28
George (Pvt.) 17, 26, 51
Gorg (Pvt.) 435, 450
Robert (Pvt.) 276, 284
William (Pvt.) 278
WIERHORN, John (Pvt.) 248
WIFE, John (Pvt.) 597
WIGAL, John 606

WILAND, Michael (Pvt.) 124
WILEY, Hugh (2nd Lt.) 521
Hugh (Ens.) 69, 77, 514, 534, 543, 584, 600
Hugh (Lt.) 105, 106
Hugh (Pvt.) 268, 382, 400
Isaac (Lt.) 628
Isaac (Pvt.) 351, 355, 357
John (Pvt.) 237, 238
Robert (Pvt.) 149, 354, 461
Samuel (Pvt.) 243, 252, 259, 472, 478, 484, 619
Thomas (Pvt.) 478
William (Sgt.) 364
WILFORD, Joseph (Pvt.) 499, 502
WILIE, Robert (Pvt.) 151
WILKESON, William (Pvt.) 111
WILKEY, Archibald (Pvt.) 105
John (Pvt.) 274, 294, 308
Thomas (Pvt.) 294, 308
WILKIN, Archibald (Pvt.) 78
John (Pvt.) 78
WILKINS, Archibald (Pvt.) 402, 418, 437, 544
John (Lt.) 3
John (Pvt.) 105, 122
WILKINSON, William (Pvt.) 291
WILKOTT, Paul (Pvt.) 651
WILL, Alexander (Pvt.) 278
Michal (Pvt.) 561
WILLAND, Michal (Pvt.) 84, 114, 129
WILLCOT, Silas (Pvt.) 509
WILLEY, John (Pvt.) 427
WILLIAM, Enoch (Pvt.) 507
James (Pvt.) 56
John (Pvt.) 81
Matthias (Pvt.) 81
Morris (Pvt.) 489
WILLIAMS, Captain 606
David (Pvt.) 291
Enoch (Pvt.) 496
Henry (Pvt.) 570
James (2nd Lt.) 537
James (Pvt.) 345, 350, 357, 573, 632
John (Capt.) 239, 243, 253, 258, 608
John (Pvt.) 98, 231, 234, 257, 275
Mathias (Pvt.) 98
Morris (Pvt.) 496
Norris (Pvt.) 508, 621
Owen (Pvt.) 269, 275, 283
Robert (Pvt.) 56, 572, 632
Thomas (Pvt.) 350, 357, 363, 455
William (1st Lt.) 241, 249, 255

William (Lt.) 26, 34, 609
William (NCO) 412, 438
William (Pvt.) 15, 17, 133, 135, 341, 361, 363, 458, 475, 507
William (Sgt.) 65, 399, 629
Windle (Pvt.) 101
WILLIAMSON (WILLIMSON), David (Lt.) 171, 173, 178
David (Pvt.) 64, 145, 147, 392, 403, 419, 437
Elliott (Pvt.) 287, 292, 296, 311, 373
George (Pvt.) 398, 430, 558
George (Scout) 626
Henry (Pvt.) 290, 380, 602, 610
Joseph (Pvt.) 411, 631, 657
Moses (Pvt.) 210, 228, 232
Thomas (Lt.) 215
Thomas (Pvt.) 159, 184, 209
WILLIANSON, Hendry (Pvt.) 280
WILLIE, John (Pvt.) 434, 449
WILLING Hendry (Pvt.) 84
Michael (Pvt.) 540, 586
WILLINGER, Jacob (Pvt.) 143
WILLS, Andrew (Pvt.) 49, 85, 120, 127, 383
David (Pvt.) 36, 40, 42, 66, 134, 401, 405, 411, 414, 440, 658
James (Pvt.) 439
John (Pvt.) 30, 33, 66, 95, 96, 134, 388, 400, 414, 440, 587, 641
WILLSON, Abraham (Ens.) 507
Abraham (Lt.) 618
Abram (Ens.) 245, 257
Adam (Pvt.) 330, 375
Alexander (Pvt.), 210, 226 ("not known")
Hugh (Pvt.), 227 ("run off")
James (Pvt.) 68, 128, 162, 174, 179, 258, 328, 411
John (2nd Lt.) 326
John (Ens.) 552
John (Pvt.) 137, 246, 327, 403, 528, 653
Joseph (Pvt.) 209, 418
Matthew (Pvt.) 375
Nathan (Pvt.) 209
Richard (Pvt.) 247, 257
Robert (Pvt.) 399, 507, 629
Samuel (Pvt.) 617
Thomas (Pvt.) 129, 460
William 605
William (Capt.) 552, 559, 629
William (Pvt.) 137, 250, 323, 329, 618
WILLY, Hugh (Pvt.) 310

116

WILSON, --- 5
Abraham (1st Lt.) 479
Abraham (2nd Lt.) 470, 602
Abraham (Ens.) 254
Abraham (Lt.) 493, 621
Adam (Pvt.) 265, 276, 283, 560, 643
Alexander (Pvt.) 220 ("not to be
found"), 356, 366
Andrew (2nd Lt.) 256
Andrew (Pvt.) 267
Archibald (Pvt.) 229, 232
Benjamin (Pvt.) 276
George (Pvt.) 567
Hugh (Pvt.) 68, 220 (1 Aug 1780 - "run
off"), 446, 448
Isaac (Pvt.) 276
James (Col.) 5
James (Committee of Observation) 4
James (Pvt.) 56, 244, 245, 280, 281,
291, 477, 479, 489, 490, 494, 502,
506, 508, 555, 560, 651, 631
John 623
John (2nd Lt.) 203, 209 ("went to the
enemy"), 320, 324, 333, 337
John (Adj.) 367, 375
John (Ens.) 489, 623, 649
John (Pvt.) 29, 54, 57, 62, 68, 91, 94,
95, 96, 97, 103, 117, 124, 136, 275,
279, 283, 287, 312, 372, 395, 420,
421, 433, 438, 446, 448, 473, 498,
506, 537, 589, 650, 654
Joseph (Pvt.) 218, 224, 402, 416, 436
Joseph 425
Mathew (Pvt.) 186, 193, 265, 270, 276,
283, 643
Matt. (Pvt.) 182
Matthew (Pvt.) 647
Nathaniel (Pvt.) 218, 224
Richard (Pvt.) 480, 494
Robert (Lt.) 71, 81, 109, 125
Robert (Pvt.) 27, 250, 271, 278, 284,
289, 302, 309, 314, 342, 354, 361,
416, 434, 449, 472, 488, 496, 619
Samuel (Pvt.) 107, 116, 162, 176, 183,
193, 276, 316, 392 (served in
Northumberland County as of Aug
1780), 403, 419, 437
Thomas (Pvt.) 182, 267, 311
William (Capt.) 319, 324, 325, 333, 559
William (Pvt.) 27, 183, 193, 270, 276,
281, 284, 309, 356, 366, 402, 418,
435, 437, 480, 494, 565, 572, 650
William (Pvt.) (Scout) 487

WILT, Michael (Pvt.) 476
WIMP, John (Sgt.) 604
WINGER, Martin (Pvt.) 280
WINGLER, Charles (Pvt.) 205
Jacob (Ens.) 216, 637
Jacob (Pvt.) 9, 207
WINING, James (Sgt.) 639
WINN, Isaac (Pvt.) 355, 366, 467
WINNING, James (Pvt.) 122, 638
James (Sgt.) 651
WINSLOW, Stephen (Pvt.) 18, 21, 57,
136, 395, 421, 433, 589
Stephon (Pvt.) 152
WINTEBARGER, Jacob (Pvt.) 112
WINTER, George (Pvt.) 341
Martin (Pvt.) 290
WINTERBARGER, Jacob (Pvt.) 89
WINTERBERGER, Jacob (Pvt.) 108, 541
WIRE, George (Pvt.) 23
WIREHAM, John (Pvt.) 101(2), 123
WIRRICK, Valentine (Pvt.) 97
WISBY, Joseph (Pvt.) 327
WISE, Christopher (Pvt.) 530
Felix (Pvt.) 219
Henry (Pvt.) 207
Jacob (Pvt.) 222, 228
John (Pvt.) 397, 416, 425, 430, 636
Phelix (Pvt.) 225
WISEMAN, George (Pvt.) 342, 361
WISHARD, Edward (Pvt.) 93, 116, 122
James (Pvt.) 74, 90, 542
John (Pvt.) 89
Joseph (Pvt.) 72, 94, 117
WISHART, Edward (Pvt.) 586
James (Pvt.) 113
John (Pvt.) 112, 542
WISNER, Ananias (Pvt.) 365, 612
WISSBEY, Joseph (Pvt.) 337
WITHEROW, Jame (Sgt.) 142
James (Pvt.) 431
John (Pvt.) 120
Samuel (Pvt.) 7, 10, 24, 48, 49, 50, 148
William 606
William (Pvt.) 121, 311
WITHERSPOON, David (Pvt.) 91, 124,
169, 575, 583, 599, 600
WITHERSPOONS, Daved (Pvt.) 103
David (Pvt.) 137
WITHNEAL, William (Pvt.) 291
WITHROW, James (Pvt.) 398, 406
James (Sgt.) 631
Samuel (Pvt.) 140, 417, 426, 637
Samuel 425

William (Pvt.) 287, 393
William (Sgt.) 620
WITZENER, Annanias (Pvt.) 629
WIVEL, Fredrick (Pvt.) 58
WODDLE, John (Pvt.) 224
WODROW, William (Pvt.) 141
WOLF, Andrew (Pvt.) 89, 112
Leonard (Pvt.) 231
WOLFE, Jacob (Pvt.) 430
WOLFKILL, William (Pvt.) 119
WOLFSKIL, Patrick (Pvt.) 128
WOLL, Isaac (Pvt.) 191
WOLVE, Leonard (Pvt.) 234
WONAHY, John (Pvt.) 86
WOOD, George (Pvt.) 292
James (Capt.) 204
James (Pvt.) 235
John (Pvt.) 246, 293, 330
Joseph (Pvt.) 329, 400
Richard (Pvt.) 158
WOODARD, John (Pvt.) 205
Thomas (Pvt.) 493
WOODART, Elias (Pvt.) 230, 234
Thomas (Pvt.) 251, 496
WOODBOURN, John (Pvt.) 617
WOODBURN, James (Pvt.) 160
John (Pvt.) 189
Joseph (Pvt.) 189
WOODEN, James (Pvt.) 20
James (Pvt.) 24
WOODMAN, William (Pvt.) 73, 80
WOODROW (Woodraw, Woodrough),
John (Pvt.) 429
Samuel (Pvt.) 416, 516
William (Pvt.) 516
WOODS, Hugh (Pvt.) 395(2), 413, 415,
421, 425, 439
Hugh (Sgt.) 636
Isaac (Pvt.) 174, 178, 186, 647
James (Pvt.) 64, 91, 104, 135, 145, 147,
230, 233, 237
Jedeah (Pvt.) 566
Jeremiah (Pvt.) 567
John (Capt.) 70, 90, 103, 104, 137, 138
John (Pvt.) 18, 21, 65, 92, 133, 134,
152, 308, 566, 567, 576, 583, 630
John (Pvt.) (Scout) 652
Joseph (Pvt.) 413, 439
Josiah (Pvt.) 508, 630
Moses (Pvt.) 252
Richard (Pvt.) 180, 189, 197
Robert (Pvt.) 181, 198
Samuel (Pvt.) 189

Thomas (Ens.) 173, 188, 190
Thomas (Pvt.) 157
William (Ens.) 154, 158, 165, 167
William (Pvt.) 15, 17, 47, 49, 65, 133,
134, 189, 400, 413, 426, 439, 627
William (Pvt.) (joiner) 188
WOODSIDE, Archebald (Pvt.) 102
WOODWARD, Thomas 606
WOOLCOTTS, Silas (Pvt.) 504
WOOLF, Andrew (Pvt.) 124
Jacob (Pvt.) 179, 428
WOOLSON, Jeremiah (Lt.) 645
John (Pvt.) 558
WOOWARD, James (Pvt.) 246
WORK, David (Pvt.) 83, 100, 111, 278
Henry (Pvt.) 270, 276, 284
James (Pvt.) 145
John (Lt. Col.) 29, 367, 375, 608
John (Pvt.) 16, 17, 47, 49, 63, 144, 146,
205, 231, 234, 265, 270, 276, 283,
402, 418, 428, 436, 627
Joseph (Pvt.) 478, 653, 654
Robert (Pvt.) 56, 496, 528, 529, 537,
572, 632, 651
William (Pvt.) 245, 258, 391, 403, 404,
419, 437, 475, 500, 505, 509, 641
WORLDLY, William (Pvt.) 643
WORMLEY, Hartley (Pvt.) 207
Jacob (Pvt.) 229, 233
WORMLY, John (Pvt.) 207, 214
WORTH, Conrad (Pvt.) 542
George (Pvt.) 542
John (Pvt.) 542
WORTHINGTON, Edward (Pvt.) By 14
March 1781 he had enlisted in the
Army. 229, 232
WORTMAN, Jonathan (Pvt.) 129
WRAY, Alexander (Pvt.) 275, 282
Daniel (Pvt.) 277
James (Pvt.) 293, 307
Robert (Pvt.) 276, 284
WREEDE, John (Ens.) 551
WRIGHT, Charles (Pvt.) 77, 82, 111, 126
George (Pvt.) 149, 151, 406, 450
James (Pvt.) 36, 40, 42, 143, 399, 406,
431
John (Pvt.) 149, 461, 482, 487, 497
Jonathan (Pvt.) 470, 602
Joseph (Pvt.) 486, 497
Malcolm (Malchum) (Pvt.) 248, 483,
485, 501
Patrick (Pvt.) 73, 78, 106
Richard (Pvt.) 84, 114, 129, 521, 540

118

William (Pvt.) 478, 490, 504, 516
WRIGHTS, Joseph (Pvt.) 482
WRITE, John (Pvt.) 450
WYLEY, Hugh (Capt.) 614
WYLIE, Hugh (Ens.) 526
Hugh (Pvt.) 302
Robert (Pvt.) 348, 349
William (Pvt.) 347, 349
WYMER, James (Pvt.) 458

-Y-
YATER, Ludwick (Pvt.) 570
YATOR, Lodwick (Pvt.) 326
YEATOR, Lodiwick (Pvt.) 579
Lodwick (Pvt.) 574
YETER, John (Pvt.) 294
Lodwick (Pvt.) 649
Ludwick (Pvt.) 338
YETERS, Lodwick (Pvt.) 561
YONG, Cowin (Pvt.) 85
James (Pvt.) 66
YOUNG, --- (Capt.) 586
Alexander (Pvt.) 80, 101, 521, 523, 572
Andrew (Pvt.) 30, 143
Daniel (Pvt.) 631
Danniel (Pvt.) 411
Gabriel (Pvt.) 523
George (Pvt.) 299

Gilbert/Gilbart (Pvt.) 84, 114, 129, 521,
540, 571
James (Capt.) 71, 81, 83, 109, 111, 512,
521, 525, 533(2), 547, 600, 614
James (Pvt.) 134(2), 174, 178, 184, 190,
205, 214, 388, 400, 414, 440, 517,
518, 542, 585
John 405
John (Ens.) 69, 93, 115
John (Pvt.) 32, 83, 108(2), 112, 114,
143, 181, 198, 390, 430, 443, 444
Jonathan (Pvt.) 129
Joseph (1st Lt.) 321, 324, 330, 335
Robert (Pvt.) 210, 229, 232
William (Pvt.) 8, 10, 142, 326, 397, 416,
429, 517, 518, 519, 558, 570, 586
William (Scout) 626
William 24, 425
YOUNGER, Conrad (Pvt.) 298, 300, 305
George (Pvt.) 298, 305
YOUNGH, John (Pvt.) 398
YOUSE, John (Pvt.) 586
YOUST, Jacob (Pvt.) 89, 112, 542
John (Pvt.), 79, 101, 123

-Z-
ZIGLER, John (Pvt.) 648

Made in the USA
Middletown, DE
24 July 2016